Queering Romantic Engagement in the Postal Age

STUDIES IN RHETORIC/COMMUNICATION
Thomas W. Benson, Series Editor

Queering Romantic Engagement in the Postal Age

A Rhetorical Education

Pamela VanHaitsma

© 2019 University of South Carolina

Published by the University of South Carolina Press
Columbia, South Carolina 29208

www.sc.edu/uscpress

Manufactured in the United States of America

28 27 26 25 24 23 22 21 20 19
10 9 8 7 6 5 4 3 2 1

Library of Congress Cataloging-in-Publication Data
can be found at http://catalog.loc.gov/.

ISBN 978-1-61117-990-3 (hardback)
ISBN 978-1-61117-991-0 (ebook)

To Jess Hughes Garrity

"What a pleasure it [is] to me
to address you

My [Spouse]"

Contents

Series Editor's Preface ix

Acknowledgments xi

Prologue 1

Introduction: Beyond Civic Engagement 6

Chapter 1
"The language of the heart": Genre Instruction in Heteronormative Relations 23

Chapter 2
"To address you *My Husband*": Addie Brown and Rebecca Primus's Queer Epistolary Exchange 49

Chapter 3
"Somehow or other, queer in the extreme": Albert Dodd's Civic Training and Genre-Queer Practices 74

Conclusion: Toward Queer Failure 99

Notes 109

Works Cited 127

Index 151

Series Editor's Preface

Pamela VanHaitsma's *Queering Rhetorical Engagement in the Postal Age: A Rhetorical Education* asks how the rhetorical genre of romantic letter writing was adapted in nineteenth-century America from the widespread notion that rhetoric had fundamentally to do with civic and public matters and was put to use in the composition of romantic relationships—and, in the cases at issue, in learning a rhetoric for composing queer romantic relationships. What she discovers fundamentally challenges the taken-for-granted supremacy and stability of the civic, the heteronormative, and the romantic, and of their composition through speech and writing—that is, through the learning, teaching, and practice of rhetoric.

Professor VanHaitsma's work is richly informed by extended archival research. Her exploration of nineteenth-century American letter-writing manuals is based largely on work she conducted at the University of Pittsburgh's Nietz Collection of American textbooks and reveals, in her account, how letter writers were guided in their treatment of class, race, gender, and other dimensions of social relations. She then turns to other archives for collections of romantic correspondence between same-sex letter writers. Here, she begins with the romantic correspondence of two African American women, Addie Brown and Rebecca Primus. She shows how the correspondents appropriate, adapt, and defy the racial and gender conventions of letter-writing manuals and romantic poetry.

VanHaitsma then turns to the case of Albert Dodd, a graduate of Yale College with training in classical and nineteenth-century arts of civic rhetorical practice, who adapted and transgressed the rules of those arts in his own extensive romantic correspondence with both women and men. VanHaitsma's exploration ends with a historically and theoretically grounded invitation to reconceptualize the conventions and expectations of rhetorical education.

This brilliant and generous book may prompt us all to reimagine our notions of the scope, the methods, and the promise of rhetorical study.

Thomas W. Benson

Acknowledgments

Special gratitude goes to two friends and mentors, Jess Enoch and Steph Ceraso. Jess offered extensive and detailed feedback on multiple drafts of the project in its earlier stages. Her generosity as a reader, in every respect, has been an incredible gift. I am equally grateful for the model of her engagement with the ideas of others in her own scholarship. Jess is a feminist mentor extraordinaire, and this book and my career would not be possible without her guidance and example.

Steph has been my peer mentor since the earliest days our time together as graduate students. As we both looked ahead to our first year on the tenure track, we set monthly goals for working on our first book manuscripts, one month and one chapter at a time. We met every other week to check our progress, and Steph read and offered feedback on every page of the draft book manuscript. Throughout the process she has been there to listen, strategize in the face of potential roadblocks, and celebrate forward movement.

This project developed throughout my time at the University of Pittsburgh, Old Dominion University, and Penn State University. As a graduate student at Pitt, I was fortunate to find a challenging yet supportive intellectual community in which to begin the archival research that grounds this book. Along with Jess, Don Bialostosky, Jean Ferguson Carr, and Nancy Glazener all offered important feedback on the early research. I am grateful to Don for conversations about arrangement and style that continue to direct my writing. I also thank Don for encouraging words about academic life that he somehow knew to offer exactly when needed. While Jean and Nancy's contributions are numerous, I especially thank them for the benefit of their expertise in archival methods and nineteenth-century U.S. culture. Other faculty also offered useful feedback as I pursued my interests in queer studies and letter-writing manuals during coursework. Here I thank Mark Lynn Anderson, Nick Coles, and Lester Olson. I also appreciate fellow grad students who joined me for writing dates and/or enlivening discussions about everything from archival research to queer theory: Erin Anderson,

Julie Beaulieu, Jean Bessette, Nathan Bryant, Jessica Isaac, Colleen Jankovich, Danielle Koupf, Peter Moe, Brie Owen, Dahliani Reynolds, and Stacey Waite. At Pitt my writing time and travel to conduct archival research were supported by an Andrew Mellon Predoctoral Fellowship as well as a grant from the College of Arts and Sciences.

I began to develop the book manuscript while an assistant professor at ODU, where several people provided crucial support. Significant portions of the manuscript materialized during weekly writing dates with Liz Groeneveld, and I am grateful for her company, shared experience, and friendship. I thank Drew Lopenzina for fielding my many questions about the process of writing and publishing a book. I am especially grateful to Lindal Buchanan, who provided feedback on the book proposal as well as mentorship that facilitated my transition from dissertator to book writer. Thanks go to Dana Heller, Maura Hametz, and Elizabeth Zanoni, who each offered research and publication guidance at key junctures, as well as Sarah Spangler, who provided assistance with secondary research. For their general encouragement and collegiality as I developed the manuscript, I thank Kevin DePew, Candace Epps-Robertson, David Metzger, Kevin Moberly, Louise Wetherbee Phelps, Alison Reed, Dan Richards, and Julia Romberger. My work on the project while at ODU was supported by a Summer Research Grant from the College of Arts and Letters, another Summer Research Fellowship from the University's Office of Research, and a Robin L. Hixon Fellowship from the Department of English.

I completed the book project while in my current position at Penn State, where I am again delighted to find a vibrant intellectual community. I thank Denise Solomon and the Department of Communication Arts and Sciences for welcoming and encouraging this work. Thank you to my colleagues in communication science—Jim Dillard, John Gastil, Erina MacGeorge, Jon Nussbaum, Lijiang Shen, Rachel Smith, and Tim Worley—for posing questions that help me to think about the interplay of interpersonal and political communication from new perspectives. I am also grateful to my fellow rhetoricians—Steve Browne, Anne Demo, Rosa Eberly, Jeremy Engels, Michele Kennerly, Abe Khan, Mary Stuckey, Brad Vivian, and Kirt Wilson—for their questions and comments about the project. It is a real treat to be surrounded by and learning from such outstanding scholars of rhetoric. Thank you especially to Michele for copious conversation about book production and publication processes. For other conversations that inform my thinking about rhetoric and archives, I thank my colleagues in the Center for Humanities and Information and the Department of English: Cheryl Glenn, Debbie Hawhee, Eric Hayot, and John Russell. I also thank the College of Liberal Arts and Department of Communication Arts and Sciences for the research summer salary and course release that supported my time when completing the final manuscript revisions.

Acknowledgments

Like all archival research projects, this one has relied absolutely on the work of archivists, special collections staff, and other historians. For their support as I conducted archival research, I thank William Daw, in Special Collections at the University of Pittsburgh; Richard Malley and Diana McCain, from the Connecticut Historical Society; and Stephen Ross, in Yale University Library's Manuscripts and Archives. I also thank Stephen Ross as well as Jeanann Croft Haas and Andrea Rapacz for additional assistance when I was navigating permissions and questions of public domain. For their groundbreaking research on letter-writing manuals, Addie Brown, Rebecca Primus, and Albert Dodd—as well as their encouragement of my work—I thank Jane Donawerth, Farrah Jasmine Griffin, Karen Hansen, Nan Johnson, Jonathan Katz, and Mary Anne Trasciatti. For the inspiration and model of his queer rhetorical and historical work, I am grateful to Chuck Morris.

At the University of South Carolina Press, I thank former acquisitions editor Jim Denton for his early support of the project and his selection of excellent readers. Both of the anonymous reviewers for this project provided constructive feedback that has made the book stronger. Also at USC Press, I thank former acting director Linda Haines Fogle and managing editor Bill Adams for their direction and guidance while seeing the project through to the production stage.

Portions of this book are derived, in part, from an article published in *Rhetoric Society Quarterly*, in February of 2014, available online: http://www.tandfonline.com/doi/abs/10.1080/02773945.2013.861009. I thank former *RSQ* editor Jim Jasinski and the anonymous reviewers for editorial guidance and feedback; I also thank current editor Susan Jarratt for assistance with acknowledgment procedures.

Speaking more personally, I would like to thank my mom, Robin Mosher, who read to me early and often and has always told me I can do anything I dream of and work for. Thank you, mom, for continuing to accept, love, and celebrate me even as my life and work took perhaps unexpected turns. Thank you for inspiring me with your example, as a true lifelong learner who remains curious and open to new experiences and perspectives. I also want to thank the chosen family and queer community—too many to name here—who have long challenged my thinking in productive ways, kept me going through uncertain periods, and cheered on my devotion to research and writing. For showing interest in this particular project, I thank Dee Giffin Flaherty and Bette Hughes. We miss you, Bette.

My greatest thanks goes to my spouse, Jess Hughes Garrity. Jess asked smart questions about my scholarship from our first date; traveled with me to the Connecticut Historical Society and, when I was running low on time my last day there, assisted with the research; checked and rechecked my citations, bibliography, and notes; listened to and offered feedback on many iterations of this work in presentation form; and took care of countless household and travel-related tasks that freed up my time and energy for research and writing. More important, Jess, you are the constant source of love, support, and sheer fun that makes this writing possible and my life pleasurable. May this book also be a love letter to you.

Prologue

This book is a queer history of rhetorical education, taking as its touchstone the teaching and learning of romantic letter writing. The genre of the letter, or epistolary rhetoric, has long occupied a place in Western histories of rhetoric. And one subgenre of epistolary rhetoric, that of romantic letters, continues to serve a crucial role as primary evidence within histories of sexuality. My own history brings together these historiographic strands, moving them in directions that are simultaneously rhetorical and queer as well as pedagogical. Through archival research, I investigate nonnormative epistolary rhetoric, seeking out the stories of diverse learners who crafted letters that subverted heteronormative forms of genre instruction in the nineteenth-century United States. But first, I begin with another story, a more normative story, the sort of story that is most often associated with romantic letters—and that nonetheless points to rhetorical and pedagogical openings for this queer history.

In 1841 *Godey's Lady's Book* presented to readers a cautionary tale about learning to compose romantic epistolary rhetoric.[1] In "Eliza Farnham; or, the Love Letters," the central conflict facing the main character is that her new fiancée, Horace, has written her a love letter and predictably expects one in return. This expectation is a problem, as she attempts to explain to the brother and grandmother entrusted with her care, for Eliza is "no great scratch at [her] pen" (Leslie, "Part the First" 218). The brother and grandmother are incredulous because Eliza was educated at a "fashionable" boarding school, and they had received many letters from her while she was away at school (217). But Eliza reveals that these letters were variously written by a friend, adapted from friends' letters, or rewritten by teachers. Unequipped to compose her own romantic epistolary rhetoric, Eliza exclaims, "I wish with all my heart there were receipts for writing love-letters. . . . How such a book would sell!" (219). Not possessing such a book, Eliza asks others to provide a love letter she may copy. Her brother refuses, insisting that doing so would amount to "deception." Her grandmother refuses initially, too, but then gives in and shares an "old" love letter. Eliza is later advised by "one of the servants, a black girl named Belinda," to avoid using the grandmother's letter (220). Belinda suggests it is "not at all fit to send . . . now-a-days," offering one of her own letters instead (Leslie, "Part the Second" 245). Eliza also decides against using Belinda's letter, calling it "nonsense" and "foolish," though admitting it contains "more ideas" than the grandmother's (246).

Setting out to write her own love letter, Eliza dates and addresses it "Dear Horace" but then labors over how to begin and end her sentences (246). Again wishing for a book to copy from, Eliza laments that because Horace is "a great reader," he may easily detect her "deception." She recalls the reading she has done, including Hugh Blair's lecture on the rhetoric of epistolary writing, yet here laments that she studied so little. Once Eliza has managed to compose a letter, she requests feedback from Belinda, who warns the letter makes "no sense" (247). Although Eliza fails to heed this warning, Belinda promises never to tell anyone "what a dreadful nonplush you've been at because you did not know how to write a letter to your sweetheart, and had to borrow patterns of every body both white and coloured." When Horace finally receives Eliza's letter, he too laments. In keeping with cultural commonplaces about romantic letters, Horace reads Eliza's letter as "a true picture" of her mind and heart (248). Of her mind, he concludes she is "shallow-headed," of her heart, that she "does not love" him truly. Horace breaks off the engagement.

While this broken engagement serves as a warning about poorly written or copied epistolary rhetoric, Eliza's story has a happy ending. She embarks on a course of study that involves daily reading as well as letter writing to her brother. Meanwhile, Horace moves abroad and, after a couple years in Europe, meets a friend of Eliza's who stays in touch by letter. Horace reads one of Eliza's letters to the friend, and he sees a new and changed "true picture" of her mind and heart. Horace is "charmed," feeling "all his love for Eliza Farnham return with redoubled warmth" (250). Horace returns to the United States, and he and Eliza marry.

Of course, the story of Eliza's love letters is a story of heteronormativity—a story in which the only happy ending imaginable is a marriage between a man and a woman. Yet the story also brings to life pedagogical and rhetorical openings that my queer history of rhetorical education mines.

First and most obvious is the question of how people like Eliza were taught rhetorical practices for crafting romantic letters. Rejecting the heteronormative presumption that Eliza's happy ending is inevitable, I ask how people *learned* to accomplish the normative rhetorical purposes she did. As exemplified by Horace's reading of Eliza's initial attempt, romantic letters are often understood simply as expressions of feeling—of one's "true" heart and mind. Even popular nineteenth-century letter-writing manuals, those very texts claiming to teach letter writing, asserted that composing a romantic letter is a matter of writing "from the heart," of speaking on paper just as one would talk to the beloved (Shields 119). But as Eliza complains in the story, "It is in vain to tell me to try and write just the same as I talk. When it comes to the pinch I can do no such thing" (Leslie, "Part the First" 219). Nor was the fictional Eliza alone. The popularity of letter-writing manuals, with their extensive instruction in the romantic subgenre of epistolary rhetoric, makes clear that writing from the heart was not automatic or simple but a practice to be taught and learned.

Manuals taught romantic epistolary practices partly through a pedagogical reliance on model romantic letters to be copied and adapted. When Eliza wishes for a book of "receipts for writing love-letters" to copy from, the story implies that such a book is unavailable. But in letter-writing manuals, chapters on the romantic subgenre consisted almost entirely of model love letters, and, as Eliza predicts, these books did "sell" quite well. As in the story of Eliza, the manuals warned that an overreliance on copying, as opposed to writing from the heart, was "deceptive." It could backfire if detected, even interfering with the learner's chances of accomplishing the heteronormative rhetorical purpose of the genre: courtship leading to the marriage of a man and woman. My queer history of rhetorical education is interested in this potential for pedagogical backfires or failures, both by learners who consulted manual models and by those who, like Eliza, turned to other kinds of educational and cultural texts.

A second opening that plays out in the story of Eliza's love letters concerns learners *not* like her. With *Godey's* addressing a readership of primarily middle- and upper-class white women, it comes as no surprise that in these articles Eliza is featured as the main character in the story. Nor would readers, then or now, be surprised that Eliza addresses her love letters to a man. Even in feminist histories of rhetoric, nineteenth-century letters are most often associated with women like Eliza. But as the story acknowledges, however implicitly and problematically, people more like Horace and Belinda also learned to write romantic letters. Moreover, as histories of sexuality and nineteenth-century romantic life document, still other people composed romantic letters within the context of same-sex and other forms of queer, as in nonnormative, romantic relationships. So, whereas the character Eliza is faced with certain options, as Belinda remarks, "to borrow patterns of every body both white and coloured," a wider range of learners diverse by gender, race, class, education, and sexuality were faced with different possibilities for borrowing and learning from the patterned models available to them. My queer history focuses on these people, considering how those least likely to find their romantic relationships represented in popular manuals learned to compose romantic epistolary rhetoric in pursuit of nonnormative relations.

Queering Romantic Engagement in the Postal Age: A Rhetorical Education seizes on both kinds of opening, even in a familiar story, even amid nineteenth-century letter-writing instruction that was predominantly heteronormative—and even though histories of rhetorical education usually treat queer romantic life as distinct from and subordinate to civic life. The book's introduction queers those binary distinctions between public and private life that have relegated queer stories to the margins in histories of rhetorical education. I theorize a new concept of rhetorical education to enable queer histories of teaching and learning, while introducing the key terms and cultural contexts for my own history of romantic epistolary rhetoric in the nineteenth-century United States. This history engages the queer openings I have described through archival research on manuals that teach the romantic letter genre, romantic letters that were exchanged between two African American women, and a white man's multigenre romantic epistolary rhetoric.

I begin with those books Eliza imagines, "receipts for writing love-letters." Through archival research in the University of Pittsburgh's Nietz Collection, I examined more than forty of these books, usually called "complete letter-writers" in nineteenth-century discourse. The complete coverage of complete letter-writer manuals included sections on the romantic letter genre. While these sections instruct that composing romantic letters is simply a matter of writing from the heart, the manuals paradoxically offer extensive modeling of the generic conventions constraining such composition. This instruction in genre conventions for romantic epistolary rhetoric embeds a heteronormatively gendered conception of romantic relations but, at the same time, teaches invention strategies for copying and adapting model romantic letters in ways that render the genre susceptible to queer rhetorical practices.

I then turn to the queer epistolary rhetoric of learners whose romantic relations were not in keeping with the genre conventions and cultural norms taught by letter-writing manuals. I consider the romantic correspondence of two freeborn African American women, Addie Brown and Rebecca Primus. I conducted primary research on Brown and Primus's romantic epistolary exchange, spanning nearly a decade and consisting of more than one hundred extant letters, at the Connecticut Historical Society. These women defied the genre conventions widely taught by manuals in order to rhetorically craft their same-sex, cross-class romantic and erotic relations. While there is no indication they consulted letter-writing manuals, Brown, like Eliza, experimented with the invention strategies manuals taught for copying and adaptation. As Belinda would put it, Brown "borrow[ed] patterns." Specifically, Brown crossed generic lines by copying romantic language from poetry and the novel and then queerly repurposing that language in order to address romantic letters to Primus. Brown and Primus's epistolary exchange pursued nonnormative rhetorical purposes that were not only romantic but also explicitly erotic and political.

From there the book's scope expands outward to explore further the overtly civic dimensions of romantic epistolary rhetoric, though by a learner culturally positioned, like Eliza's fiancée, Horace, as an upper-class white man. In the third chapter I focus on the formal rhetorical education and romantic epistolary practices of Albert Dodd, who was a student at Washington College and then at Yale. Dodd's multigenre epistolary practices included a commonplace book turned diary and a poetry album that I consulted in the Yale University Library's Manuscripts and Archives. In the commonplace book turned diary, Dodd described his formal educational experiences and accounted for the romantic letters he addressed to and exchanged with both men and women. These accounts, along with an album of his poetry, suggest that Dodd transferred his college-level civic training in order to develop multigenre forms of epistolary address and exchange across a network of genres related to the letter. Dodd used these multigenre practices to queerly compose his nonnormative romantic relations with multiple men and women.

Across these archival studies, I argue that rhetorical education shaped learners as romantic subjects in predictably heteronormative ways and simultaneously opened up possibilities for queer rhetorical practices that transgressed cultural norms while subverting genre conventions and boundaries. In framing such teaching and learning as specifically *rhetorical,* I am conceiving of rhetorical education in atypical ways. Indeed, what makes this history of romantic epistolary instruction and practice *queer* has as much to do with its conception of rhetorical education as with its emphasis on the practices of learners in same-sex relationships. This project is not simply a recovery of queer rhetorical practices from the nineteenth-century United States, in other words, but a reconception of rhetorical education and the normative frames that continue to direct historiography to this day.

Introduction

Beyond Civic Engagement

> The purpose of education in the rhetorical tradition was to prepare such [civic] leaders. As an art of effective communication, then, the tradition of classical rhetoric gives primary emphasis to communication on public problems, problems that arise from our life in political communities. The many other sorts of problems that might be addressed through an art of communication—problems of . . . personal relationships . . . for example— are in the tradition of classical rhetoric subordinate.
>
> S. Michael Halloran (1982)

To develop a history of rhetorical education that centers romantic epistolary rhetoric requires queer methodological moves. As Charles E. Morris III has urged, queer histories of rhetoric call for methodologies of "*queer movement . . . mobilization and circulation of meanings that trouble sexual normalcy and its distinctions*" ("Archival Queer" 147–48).[1] This book's history is methodologically queer in that I join queer as well as feminist scholars in troubling normative, hierarchical distinctions—between public and private, political and personal, civic and romantic—that often frame histories of Western rhetoric and rhetorical education. S. Michael Halloran has acknowledged this framing and its consequences. His history of nineteenth-century rhetorical education is forthright about the types of rhetorical concerns subordinated through a series of distinctions handed down from Greco-Roman rhetorical traditions: between the "public problems" of "political" life and the "other sorts of problems that might be addressed through an art of communication," including "problems of . . . personal relationships" (94).[2] Historiography directed by these normative distinctions occludes questions about how people teach, learn, and practice "an art of communication" for addressing problems of intimate relationships in general and queer relationships in particular. In order to investigate rather than subordinate such questions, I queer the binary distinctions of public/private, political/personal, and civic/romantic.

In doing so, my historiography unsettles a close and enduring relationship between Western rhetoric and citizen education. The history of rhetoric may be understood, according to Arthur Walzer, "as a twenty-four-hundred-year reflection on citizen education" ("Teaching 'Political Wisdom'" 113).[3] In keeping with this history, the predominant concept of rhetorical education is that it prepares people for civic engagement, for active participation in the public discourse of political life (Atwill; Denman; Glenn; Hauser; Poulakis and Depew; Walker). As Karma R. Chávez's reflections on the intellectual history of rhetoric underscore, this concept of rhetorical education is tied to "our field's long standing investment in the normative formation of citizenship" ("Beyond Inclusion" 163). Operating in keeping with such an investment, "we issue a normative claim about what rhetoric does": it "educates the citizenry and helps citizens promote their interests" (164).

Usually traced back to the classical Greek and Roman rhetorical theory of Isocrates and Cicero, this interest in civic instruction has been revived within histories of rhetorical education in the nineteenth-century United States. On the one hand, early histories of college-level instruction characterize the period by a shift away from the classical model of education. This shift involved downplaying public, political oratory and emphasizing private, individualistic modes of writing instead (Brereton; Connors, *Composition;* Halloran and Clark; Kitzhaber). On the other hand, more recent histories by Jessica Enoch, David Gold, Susan Kates, and Shirley Wilson Logan consider instruction at a wider range of pedagogical sites, both institutional and extracurricular.[4] These historians show instead that, over the course of the century and especially after the Civil War, increasingly diverse groups of people did teach and learn spoken as well as written rhetoric in order to bring about social and political change. Such differing accounts of nineteenth-century rhetorical education productively point to its complexity, to an ongoing need to reexamine both what may constitute a site of rhetorical education and what its pedagogical purposes may be. Still, as much as historiographic practices have been reexamined in order to consider new pedagogical sites, civic engagement remains *the* framing term for investigations of rhetorical education.

An unfortunate effect of this long-term coupling of rhetorical education and civic engagement is the methodological marginalization of questions about other potential pedagogical purposes, especially those concerned with romantic and sexual life. Certainly historical discourses of sexuality have been examined by a number of queer rhetorics scholars including not only Morris but also Jonathan Alexander and Jacqueline Rhodes, Jean Bessette, Thomas R. Dunn, Morris and

K. J. Rawson, Lester C. Olson, Eric Darnell Pritchard, Erin J. Rand, and Rawson. Other scholars such as Alexander, Zan Meyer Gonçalves, Karen Kopelson, Harriet Malinowitz, Rhodes, and Stacey Waite have explored present-day queer pedagogies.[5] But there has been no history of sexuality *and* rhetorical pedagogy (no queer history of rhetorical education) focused on the nineteenth-century United States. Indeed, this historiographic effect within the fields of rhetoric, communication, and composition mirrors the function of normative distinctions with respect to maintaining heteronormativity in the culture at large.

Addressing this problem, queer and feminist theorists show how operating according to normative distinctions oversimplifies the relationships between so-called public and private life. In fact, what gets deemed private holds political implications for the culture of a nation. As Lauren Berlant and Michael Warner proclaimed, "there is nothing more public than privacy" (547).[6] The concept of privacy is itself public with respect to sexuality, and the figuring of sexuality as private is a political move with widespread significance for civic life at community and national levels. Crucial to heteronormativity in the United States, for instance, is how the presumptive distinction between private and public has been used to simultaneously obscure the relevance of sexuality to the nation and, at the same time, afford basic rights and responsibilities of citizenship on the basis of accordance with romantic and sexual norms (for example the public performance of legally sanctioned, monogamous and, until recently, opposite-sex marriage).[7] Where this sexualization of the nation is cloaked as private, questions of sexuality are deemed irrelevant to citizenship, to a national public, and to matters political, and yet so-called private romantic relations are mediated by public norms, political decisions, and laws.[8]

Alongside greater acknowledgment of the relations between sexuality and nation, however, there is a need to recognize that what is of public and political significance is by no means limited to that which can be linked to questions of nation or citizenship. This need is especially exigent in the field of rhetorical studies where, as Chávez has pointed out, the entwining of rhetoric with citizenship "is so ubiquitous as to be taken for granted" ("Beyond Inclusion" 163).[9] In keeping with this ubiquity, national citizenship functions as a normative frame for engagement, such that rhetorical practices become defined, whether explicitly or implicitly, as practices of civic engagement. Countering this normative frame requires not simply that rhetoric become "more inclusive"—in this case, including queer rhetorical practices within histories of rhetorical education for civic engagement—but that "we imagine alternatives to the citizenship discourses that [have] oriented our discipline's history" (163)—that we imagine, in other words, alternate histories of rhetorical education that envision relations between intimate and political life without being oriented primarily or exclusively to citizenship. It is possible to realize the political, public, and even civic implications of romantic life while understanding these terms as pointing to the power dynamics of not just national but collective life.

In order to attend to both romantic and civic life, my queer history advances a new concept of rhetorical education as serving a broader range of pedagogical purposes that involve not only civic engagement but also what I call "romantic engagement." I define rhetorical education for romantic engagement as *the teaching and learning of language practices for composing romantic relations*. Within this definition, the term "composing" is used in a dual sense: people learn how to compose with language in order to participate in romantic relations, and this rhetorical practice simultaneously composes the romantic relations themselves. In this way, instruction and practice are rhetorically constitutive of romantic relations and even subjects.[10] Moreover, while this concept of rhetorical education emphasizes romantic life, it does so with the understanding that the pedagogical shaping of romantic subjects is indeed a profoundly public process imbricated in civic life.[11]

Of course, the shaping of subjects through pedagogy is already a primary concern animating histories of rhetorical education for civic engagement. As Jeffrey Walker argued, rhetoric may be understood "as a pedagogical tradition," "an art of producing rhetors" (3, 223). In Walzer's terms, "Historically rhetoric is a *complete* art for shaping students" ("Rhetoric" 124, my emphasis). Rhetorical education is a process of "acculturation," in that instruction shapes "historically appropriate" citizen subjects (124); this "inevitable" acculturation both "limits" and "liberates" (132). In the words of Cheryl Glenn, "rhetorical education enables people to engage in and change American society—but not always" (viii). I share with Glenn and Walzer an interest in this dynamic tension within education that is culturally limiting but potentially liberating. Taking Walzer's remarks further, toward a more complete understanding of the complete art, I consider how rhetorical education for romantic engagement acculturates where its instruction is heteronormative and liberates where it invites queer practices. I ask, how does instruction in language arts for participation in romantic relations shape historically appropriate, or heteronormative, romantic subjects? At the same time, how does it enable nonnormative, or queer, rhetorical practices and romantic relations?

Genres for Romantic Epistolary Rhetoric

The centerpiece for my investigation of these questions is the teaching and learning of romantic epistolary rhetoric. As readers might expect given this project's emphasis on romantic instruction and practices, I define "rhetoric" in terms more Burkean than classical, such that rhetorical practices are symbolic actions by humans to not only influence each other but also create identifications and compose relationships. I use the term "epistolary" as typically defined, to mean of or relating to the epistle, or letter. As such, I emphasize rhetorical practices in the form *of* the romantic letter genre, but I also attend to rhetorical practices in other genres that my archival research indicates were *related to* the romantic letter during the nineteenth century.

Heteronormative Genre Instruction and Queer Practices

In first focusing on education in romantic epistolary rhetoric that takes the form *of* the romantic letter, I treat rhetorical education for romantic engagement as an instance of genre instruction. Following rhetorical genre theorists, I conceive of genre as rhetorical and social action that emerges through repeated response to rhetorical situations that recur within broader cultural and historical contexts (Bakhtin; Bazerman; Devitt; C. Miller). As Carolyn Miller has theorized, this rhetorical and social action becomes "typified" through repetition, so that genres are "interpretable by means of conventions," and generic purpose is "conventionalized social purpose" rather than "private or idiosyncratic" (151, 158, 161–62). Thus rhetorical education teaches "not just a pattern of forms or even a method of achieving our own ends" but, "more importantly, what ends we may have" (165); it teaches "not just forms" but "forms of life, ways of being" (Bazerman 19).[12]

Through such rhetorical instruction, popular letter-writing manuals taught not only the genre or form of the romantic letter but also heteronormative ends and even ways of being. Following Berlant and Warner, I use the term "heteronormativity" to refer to processes of normalizing heterosexual romantic relations. This normalization of heterosexuality presumes that it is coherent as a sexuality and treats it as the privileged sexuality; it is characterized primarily by the commonsense understanding, however implicit, that this so-called heterosexuality is natural, that it is just plain right.[13] Instruction in romantic epistolary rhetoric was heteronormative because manuals modeled the conventions for gendered epistolary address in ways that naturalized exclusively opposite-sex relations between writers and readers.

However, there is more to heteronormativity than the naturalizing of opposite-sex relations, and heterosexuality is not synonymous with heteronormativity. Rather, particular forms of heterosexual coupling are normalized in accordance with historically and culturally specific notions of "propriety" with respect to relationship development (Berlant and Warner 548). Opposite-sex relations that are normative develop in keeping with what Jack Halberstam called "straight time"—a normative temporality for when and how people proceed from one stage of relationship and life to the next (*Queer Time*).[14] In a nineteenth-century version of "straight time," manuals taught heteronormative genre conventions for not only epistolary address but also letter pacing and rhetorical purpose. This genre instruction normalized opposite-sex relations that were characterized by the exercise of restraint, with letter writers moving slowly and carefully from the courtship stage to engagement as directed by a marriage *telos*.

While manual instruction in the romantic-letter genre was predominantly heteronormative, this same instruction was also subject to nonnormative practices. Even as genres are normative, they are also "changeable, flexible, and plastic" (Bakhtin 80). Learners are not entirely constrained by genre conventions, as they "may . . . combine different genres or may 'violate' the norms of an existing genre" (Devitt 579–80). In keeping with this understanding of generic flexibility, my analysis of manual pedagogy identifies the subtle ways that instruction in genre conventions was predisposed to nonnormative violations, challenges, and adaptations with what Kate Thomas has called "queer effect" (37). I use the phrase to refer to the potential effects of genre instruction that subvert the very conventions emphasized by that instruction. In the case of letter-writing manuals, they taught conventions with "queer effect" in that their instruction in invention strategies for copying and adapting model letters made the genre susceptible to gender-crossing address, unrestrained outbreaks, and queer repurposing. In this sense, even as manual pedagogy taught heteronormative conventions, its queer effects reflected what Halberstam theorizes as "the queer art of failure." The predominantly heteronormative pedagogy failed insofar as learners developed rhetorical practices to artfully "resist mastery" and instead accomplish queer ends (*Queer Art* 11).

Whereas my analysis of letter-writing manuals anticipates the potential for queer effects and failures, my research on romantic epistolary rhetoric identifies actual queer practices by learners Addie Brown and Rebecca Primus. As is often the case, only Brown's half of the romantic correspondence with Primus is extant, so the main primary materials I examine are Brown's letters to Primus, along with notations that Primus made on the envelopes. It is crucial to clarify that my research does not "recover" Brown and Primus as LGBTQ-identified rhetors; nor do I ascribe any sexual identities to them. Informed by queer theory, queer historiography, and queer rhetorics scholarship, I understand Brown and Primus's romantic epistolary exchange and relations as "queer" not in keeping with present-day categories of sexual *identity*—such as bisexual, lesbian, or heterosexual—which are generally understood as having emerged after the period under study. Rather, I use the term "queer" in reference to nonnormative or unconventional *practices* (Alexander and Rhodes, "Queer Rhetoric").[15] Instead of framing Brown and Primus as queer women, I characterize their romantic epistolary practices as queer insofar as they subverted the genre conventions and cultural norms taught by nineteenth-century letter-writing manuals. In teaching genre conventions for romantic epistolary address, for instance, manuals embedded a culturally normative conception of romantic relations as between a man and woman. By addressing romantic epistolary rhetoric to each other, Brown and Primus obviously defied the genre conventions taught, but their queer rhetorical practices do not make them queer-identified. As in this example, what I mainly define as queer are *relational and rhetorical practices that were nonnormative within the context of nineteenth-century manual instruction in cultural norms and genre conventions.*

Moving forward with this first definition of queer practices, I also want to clarify that I do not use "queer" as an interchangeable term for "same-sex." Although what makes Brown and Primus's practices queer includes their composing of same-sex romantic epistolary address, their practices were nonnormative in still other ways that were not limited to writers in exclusively same-sex relations. Again, manuals not only taught norms and conventions for opposite-sex epistolary address but also instructed that normative letters proceeded slowly and cautiously from courtship to proposal to marriage. Any letter writers, regardless of sex or gender, could participate in the queer rhetorical practice of composing nonnormative epistolary rhetoric that was rushed, uncoupled, or not in pursuit of a marriage *telos*. I highlight exactly these kinds of "queer effect"—that is, the ways manual instruction offered at least some resources for rhetors who resisted mastery of the widely taught genre conventions in order to compose nonnormative romantic relations, whether same-sex or not. As I acknowledge that all queer practices are not same-sex practices, I understand that doing so may raise concerns for readers. Some readers are likely hesitant about uses of the term "queer" that, in seeming to stray too far from same-sex romantic and sexual life, become emptied of significance. I share similar concerns. Therefore, even as I characterize a broader cultural context that included a range of potentially queer practices, my research focuses largely on rhetors who did participate in same-sex relations.

Epistolary Address, Exchange, and Genre-Queer Practices

This distinction between "same-sex" and "queer" is key to the secondary definition of queer rhetorical practices that operates in my analysis of college student Albert Dodd's epistolary rhetoric. Unfortunately, none of Dodd's romantic letters are extant. But in his commonplace book turned diary, he wrote about his romantic epistolary exchanges with other men and women. In addition, within his poetry album, he addressed epistolary rhetoric to his romantic interests. In terms of the first definition of queer that I offered earlier, Dodd's rhetorical practices were queer insofar as he defied the cultural norms and genre conventions taught by nineteenth-century letter-writing manuals. For instance, Dodd's diary writing about his romantic epistolary rhetoric suggests that he queerly defied conventions by exchanging romantic letters with other men, as well as writing romantic letters to both men and women that did not pursue marriage. But there is a second way Dodd's practices were queer: he composed his romantic relations by transgressing not only normative boundaries of gender and sexuality but also conventional boundaries of genre. Dodd's rhetorical practices crossed generic boundaries between the commonplace book and diary, between the diary and diary writing about romantic epistolary address, and between romantic address in letters, poetry, and epistle verse. Such practices were what Dodd himself termed "odd" and "queer," even where he addressed women (Apr. 1836).

Along with Dodd's own characterization, I engage with theories of epistolary address, epistolary exchange, and genre-queer writing in order to account for how his rhetoric was both epistolary and queer. In analyzing Dodd's practices within a broad network of other genres related to the letter, I am informed by Suzanne B. Spring's notion of "epistolary logic" ("'Seemingly Uncouth Forms'" 638). Spring has described early-nineteenth-century student writing that resembled features of the letter genre even when it did not take the form of a letter. She characterized these "complex generic hybrids" as operating according to an "epistolary logic" insofar as "address and exchange are central aspects" (633, 638). I understand Dodd's rhetoric across generic boundaries as operating according to this logic: as taking the form of multiple genres other than the letter, yet framed by address to and exchange with the romantic interests who were his audiences.[16]

I also understand Dodd's romantic epistolary rhetoric across a network of genres related to the letter as "genre-queer." Scholarship on genre and queerness, much like that on gender and queerness, takes interest in practices that transgress normative categories and the reductive binaries and boundaries often associated with those categories.[17] Along these lines, Kazim Ali has refashioned the term "gender-queer" to theorize "genre-queer" texts. Genre-queer texts are those "whose genre is unto themselves, whose whole texts live with bodies ungenred as genderqueer bodies, take their own gender unto themselves, neither accepting one category or another" (36).[18] However, "cross-genre" or "mixed-genre" texts are not necessarily genre-queer: "even to move from one form of writing to another is not transgressive in the purest sense—you are still stuck in a sense of separation between genres, as in gender binaries" (36). I characterize Dodd's multigenre romantic epistolary rhetoric as genre-queer because he did not simply move from one genre to another but did so with a critical awareness that refused to pin down generic separations. My second definition of queer refers, then, to *rhetorical practices that were unconventional in their transgressions of generic boundaries while pursuing nonnormative romantic relations.*

In this second definition of queer, the reference to pursuing nonnormative romantic relations is central. While my approach to queerness is expansive, I do not go so far as to argue that any generically unconventional rhetorical practice is queer.[19] Again, my archival research intentionally focuses on primary materials composed by people who participated in nonnormative romantic relations that included but were not limited to same-sex relations. What Dodd, Brown, and Primus have in common across their different kinds of queer rhetorical practice is that they composed within cultural contexts and rhetorical situations that rendered their romantic relations nonnormative and called for unconventional uses of the genres available.

Romantic Letters as Epistolary Rhetoric

This project's focus on romantic epistolary rhetoric not only challenges predominant conceptions of rhetorical education but also complicates commonplace understandings of the romantic letter. As Carol Poster has explained, letters are often and inaccurately assumed to be "products of unconstrained personal creativity resulting from an untutored and spontaneous overflowing of language or emotion" ("Introduction" 1). Romantic letters in particular are presumed to be natural and unstudied expressions of heartfelt love. Perhaps because of this presumption, even historians of rhetoric, communication, and composition who study letter-writing instruction have yet to explore how it shaped specifically romantic letters, relations, and subjects in the nineteenth-century United States.[20] In turning attention to the romantic subgenre, I understand the so-called language of the heart not simply as an unstudied and natural expression of feeling but as a rhetorically taught, learned, and crafted practice (*Fashionable American Letter Writer* iii).

That romantic letters are more often understood as unstudied is evident throughout histories of romantic and intimate life. Many of these histories draw on romantic letters as primary sources but downplay or even ignore how instruction through manuals may have influenced letter-writing practices. Karen Lystra's history of nineteenth-century romantic love is an especially suggestive instance, because she *has* raised the "obvious question" about the "availability of model love letters in letter-writers and etiquette manuals" and "the originality and reliability of love letters as scholarly sources" (13). Lystra asked, "How much did native-born middle-class [opposite-sex] correspondents rely upon standardized book copy?" But she answered, "probably very little" (13–14). Certainly there were letter writers who relied "very little" on "the standardized book copy" of model romantic letters in manuals. Indeed, in Brown, Primus, and Dodd's extant writing, there is no evidence they consulted letter-writing manuals. But they did learn romantic epistolary rhetoric through their study of other kinds of texts; even those writers who did not copy their romantic letters from manual models were still, in one way or another, learners. Moreover, the widespread publication and popularity of manuals offering instruction in romantic-letter writing indicates it was taught. Romantic letters were far from unstudied, in other words. They were taught and learned through the rhetorical education for romantic engagement of manuals as well as other means.

These romantic letters were not natural expressions of feeling and affection but rhetorically crafted writing. That romantic letters are more commonly treated as natural expressions is also evident throughout popular as well as scholarly histories of intimate life. Of course historians rely fundamentally on letters (and diaries) as evidence of past romantic relations. As explained by Lystra, letters "provide as genuine a record as possible of feelings, behaviors, and judgments as they occurred in romantic relations" (4–5). The idea that letters offer "genuine" records may be especially seductive for historians of sexuality who study those relations met with denial or outright hostility within both their contemporary moment and later historiographic and archival practices. As Patrick Paul Garlinger has maintained, "The association of letter writing with intimate secrets and sexuality has motivated . . . critics to investigate *authentic* letter correspondence for *evidence* of homoerotic and homosexual relationships" (ix, my emphasis).[21] Such investigation becomes misdirected, however, when Lystra's "as genuine as possible" becomes, simply, "genuine"—when letters are approached as "authentic . . . evidence" of romantic feeling, desire, and even sexual identity within a given period—when letters are read as mere transcriptions that transparently reflect feelings and relations from the past.[22]

I instead read romantic letters as epistolary rhetoric that, however heartfelt, was crafted. There are precedents for understanding romantic communication as rhetorical. Kenneth Burke, in expanding rhetoric to include not only persuasion but also identification, conceived of the "rhetoric of courtship" as a form of identification (208–09). He defined the rhetoric of courtship as "the use of suasive devices for the transcending of social estrangement" (208). Burke was interested in forms of courtship both literal and metaphoric, both romantic and social.[23] I join Burke in understanding romantic communication as a form of rhetoric, one with intimate as well as social dimensions.

But I also want to emphasize: to assert that romantic letters are rhetorically crafted is not to suggest they are necessarily crafted in inauthentic ways. This point matters because of rhetoric's other connection to courtship—because of how rhetoric itself gets dismissed precisely for its association with seduction. This dismissal can be traced to Plato, for whom the differences between dialectic and rhetoric were analogous to those between a search for true love and a deceptive craft of flattery and seduction. Plato's association of rhetoric with seduction has been accepted, rejected, and celebrated by scholars across the humanities.[24] In Catherine Bates's history of the rhetoric of courtship in Elizabethan language and literature, for instance, rhetoric by definition consists of "flattering, dissembling, deceitful, and tactical discursive strategies" (9).[25] But manuals from the nineteenth-century United States actually defined the language of the heart against the potential for romantic letters to be used toward dangerously seductive ends (Halttunen; Hewitt; Zaczek). Moreover, as in the story of Eliza's love letters, warnings about the dangers of deceptive letters circulated not only in manuals but throughout the culture. While I insist that romantic letters were rhetorically crafted, then, I am not implying they were deceptively seductive (though they certainly could be).²⁶ Instead, manuals represented romantic epistolary rhetoric as a crafted practice that, while not necessarily coming naturally, could be learned.

This book thus alternates between considering how language practices for romantic engagement were taught and learned through rhetorical *instruction* and how they were crafted through rhetorical *practice*.²⁷ Whereas my analysis of letter-writing manuals focuses on instruction in the romantic letter genre, I also anticipate potential uses of this instruction by learners participating in queer romantic relations. And, whereas my archival research on Addie Brown, Rebecca Primus, and Albert Dodd examines their rhetorical practices, I focus on them as learners. Romantic letter writing is approached as epistolary rhetoric—as a crafted rhetorical practice that is taught and learned through rhetorical education for romantic engagement.²⁸

Education, Gender, and Sexuality in the Postal Age

My studies of romantic epistolary rhetoric by Brown and Primus (1859–68) and Dodd (1836–38) locate this history across the mid-nineteenth century, but in a baggy sense that includes the period before, during, and after the Civil War (elsewhere termed "Victorian America"). So, although I examine manuals spanning the nineteenth century (1807–97), I focus primarily on books printed between the 1830s and the 1870s. The midcentury is rich for my study of rhetorical education for romantic engagement because, in addition to being a time of profound national change, the period is significant as what David Henkin termed "the postal age" in his book by the same name. This period is marked by a democratization of the post, as the ability to send and receive letters through the mail became more accessible. Already the national postal service had expanded with the Post Office Act of 1792. But infrastructure was improved in the 1820s and 1830s, and, with the Postal Acts of 1845 and 1851, the post came into "popular" use by "a critical mass of Americans" (Henkin 3, 9).²⁹ While practices of sending and receiving letters became available to those who previously could not afford postage, such practices were also facilitated by a broader democratization of literacy through common schools (Decker 11). Situated across the postal age, my book considers rhetorical education and practice at a time when both postal services and literacy instruction became more widely available in the United States, particularly in the New England region. In fact, the extensive correspondence written and mailed by Brown, an African American woman employed as a domestic, probably could not have existed prior to the postal age. Letter-writing manuals also became more affordable because they were often purchased via the mail. In addition, there were other important shifts during the postal age with respect to education, gender, and sexuality.

Letter-Writing Instruction during Rhetoric's Period of Decline

Historians of rhetoric generally understand the postal age as a period of decline for college-level instruction in service of civic engagement. While much of my research examines "extracurricular" teaching and learning, this narrative of decline is important because of how letter-writing instruction has been implicated in it. At the onset of the century, college-level rhetorical education remained classically oriented to the public discourse of political life. Facilitated by broader shifts in higher education, however, this form of instruction declined during the second half of the century. With colleges and universities increasingly emphasizing specialization, disciplinarity, and research, rhetoric was demoted from its central place in the curriculum. The emphasis on oral delivery dwindled as the importance of print culture grew; the writing assignments that gradually replaced recitations and exhibitions were more individualized, less concerned with overtly political questions, and less likely to be addressed to audiences beyond tutors, teachers, and classmates.[30]

In part, it is this increasing emphasis on written as opposed to oral rhetoric that implicates epistolary instruction in the decline of rhetorical education. Epistolary rhetoric for business and personal (but not romantic) purposes was a standard subject of study in college-level rhetorical education. It was covered in rhetorical treatises and, later in the century, in composition textbooks. On the one hand, this inclusion of letter writing within rhetorical education was merely a continuation of the classical tradition of epistolary rhetoric, from Cicero's letters to the medieval *ars dictaminis* to Hugh Blair's *Lectures on Rhetoric and Belles Lettres*.[31] On the other hand, letter writing's ubiquity within college-level education was a particularly nineteenth-century function of the rise in writing instruction. For example, Albert Kitzhaber characterized the decline of rhetorical education as marked by "the appearance of specific instructions in [textbooks] for the writing of such things as letters" (207–08). John Brereton, in describing the late nineteenth-century shift away from publicly delivered speeches to relatively private writing, cited as an example "such mundane subjects as letters," asserting that the "amount of space that texts, particularly handbooks, devoted to letter writing . . . indicated the presence of a new type of student" (438).

As this reference to "a new type of student" suggests, epistolary instruction has also been associated with the decline of rhetoric in terms of increasing enrollments of students who did not previously have access to higher education. More men as well as women gained access to institutions of higher education.[32] The types of individualized attention and occasions for public speaking that had characterized rhetorical education for civic engagement at elite institutions earlier in the century became practically impossible, because each tutor or professor was responsible for a greater number of students. Amid these shifts, letter writing was "considered an appropriate educational practice as education aimed to reach a broader segment of society" (Gage 202).[33] Epistolary instruction played a role, in other words, in the broader project of democratic education, of teaching increasingly diverse groups of people to be rhetorically active through letter writing for business and personal life.

Given the simultaneous democratization of higher education and the decline of rhetorical education for civic engagement, the mid-nineteenth century is an ideal period for investigating rhetorical education for romantic engagement in its complexity. But my project does not merely confirm existing historical narratives of democratization or decline. I do not develop another linear argument consisting of claims about changes over the course of the period, for instance by associating a decline in oratorical instruction and civic engagement with a rise in letter-writing instruction and romantic engagement. Instead, I examine multiple instances of instruction and practice, including both the letter-writing manuals that reached people without access to higher education and the classically modeled rhetorical education of institutions such as Washington College and Yale, where Albert Dodd studied. This approach allows me to flesh out a textured understanding of how diverse people learned and practiced romantic epistolary rhetoric, even before the late-century peak of the shift away from rhetorical education for civic engagement.

Gender, Letters, and Nineteenth-Century Women's Rhetoric

The postal age is also noteworthy as a period in which the letter was often associated with women's rhetoric. Books and periodicals made direct claims about letter writing being a woman's "positive duty," "especially feminine," and the "one species of writing which seems to belong appropriately to the lady" (Mahoney 411, 415). These claims took on real significance because of the restrictions nineteenth-century women faced as rhetors. Even with education and literacy increasingly democratized, women's access to college-level rhetorical training was limited, as were traditional opportunities for public speaking via the pulpit, bar, and assembly. Within this context of limitations, epistolary rhetoric was understood as a genre through which it was suitable for women to address at least some audiences. Letter-writing instruction via home manuals was vital, therefore, to women's rhetoric.

Not surprisingly, then, epistolary instruction has been widely studied by feminist rhetoricians, who explore how it constrained (white middle- and upper-class) women's rhetorical participation, limiting it to a private, domestic sphere. As Jane Donawerth has explained, letter writing, conversation, and reading aloud— but not speeches and essays—were the forms of rhetorical practice culturally sanctioned as appropriate for women ("Nineteenth-Century United States" 16).[34] Nan Johnson's analysis of letter-writing manuals shows how subgenres of letters were gendered: while both women and men were taught to write familiar and romantic letters, women were not taught to write letters with "agency in arenas of public or professional opinion" (*Gender and Rhetorical Space* 81). Other scholars have considered how epistolary instruction enabled women's rhetoric, providing a training ground for entry into public discourse (Gring-Pemble; Mahoney; Spring "Meditation"). Even as letter-writing manuals instantiated those constraints limiting nineteenth-century women's rhetoric, some women were able to use the epistolary genre to advance political positions precisely because of the presumption that letters were relatively personal or private and thus suitable forms of expression for women.

While the letter is often associated with women's rhetoric, men were also trained to compose epistolary rhetoric. In fact, as Mary Favret has argued, it is a "fiction" of nineteenth-century letters that they are feminine (as well as private and romantic).[35] So, whereas studies of nineteenth-century epistolary rhetoric tend to focus on women like the character Eliza, whose story I opened with, my history intentionally includes rhetors like Horace. In analyzing manuals, I consider how both women and men were taught the cultural norms and genre conventions for romantic epistolary rhetoric. And, as will be clear in my analysis of Albert Dodd's romantic epistolary rhetoric, he took an avid interest in romantic letter writing and other genre-queer epistolary practices. In these ways, my archival research on romantic engagement during the postal age challenges long-standing associations between women and letters—between women and romantic letters in particular—while turning to questions of sexuality.

Same-Sex Romantic Friendships before Sexual Identity Categories

The nineteenth century was marked by significant changes in the organization of same-sex romantic relationships, particularly late in the century. Following Michel Foucault's *The History of Sexuality*, it is generally understood that categories of sexual identity, such as "homosexual," emerged in the West with the rise of sexological discourse during the late nineteenth and early twentieth centuries.[36] This dominant historiographic account of the emergence of sexual identity categories has been complicated, because it overemphasizes simple models of historical succession and ignores the significance of racial categories.[37] What remains powerful, however, is the distinction between present-day understandings of sexuality as a category of identity (what people are) and earlier practices (what people did). Again, it is in keeping with this distinction that my research explores queer epistolary practices rather than "homosexual," gay, lesbian, bisexual, or queer identities.

While I do not approach midcentury same-sex romantic relations as suggestive of a particular sexual identity, they have been characterized as consisting of historically specific relational practices, namely those of "romantic friendship." Historians widely debate the features of these so-called romantic friendships. Especially in their early scholarship on romantic friendships between women, Lillian Faderman and Carol Smith-Rosenberg argued that, prior to the late nineteenth-century invention of sexual identity, romantic friendships were socially acceptable and nonsexual. While this early conception of same-sex romantic friendship continues to be cited, it too has been widely challenged.[38] Complicating accounts in which the early and mid-nineteenth century was described as "a 'golden age' of romantic friendship," scholars have described instead "a period of contentious struggle," during which same-sex relations were pathologized even before late in the century (Diggs 321). These scholars have also argued that it is a mistake to presume all same-sex relations during the period were necessarily nonsexual.[39]

Of particular interest to my queer history of romantic epistolary rhetoric, disagreement about whether same-sex romantic friendships were sexual usually turns on how diaries and especially letters are interpreted.[40] As Marylynn Diggs has pointed out, where Faderman argued that women probably did not act on their love through sex, she "cites as evidence the dearth of explicit references to sex between women in correspondence or diaries, ignoring the similar lack of such discussions of heterosexual sex" (337 n. 2).[41] Indeed, histories of heterosexual or opposite-sex relations also grapple with questions about how to interpret the romantic affections expressed in nineteenth-century letters, about how to extrapolate information about erotic and sexual behavior from the highly sentimental and often cloaked language of the period.[42] Nor are such questions irrelevant in histories focused on same-sex relations and romantic letters between men. Morris's work on the friendship between Abraham Lincoln and Joshua Speed makes clear, for instance, that debates about how to understand their relationship center around the available letters between the men, around how the sentiments expressed in those letters are interpreted and whether they are read as suggestive of physical contact and orgasm ("My Old Kentucky Homo").

Similar questions arise about the nature of the romantic relations between Addie Brown and Rebecca Primus and between Albert Dodd and other men. I acknowledge such questions where relevant. But my goal is not to read Brown, Primus, and Dodd's epistolary rhetoric in search of evidence that proves the nature of their romantic, erotic, or sexual relations. Rather, I focus on what their writing suggests regarding their rhetorical education and practices for romantic engagement—what the writing suggests, in other words, about how they learned to use romantic epistolary rhetoric to compose their queer relations.

Expanding Histories of Rhetorical Education for Civic and Romantic Engagement

As my queer history of epistolary instruction and practice moves from the story of Eliza's love letters to letter-writing manuals, from Addie Brown and Rebecca Primus's correspondence to Albert Dodd's genre-queer epistolary rhetoric, I expand on histories of rhetorical education by considering not only civic but also romantic engagement. Methodologically queering binary distinctions between public and private life, my archival research turns historiographic attention to romantic engagement while exploring its civic implications within instruction and practice.

Letter-writing manuals treated the romantic subgenre of epistolary rhetoric as apart from civic life. However, insofar as these manuals were widely circulating books, romantic epistolary instruction was a public concern. The public instruction through manuals, by teaching what was considered appropriate within the culture at large, shaped not only romantic letters but also romantic relations and even citizen subjects. In contrast with this popular extracurricular instruction, Albert Dodd's formal rhetorical training at Washington College and at Yale was classically oriented. His position as an upper-class white man meant he had full access to rights of citizenship as well as those forms of public speaking and political participation imagined by a classically modeled rhetorical education. While this education prepared him for an expected career in law and politics, Dodd also transferred what he learned as a college student to develop genre-queer practices for composing romantic relations. Unlike Dodd, Brown and Primus were not granted full rights of citizenship in basic ways: as African Americans and as women, they were legally barred from voting; as women, they were denied many other rights unless secured through marriage to men. But, even in the face of limits on their full civic participation, these women repurposed the romantic letter genre to explicitly political ends. In the same letters that composed the women's romantic relationship, they commented on political figures, electoral politics, voting rights, and especially racial politics.

This expanded view of rhetorical education for romantic and civic engagement positions scholars of rhetoric not only to queer our own histories but to contribute to interdisciplinary histories of sexuality. In understanding the romantic letter as epistolary rhetoric—as a genre rhetorically learned and crafted in relation to other genres—we may nuance approaches to reading romantic letters and other intimate texts as evidence of romantic friendships, erotic practices, and sexual identities from the past. Nor is this question of how romantic life gets composed via rhetorical practice and education limited to the postal age. Diverse groups of learners—including those who take and teach undergraduate and graduate courses in rhetoric, communication, and composition—continue to shape and be shaped by public and politically weighted pedagogies that instruct us in multimodal and digital technologies for composing our romantic, erotic, and sexual selves and interactions. Ultimately, *Queering Romantic Engagement in the Postal Age: A Rhetorical Education* demonstrates how such pedagogies have long played a culturally significant role in inventing both civic and romantic life.

Chapter 1

"The language of the heart"

Genre Instruction in Heteronormative Relations

> Had letters been known at the beginning of the world, epistolary writing would have been as old as love and friendship; for, as soon as they began to flourish, the verbal messenger was dropped, the language of the heart was committed to characters that faithfully preserved it, secresy was maintained, and social intercourse rendered more free and pleasant.
>
> *The Fashionable American Letter Writer* (1832)

Nineteenth-century people seeking to learn romantic epistolary rhetoric could consult a wide range of texts. They could learn from periodical articles, such as the already discussed *Godey's Lady's Book* piece about Eliza's love letters (Leslie, "Part the First," "Part the Second").[1] People could learn from literary texts that represented epistolary exchange, including not only epistolary novels but also sentimental literature and slave narratives.[2] Also available to learners were models of epistolary rhetoric in the published letters of literary and political figures, as well as the more ordinary letters read aloud and shared within familial circles.[3] While less explicitly pedagogical than letter-writing manuals, all of these texts offered lessons about the potential relational consequences of composing letters. Moreover, in terms of overtly pedagogical texts, single chapters about epistolary rhetoric were included within instructional manuals of different types: rhetoric and composition textbooks assigned in schools and colleges, as well as universal instructor manuals and conduct and etiquette guides designed for home use.[4]

But the most extensive instruction in specifically *romantic* epistolary rhetoric was provided through popular manuals that focused entirely on letter writing. Often called "complete letter writers," these manuals devoted entire chapters to the romantic subgenre, or what *The Fashionable American Letter Writer* (1832) calls "the language of the heart" (iii). While complete letter writers constitute just one strand of a rich epistolary culture ripe with opportunities for learning romantic epistolary practices, my archival research focuses on these manuals because of their popularity. Widely available and intended for home use, the manuals amounted to what Anne Ruggles Gere has termed an "extracurriculum" of rhetorical instruction, which "extends beyond the academy to encompass the multiple contexts in which persons seek to improve their own writing; it includes more diversity in gender, race, and class among writers" (80).[5] Popular letter-writing manuals reached more diverse audiences of adult learners, including those with little access to schooling and especially to formal college-level training in rhetoric, than did college and university textbooks.

After further introducing the features of complete letter writers as sites of rhetorical education for romantic engagement, my analysis asks how these manuals taught language practices for composing romantic epistolary rhetoric and, by extension, cultural norms for participating in romantic relations. While manuals advised simply writing "from the heart," they extensively modeled the genre conventions constraining such composition. In modeling conventions for the romantic subgenre of the letter, manuals embedded a heteronormative conception of romantic relations. At the same time, however, manual instruction emphasized rhetorical strategies of invention through copying and adaptation, which rendered the same model letters susceptible to more queer effects and failures.

Complete Letter Writers

Letter-writing manuals in the nineteenth-century United States continued a long rhetorical tradition, detailed in Carol Poster and Linda C. Mitchell's *Letter-Writing Manuals and Instruction from Antiquity to the Present*. In the West this rhetorical tradition may be traced from Cicero to the medieval *ars dictaminis*, from Erasmus to seventeenth- and especially eighteenth-century British manuals.[6] Two features of the tradition were carried forward in nineteenth-century manuals with significant implications for their instruction in romantic epistolary rhetoric. First and foremost, the letter continued to be defined in ways consistent across Western rhetorical history. Cicero defined the letter as "written conversation," Erasmus as "a conversation," and Blair as "conversation carried on upon paper."[7] Cicero's definition was rehearsed across late seventeenth- to early nineteenth-century British and U.S. manuals. Second, in keeping with this definition, manual instruction was marked by what Eve Tavor Bannet called a "paradox": between the commonplace, even clichéd, instruction to compose letters *simply* by writing as though one would speak to the audience and the existence of manuals offering elaborate recommendations and models teaching *how* to do so—not so simply after all, as the story of Eliza's love letters suggests when she wishes for such a manual (53, 276). As I discuss, this pedagogical paradox of letter-writing manuals and definition of the letter played out in particular ways within nineteenth-century instruction in the so-called language of the heart.

My analysis of such instruction is based on archival study of letter-writing manuals in the University of Pittsburgh's Nietz Collection. One of the largest of its kind, the Nietz Collection consists of about nineteen thousand textbooks from the United States, including nineteenth-century letter-writing manuals as well as etiquette guides with sections on letter writing. While I reference etiquette guides containing instructions consistent with popular letter-writing manuals, my analysis focuses on the latter.[8] I concentrate especially on the most popular type of extracurricular letter-writing manual, the "complete letter writer." Books with variations of the title *Complete Letter-Writer* have been republished countless times in the United States since at least 1790. These "complete letter writers," like their eighteenth-century English predecessors, were named for their inclusion of a wide range of model letters, often hundreds of them, and related claims to assist with every situation in which any person might write a letter (Bannet 22). In the words of Henry Loomis's manual *Practical Letter Writing* (1897), "*Complete letter-writers* are books giving model letters, so-called, on all subjects" (67). Whether or not a manual was titled *Complete Letter-Writer,* the book was understood as such if it attempted completeness through the provision of model letters.

The contents of complete letter writers were structured in keeping with their objective to provide models "on all subjects" (Loomis 67). *The Fashionable American Letter Writer* exemplifies the characteristic organization of manual contents. The manual begins with a "Preface" emphasizing the importance of epistolary rhetoric (iii–iv). Its "Introduction," while including instruction in principles of spelling, grammar, punctuation, handwriting, letter folding, and style, claims that the best way to study epistolary rhetoric is through "fair examples" and "specimens" that illustrate those principles (xiii–xx). Another section, "Directions for Letter-Writing, and Rules for Composition," actually says nothing of letter writing in particular but instead offers more general instruction in rhetorical principles and style (xxi–xxxii). Following these short initial sections, or chapters, the manual consists mainly of model letters. The models are divided into chapters titled "On Business," "On Relationship," "On Friendship," and "On Love, Courtship, and Marriage." The titles of the multiple models within these chapters are listed above each model as well as in the manual's table of contents. To varying degrees, the contents of most complete letter writers were organized similarly: manuals opened with a relatively brief introduction to principles of rhetoric and writing in general and/or epistolary rhetoric in particular. The rest of the manuals consisted primarily of model letters. These models were organized by subgenre and labeled with titles suggestive of variations within each subgenre, in terms of the specific rhetor, audience, and purpose.

The characteristic contents and organization of complete letter writers leave no question that their instruction in letter writing was a form of rhetorical education, even if distinct from formal college-level training. Manual instruction amounted to rhetorical education because it treated language and meaning as produced, understood, and negotiated in ways inseparable from rhetorical situations involving rhetor, audience, purpose, and the larger social context. As complete letter writers filled the majority of their pages with titled model letters, the features of rhetorical situations were marked over and over again, on page after page. In *The Fashionable American Letter Writer*, for instance, pages 39 to 179 present nothing but model letters. Sample titles for these models include "From a Tenant to a Landlord, excusing delay of Payment" (45), "From a young Woman, just gone to service in Boston, to her Mother in the country" (110), and "From a Gentleman to a young Lady of a superior fortune" (62). As such, readers could learn to become rhetorically minded as they found one example after another, for well over a hundred pages, of models that called attention to the audience being addressed in the salutation, the rhetorical purpose articulated in the initial lines of the letter, and the rhetor signing the letter.

While structured much like their English predecessors, "American" complete letter writers sought to distinguish their models as fitting for the rhetorical situations distinctive of "an enlightened and educated country like the United States" (Shields 15).[9] These manuals marked their model letters as not "English" but "American," not "savage" but "civilized." In one troubling but perhaps expected instance, *Frost's Original Letter-Writer* (1867) acknowledges the widespread practice of letter writing in "every country" but differentiates the practices of "the savage" from those "marked" by "the progress of civilization." *Frost's* even describes this "progress" through a narrative about the colonization of "the rough Western wilds" (Shields 14). The preface to *The Complete American Letter-Writer* (1807) insists that, because it is addressed to "this country" and what is "important in the life of a young American," its models "are not taken from the English books of forms" (iii). *The Complete Art of Polite Correspondence* (1857) claims that its "letters are all carefully adapted to the circumstances of our own country, and a considerable number are taken from approved American writers" (10).

In keeping with this emphasis on "American" letters, manuals also left no question that they modeled culturally specific social relations as much as epistolary rhetoric. Social markers listed in model letter titles explicitly called attention to the ways that rhetors and audiences were positioned by class, age, family, gender, education, and region (as well as race, in a few instances). Moreover, the organization of the models by subgenre emphasized what Carolyn Miller referred to as each subgenre's "recurrent situation" and, within that situation, "typified rhetorical action" and "conventionalized social purpose" (162). In short, complete letter writers modeled social conventions for who was to write what to whom, with what purposes, and within which situations. They offered, in the words of Elizabeth Hewitt, "a veritable how-to manual for depicting and enforcing appropriate social relations" in the nineteenth-century United States. (11).

Before turning to my focus on the heteronormative dimensions of these "appropriate social relations," I want to acknowledge how this epistolary instruction in gender and sexuality intersected with normative ideas about class and race. Class was central to the culturally approved romantic relations modeled by complete letter-writer manuals. Manuals marked class with model letter titles that distinguished between the epistolary rhetoric of a "servant," a "woman," and a "lady"—and between the epistolary rhetoric of a "tradesman," a "man," and a "gentleman."[10] These titles suggested the genre's potential, however limited, to enable romantic address across at least some class differences. *The Complete Letter Writer* (1811) includes a "Letter from a young Tradesman to a Gentleman, desiring Permission to visit his Daughter," and then a "Letter from the same to the young Lady, by permission of the Father," indicating that this particular cross-class romantic relation was culturally sanctioned through the patriarchal structure of the family. Other models instructed learners against participation in cross-class epistolary rhetoric. *The Fashionable American Letter Writer,* for instance, contains a letter "From a rich young gentleman to a beautiful young lady without a fortune," to which the lady responds, "You know that I have no fortune; and were I to accept your offer, it would lay me under such obligations as must destroy my liberty," concluding, "let me beg, that you will endeavor to eradicate a passion, which if nourished longer, may prove fatal to us both" (79–82). Through model exchanges like these, readers were taught what sorts of cross-class romantic relationships to pursue or avoid through romantic epistolary rhetoric.

Whereas complete letter writers marked class distinctions explicitly, racial categories were rarely noted. Instead, manuals taught romantic relations as racialized, though less obviously so, in the silent way that renders whiteness as an unremarkable norm. As Julian Carter wrote in his study of late nineteenth- and early twentieth-century sex advice manuals, "one of the hallmarks of . . . 'normal whiteness' . . . was the ability to construct and teach white racial meanings *without appearing to do so*" (2).[11] Given the relative absence of racial markers in most letter-writing manuals, it is likely that model letters were understood as written by and addressed to white people of various genders and classes but that whiteness was privileged to the point of being taken for granted, that "American" was taken to mean "white." This reading of unmarked race as whiteness is confirmed by the few mentions within guides of racial or ethnic markers other than "American." For example, *The Parlour Letter-Writer* mentions "the Irish laborer who . . . writes . . . to his kinsfolks across the wide ocean," as well as letters to and from an "English gentleman" (Turner xiii–xv, 116). *The Pocket Letter Writer* includes a model marking blackness—"From a colored laboring man to a gentleman, soliciting a situation for his son"—though this letter does not model romantic epistolary rhetoric (xviii). Thus it is highly probable that, with marked exceptions, manuals offered instruction in epistolary rhetoric designed for those presumed to be white "Americans."

Not surprisingly, given the ways complete letter writers modeled social relations, historians of rhetorical education as well as cultural historians have studied how manual instruction in epistolary rhetoric taught the cultural norms governing social relations. In the most developed line of inquiry, already discussed, feminist historians of rhetoric have explored questions about gender and genre. Jane Donawerth, Nan Johnson, and Deirdre M. Mahoney investigated whether and how instruction in the epistolary genre enabled or constrained women's rhetorical practices and participation in civic life. In other studies, Mary Anne Trasciatti explored how bilingual, bicultural manuals modeled U.S. norms for social and business life to Italian immigrants. Bannet examined how complete letter writers appealed to readers across class lines but inscribed differences between social classes. And Lucille M. Schultz studied how school-based textbooks inculcated children in dominant cultural norms for upper-middle-class morals and manners.

Even as scholars have considered this range of questions about how complete letter writers taught cultural norms for social relations, there has been no extended attention focused on instruction in the romantic subgenre.[12] Complete letter writers are ripe for an in-depth analysis of how they scripted model relations through their instruction in romantic epistolary rhetoric. Especially in separating sections on the romantic subgenre from the others, manuals modeled what was distinctive about the conventions for composing social relations through romantic letters. Analysis of this manual pedagogy is needed in order to more fully understand what Arthur Walzer characterized as rhetoric's "complete art for shaping students," because the "politically appropriate subjectivity" taught by rhetorical education includes the enactment of heteronormative romantic relations ("Rhetoric" 124).

Genre Conventions in Heteronormative Models

Rhetorical education through complete letter writers amounted to more than instruction in genre conventions; it functioned as instruction in model romantic relations. Manuals taught not just genre conventions for achieving one's "own" romantic ends but what romantic "ends [one] may have" (C. Miller 165). I argue that manuals taught heteronormative ends for romantic epistolary rhetoric. Instruction in genre conventions for epistolary address taught normatively gendered romantic coupling, instruction in conventions for the pacing of exchange taught normative restraint, and instruction in conventions for rhetorical purpose taught a normative marriage *telos*.[13] Importantly, however, manual instruction in the romantic letter reflected the broader paradox discussed earlier: in spite of extensive modeling in conventions for the romantic subgenre, manuals claimed that writing a romantic letter, like composing any other, was a matter of speaking on paper and, in the case of the romantic subgenre, doing so "from the heart."

Romantic Letters and Writing from the Heart

The most basic instruction for the romantic subgenre of epistolary rhetoric was to write "from the heart." In keeping with *The Fashionable American Letter Writer*'s designation "the language of the heart," complete letter-writer manuals taught learners to write romantic letters that sincerely conveyed their heartfelt feelings. For example, in model romantic letters from *The Natural Letter-Writer* (1813), "the language of [the] heart" is described as marked by "sincerity," particularly in terms of communicating "emotions of the heart" (Shepard 27–29, 55–57). *Frost's Original Letter-Writer* (1867) spells out the potential pedagogical implications of such characterizations of the language of the heart: "Love Letters written in sincerity and faith need but little guidance except from the heart of the writer. The true lover will find the words he seeks flow easily from his pen" (Shields 119). If one truly loves, in other words, he needs no rhetorical training, his letters no rhetorical crafting. The obvious paradox of this instruction is that, if composing romantic epistolary rhetoric relied so simply on feelings, if it required so "little guidance," then there would be no need for complete letter writers like *Frost's*, which went on to offer no fewer than thirty-seven model romantic letters. In spite of *The Natural Letter-Writer*'s title, its similar elaboration of model letters suggests that sincerely communicating from the heart was no simple or "natural" matter.

Models of the romantic subgenre were necessary, these same manuals taught, because of the twin threats of deceit and flattery. *The Natural Letter-Writer* further defines the language of the heart by contrasting its sincerity with "deceit and flattery." Because deceit and flattery are "used to betray the innocent," the manual continues, rhetors should not simply write from the heart or read letters as transparent windows into the writer's heart. Instead, writers need to learn how to rhetorically craft language in ways that will "prove the sincerity of [the] heart" so that readers will "have . . . reason to believe"; readers need to become rhetorically savvy in order to distinguish between "apparent sincerity" and "ample proof of . . . sincerity" (Shepard 27–29, 55–57).

Outright deception was the most obvious threat to sincerity. Manuals usually represented the risks of dishonesty about love as though men were more likely to deceive women than the other way around. This gendered representation was in keeping with the "rake" figure of epistolary novels and reflected broader cultural anxieties about men deceptively seducing women through letters.[14] Still, manuals advised both men and women to avoid dishonesty. *Letter-Writing Simplified*

(1844) instructs men that "the lover should promise nothing the husband would hesitate to perform . . . all promises should be carefully made, and always with strict regard to truth" (61). Women were instructed through a lengthy series of letters, titled "From a Father to his Daughters," which was widely reprinted in countless manuals. In this series, the father warns his daughters against both deceiving and being deceived: "I wish you to possess such high principles of honor and generosity as will render you incapable of deceiving, and at the same time to possess that acute discernment which may secure you against being deceived" (*Fashionable American Letter Writer* 84).[15]

As much a threat as deceit was its twin, flattery. Manuals taught that, because writing from the heart involves communicating feelings of affection, such communication can easily veer into the risky territory of flattery. *Letter-Writing Simplified* advises, "Extravagant flattery should, by all means be avoided" (61). *Frost's* goes further, claiming, "It is best to entirely avoid flattery in such letters" (Shields 119). One risk with flattery, according to *Frost's*, is it may undermine actual sincerity and proof of true feeling: "The fact that you love the person to whom [the letters] are addressed is a sufficient proof of your appreciation of any merit or beauty he or she may possess, and the praises of lovers are apt to become too warm to appear perfectly sincere" (119). Rhetors who sincerely felt love were taught to avoid flattery because, however sincere flattering romantic letters were, they may not "appear" as such.

In most cases, though, the risk manuals warned learners about was flattery combined with the intention to deceive. Here especially, men were admonished not to deceive through flattery, women to avoid being deceived by flattery. For example, while complete letter writers consisted primarily of model letters, *The Natural Letter Writer* includes a poem, "To Young Ladies," which warns women who "are . . . beset on every side" by "flattering men" to "believe them not, / The rake, the beau, the drunken sot, / Although they are flattering to your face, / They will leave you in disgrace" (70). Similarly, *Letter-Writing Simplified* prefaces its models by instructing women to guard against deception through flattery: "The sincerity of the writer is questioned when his language is exaggerated, and ridicule or disgust is excited toward him in the bosom of a woman of sense" (61). *The Art of Correspondence* (1884) affirms that sensible readers, even if deceived initially, will eventually see through mere flattery: "Hypocritical letters, abounding in overwrought expressions of love, may possibly, for a while, deceive the inexperienced . . . but the . . . sensible will penetrate the deceptive film, and expose the treacherous writer to deserved contempt" (Locke 140). Of course, this particular warning was likely intended not for already "sensible" readers but for writers hoping to get away with deceit through flattery.

In spite of the presumptions about gender that underlay such manual instruction, the lessons for both women and men were clear: be wary of deception and even of flattery, but otherwise write from the heart, sincerely expressing your heartfelt feelings. To write from the heart was the most basic advice manuals gave about romantic epistolary rhetoric. But writing from the heart did not amount to natural or spontaneous expression. Instead, manuals taught that such expression was governed by at least three generic conventions, all with implications for the cultural shaping of heteronormative romantic relations.

Epistolary Address and the Gendered Coupling of Romantic Relations

The first and most elementary of these heteronormative genre conventions concerns romantic epistolary address. Manuals taught conventions for addressing not just romantic but all epistolary rhetoric: composers were to begin with a left-aligned salutation line, placed just below the right-aligned date and above the body of the letter, and address the immediate, intended audience, usually using the words "Dear" and/or "My." Instruction in terms of epistolary address amounted to a lesson in what forms of exchange were culturally approved according to the social rank of writers and readers and the intimacy of their relations (Bannet 64–66). In the case of manual chapters focused on romantically intimate letters, instruction in the simple and still familiar conventions for epistolary address offered a lesson in heteronormative exchange. By marking rhetor and audience positions as masculine or feminine, manuals gendered romantic epistolary relations in keeping with heteronormative coupling.

Simply put, in the thousands of model letters categorized as romantic in complete letter writers, every model I have studied is addressed to a reader gendered feminine if the writer is gendered masculine and is addressed to a reader gendered masculine if the writer is gendered feminine (or is about a relationship between one person gendered feminine and another gendered masculine). In other words, manuals normalized opposite-sex couplings between writers and readers—or what are now understood as "heterosexual" relations. To normalize this particular form of relations, manuals needed to mark gender as an organizing feature of romantic epistolary rhetoric. Indeed, while many manuals also marked class (and very few race) in the titles to selected model letters, all manuals consistently marked gender as a defining feature of virtually every model letter. Gender was attributed primarily in the titles above model letters, which framed the terms of address through third-person pronouns as well as gendered nouns. For example, *The Useful Letter Writer* (1844) includes "From a young Gentleman to a Lady with whom he is in love," "From a Gentleman to a Lady," and "From a rich young Gentleman, to a beautiful young Lady with no fortune." Because manuals listed such titles in the tables of contents and repeated the titles above each model, their gendering of romantic epistolary address occupied a prominent position in the framing of models at the level of both the entire manual and the specific chapter.

In what is perhaps the most striking example, *The American Lady's and Gentleman's Modern Letter Writer* [185-], the entire manual is organized first and foremost by the gender of model rhetors. Whereas most manuals followed their introductions with models organized into multiple chapters by subgenre, this one follows its especially brief introduction with only two sections: "The Ladies' Hand-Book of Letter-Writing" and "The Gentlemen's Hand-Book of Letter-Writing." Within the "Ladies'" half of the book, the gendering of rhetors and their addressed readers is marked in titles to model romantic letters such as "A Lady on Receiving a Letter from a Gentleman, in which He Proposes a Meeting" (28); in the "Gentlemen's" half, the gendering is made clear through titles such as "A Gentleman to a Lady, Proposing to Pay His Addresses" (20a). Titles aside, however, the overall organization of the book by gender offered a lesson, however inductive, on the organization of gender within heteronormative romantic relations: there were two genders for rhetors and readers, lady and gentleman; they were markedly different from each other, to the point of requiring two separate sections; and, like two halves, they together made up a whole. In this sense, manuals did not merely gender romantic relations as opposite-sex. Manuals also privileged the "couple" form of such opposite-sex relations as "the referent or the privileged example" of what Lauren Berlant and Michael Warner characterize as a culture of "national heterosexuality" (548–49).

This predominantly heteronormative conception of romantic relations as defined by coupling across gender difference carried forward into the model letters themselves. While model titles and manual organization clearly gendered epistolary address, it was in the actual letter models that this address occurred, and it occurred most directly in salutation lines. In chapters focused on romantic epistolary rhetoric, salutations consisted of not only the familiar "Dear" but more gendered terms of address. In *The Pocket Letter Writer* (1840), for example, the gendered terms of address in salutation lines for initial romantic letters and their subsequent replies include the following: "My Dearest Harriet" and "Sir" (65–66); "Madam" and "Sir" (70–71); "Dear Mary" and "Dear James" (81–82); "My Dear Anne" and "Dear George" (90–91); and, finally, "My Dearest Mary" and "My Dearest John" (96–97). Again, these terms made gender central to epistolary address and normalized opposite-sex address and the heterosexual couple form as characteristic of romantic epistolary rhetoric. Gender was marked so as to make opposite-sex couplings unremarkable—(un)marked by "a tacit sense of rightness and normalcy"—so these relational forms were treated as normative, natural, right, and even inevitable (Berlant and Warner 554).

Letter Pacing and the Exercise of Restraint

A second genre convention taught by complete letter-writer manuals was that for dating letters and, by extension, pacing romantic epistolary exchange. Like the conventions for epistolary address, those for dating letters were taught through modeling across the subgenres of epistolary rhetoric: most models included a date in the upper right corner of the letter.[16] Embedded within the bodies of the letters categorized as romantic, however, were more interesting lessons about the relationship between the dating and pacing of letters and the normative temporality of romantic coupling. In a nineteenth-century version of "straight time," manuals modeled a temporality for romantic epistolary exchange proceeding slowly and cautiously, so as to avert "base" relations.

Jack Halberstam has theorized "straight time" as a normative timeline for the development of relationships (*Queer Time*). Within straight time, futures are imagined not only to be heterosexual but also to operate according to heteronormative bourgeois logics. One moves, over time and through so-called stages of life, from birth to marriage to reproduction to death. One lives so as to enable certain forms of reproduction and family, reduce risk and maintain safety for the sake of longevity, and plan and save for the inheritance that will ensure further reproduction. Within "queer time," in contrast, futures are imagined as operating in ways "unscripted by" such "conventions" (2).[17] Related questions of temporality figure across queer studies in a number of ways as detailed by Thomas R. Dunn: at the micro level of daily life, in terms of the straight time of schedules and routines for normative family formations, and, at a more macro level for scholarly work, in terms of queer temporalities in historiography itself ("(Queer) Family").[18] My analysis of genre instruction approaches temporality specifically in terms of normative timelines for moving from one stage of relationship development to the next. Nineteenth-century letter-writing manuals, in their instruction in genre conventions for dating letters and pacing epistolary exchange, scripted such development in keeping with a "straight time" that required restraint.

The exercise of studied restraint with respect to timing was taught as a way to keep in check "base" passions. In *The Pocket Letter Writer* a series of model letters represents a temporal slowing of romantic relations as a virtuous response to and even a punishment for baseness. The series begins with a letter titled "From a lady to a gentleman, in answer to a dishonorable proposal," in which the lady "scorn[s]" the gentleman's "highly improper letter" and its "baseness," insisting on her own "virtue" (92–93). Following "The gentleman's apology," the lady answers again, this time expressing her willingness to continue relations in the future, but only after a period of time in which she may study his conduct. She writes, "If . . . at the expiration of six months, your conduct has been that which I hope and expect . . . you may then return, and claim both my heart and my hand. But any efforts on your part to shorten this period will be unavailing, my resolution being not to see you till the period I now mention, which, permit me to add, is a very mild punishment when compared with your offence" (94–95).

Through this model and its emphasis on timing, *The Pocket Letter Writer* teaches a normative temporality for romantic relations, in which the slowing of relations is a virtuous punishment for baseness, one that allows time to study the gentleman's conduct further. This temporality is also predictably gendered: it presumes an opposite-sex relation defined by gender difference, such that the base letter was from a rhetor gendered masculine and the virtuous and punishing response from a rhetor gendered feminine.[19]

Manual instruction in heteronormative relations also taught rhetors to use studied restraint as a precaution against hastiness. *The Art of Correspondence* asserts, "Of all letters those on matters of love and marriage should be written with mature deliberation—not under the influence of hasty impressions, nor sudden impulses" (Locke 141). *Chesterfield's Art of Letter Writing Simplified* (1857) is especially cautious about epistolary rhetoric deemed "hasty" or "precipitate" (63). *Chesterfield's* spells out what *The Pocket Letter Writer* implies about the relationship among cautious restraint, timing, and the study of conduct. In one model, a "lady" writes, "Let us not . . . be too hasty in our conclusions—let us not mistake momentary impulse for permanent impression; let us seek rather to know more of each other, to study each other's tempers, and to establish . . . sincere esteem" (64).

Such slow study was crucial to crafting epistolary rhetoric restrained in both timing and intensity, so as to avoid passionate outbreaks. In another model titled "To an acquaintance of long standing," the rhetor preempts concerns about potential haste by explaining as follows: "From constantly meeting with you, and observing the thousand acts of amiability and kindness which adorn your daily life, I have gradually associated my hopes of future happiness with the chance of possessing you as their sharer. Believe me, dear Miss ——, this is no outbreak of boyish passion, but the hearty and healthy result of a long and affectionate study of your disposition. It is love, founded on esteem" (*Chesterfield's* 64). This rhetor insists that he engages in constant observation, observation of a thousand acts, and so his expression of affection is based on long study, and his love is true. His writing from the heart is far from an unrestrained expression, a momentary impulse, or a passionate outbreak. Complete letter writers thus instructed learners in how to date their romantic letters as well as how to pace their romantic relations. In teaching genre conventions for the pacing of romantic exchange, manuals also taught cultural norms for the exercise of restraint with respect to heteronormative relationship timing and even intensity.

This exercise of restraint within romantic epistolary rhetoric was normative not merely because it facilitated a particular timing for relationship development. Nor was this timing normative only because of its association with a conventional script that, if followed, could aid rhetors in averting "baseness" or "passionate outbreaks" (though certainly the cultural and material risks were real, especially for women, if letter writers moved too quickly—if "base" passions interrupted the normative progression with pregnancy occurring before marriage). Rather, what made the "straight time" taught by manuals most significantly normative was its orientation to a heteronormative *telos* for romantic epistolary rhetoric.

Rhetorical Purpose and the Marriage Telos

Third and finally, complete letter writers taught the generically conventional rhetorical purpose for romantic letters. The rhetorical purposes taught for other subgenres concerned with business, friendship, and family were varied. But in the case of the romantic subgenre, the purpose was quite limited. Even as manuals advised that romantic epistolary rhetoric was to express heartfelt feelings of love, model letters were directed to a narrowly defined type of love relationship. Manuals taught learners to compose letters not to develop just any sort of romantic correspondence or relationship but with the particular goal of courting and being courted in pursuit of a heteronormative *telos* and generic end: union through marriage between a man and a woman.

This normative *telos* is apparent throughout the various elements of manual instruction in romantic epistolary rhetoric. Consider, for instance, these typical titles to chapters about the subgenre: "Love, Courtship, and Marriage" (*Pocket Letter Writer* 65), "On Love, Courtship, and Marriage" (*Fashionable American Letter Writer* 56), "Letters on Love, Courtship, and Marriage" (Turner 95), and "Letters of Love, Courtship, and Marriage" (*Useful Letter Writer* 91). Some of this repetition within and among chapter titles was a function of nineteenth-century textbook production and compilation practices.[20] But the consistent ordering of the key words in chapter titles—love, courtship, and then marriage—characterized romantic love, however heartfelt, as teleological. This ordering figured romantic epistolary rhetoric as a subgenre for moving from love through courtship to marriage.

Chapter contents were predictably in keeping with these common titles, in that most model romantic letters were concerned with marriage. In those few manuals that did not include the word "marriage" in the chapter title, such as *Frost's* chapter "Love Letters," more than half of the models link love and courtship to the end of marriage. Among *Frost's* thirty-seven models, a majority of twenty are unquestionably oriented to marriage proposals and responses to those proposals or to maintaining, fortifying, or terminating an engagement to be married. Consistent with other complete letter writers, for example, the first model in *Frost's* chapter is a "Letter from a Gentleman to a Lady Offering her his Hand," followed by a "Favorable Reply to the Foregoing" and an "Unfavorable Reply" (Shields 119–21). Other models include a letter "From a Gentleman to a Lady Seeking to Renew a Ruptured Engagement," also followed by both a favorable and an unfavorable reply (133). Moreover, even in romantic models less obviously directed toward the rhetorical purposes of negotiating marriage proposals and engagements, the exchange in process is oriented to the normative *telos* of marriage. The content within a model reply to a "Letter from a Gentleman to the Father of the Lady he loves, Requesting Permission to Pay his Addresses" makes clear, for instance, that "addresses" is simply a euphemism for "marriage proposal," because in the favorable response, the father answers that the gentleman is "acceptable . . . as a son," welcoming him into the "family" (121–22).

In actuality, romantic epistolary exchange could facilitate a range of relational acts occurring alongside or entirely outside the heteronormative progression from love to courtship to marriage: the development of any romantic relationships that does not pursue (or is not allowed to pursue) marriage; the enjoyment of flirtations that do not develop into anything more; the facilitation of extramarital affairs; the construction of discursive realms for discussion of extraromantic concerns such as politics; the arrangement of meetings in person for erotic or sexual encounters; or the appreciation of romantic language for its own sake. But this range of possibilities was not represented within the many generic models provided by heteronormative manual instruction.

The normative teleological orientation of romantic epistolary rhetoric was reinforced not only by the narrow presentation of manual models but also through direct commentary about the genre. In *Chesterfield's* account of the romantic letter's rhetorical purpose, the manual includes a reference to writing "of the heart" but specifies that this writing is directed to marriage: "Affairs of the heart—the delicate and interesting preliminaries of marriage, are oftener settled by the pen than in any other manner" (54). That romantic epistolary rhetoric conventionally settled marriage is more bluntly put by *Hill's Manual of Social and Business Forms* (1883): "The love letter is the prelude to marriage" (110). Manuals clearly taught that romantic letters were composed not for the sake of themselves or romantic love or "the heart" but for marriage.

This goal of heteronormative marriage was prioritized even over the cultural valuing of sincerity and honesty, though manuals emphasized the importance of writing from the heart, being sincere, and avoiding deception. In fact, manuals warned against deceptive romantic rhetoric *because* of its potential to interfere with a relationship's culmination in marriage. Where *Letter-Writing Simplified* advises a "strict regard to truth" and avoidance of "extravagant flattery," the manual reminds readers that "In honorable minds courtship is always regarded as the porch to marriage" (61). Similarly, in one of *The Natural Letter Writer*'s many models of fathers warning daughters to be wary of deception and flattery, the father writes, "guard yourself against the snares and temptations designing men throw in the way of young inexperienced girls. Young girls are too apt to persuade themselves that young men who fawn over, and flatter them, wish to make wives of them; but no mistake can be more fatal" (Shepard 72). This model reinforces advice throughout complete letter writers to resist being persuaded by flattery, not simply because of its questionable sincerity but because flattery within romantic epistolary rhetoric did not lead to the *telos* of marriage.

Ultimately, manuals taught learners to compose romantic epistolary rhetoric from the heart, sincerely expressing their love but in keeping with generic conventions for the gendering of epistolary address and the temporality of exchange. These generic conventions were significant, manuals instructed, so that rhetors could learn to craft romantic exchanges that accomplished rhetorical purposes in keeping with cultural norms. As a generic means of accomplishing the "ends [one] may have" in the nineteenth-century United States, romantic letters were to constitute opposite-sex relations that developed in keeping with "straight time" and its progression toward the heteronormative *telos* of marriage between a man and woman.

Invention Strategies with Queer Effects

While manuals predominantly taught heteronormative genre conventions for romantic epistolary rhetoric, this instruction more subtly suggested how the same generic conventions were subject to challenge (Bakhtin; Devitt). My point is not merely that the romantic subgenre was inherently susceptible to queer challenge by writers whose nonnormative desires and relations motivated inventive rhetorical practices (though it was). Rather, complete letter-writer manuals themselves enabled such rhetorical practices, because of how the manuals taught invention strategies.[21] Complete letter writers taught that learners who pursued normative romantic relations through epistolary rhetoric did so by becoming model adapters: by using invention strategies such as copying and adapting the model letters provided. In the hands of at least some manual users, however, these models could be reinvented through copying and adaptation with nonnormative or "queer effect." Borrowing the phrase from Kate Thomas, I use "queer effect" to refer to potential effects of manual instruction that subvert the very conventions and norms taught (37). In doing so, I turn my attention to potential *uses* of manuals. Here I argue that the same three genre conventions already examined—for gendered epistolary address, pacing of exchange, and rhetorical purpose—were prone to challenge through gender-crossing address, unrestrained outbreaks, and queer repurposing. Manuals enabled such challenges by teaching learners to invent letters by copying and adapting the language of the heart as composed by others.

Copying from Others' Hearts

The most basic instruction for romantic epistolary rhetoric—to write from the heart with sincerity—was especially open to queer challenge given manual instruction in the invention strategy of copying model letters. Certainly a manual such as *Frost's* provided a model "Letter from a Gentleman to a Lady Offering her his Hand" so that readers could study it in order to learn how a gentleman proposes to a lady. Whereas the model rhetor expresses his "true, abiding love," asks if his feelings prompt "any response in [the lady's] heart," and then proposes, learners were expected to write their own letters, from their own hearts (Shields 119–20). They were to express their true feelings, though in keeping with genre conventions for heteronormatively proceeding toward marriage. But, while the letter may have been offered as a model of conventional rhetorical practice, written from the heart, this model could be copied outright. In other words, a learner could copy what was allegedly written from another's heart as though it were his own. This susceptibility to copying is important to understand because of its role in making possible the forms of queer generic invention I discuss next.

The practice of inventing romantic letters by copying what was written from another's heart was widely discussed across nineteenth-century epistolary culture, especially within other manuals that did *not* take the complete letter-writer form. Not surprisingly, much of this acknowledgment appeared as criticism that complete letter writers and their provision of models were culturally suspect. Consider, for instance, Loomis's *Practical Letter Writing*, which was structured by parts of letters and clusters of numbered tips, rather than chapters of models in each subgenre. Loomis criticized the more common complete letter-writer form because learners "fall into the habit of copying these almost word for word, instead of writing original letters. This is a bad practice; it is better to send a poorly constructed letter, of which you are the author, than a copied 'model'" (67). Bothered by this copying of models, Loomis warned of its consequences, particularly in the case of romantic correspondence: "A young man who copied and used such a letter proposing marriage, received a reply saying, 'You will find my answer on the next page.' It was a polite refusal" (67). In other words, because the letter's recipient discovered that this man had copied his proposal from a manual, he was directed to view the next letter in the manual, which was a model for how to reject that proposal. In another manual, *The Youth's Letter-Writer* (1836), the conduct author Eliza Ware Rotch Farrar offered an even stronger critique, claiming that complete letter writers "are filled with absurdities, vulgarisms, and the flattest nonsense," with "models calculated to mislead the rising generation and pervert their taste" (vi, 125). Nor were Farrar and Loomis alone in their criticism.[22] Manuals frequently warned of model copying gone wrong and, in the case of romantic epistolary rhetoric, almost always with the same consequence: a marriage proposal declined.[23]

Complete letter writers themselves acknowledged the susceptibility of their models to invention through outright copying and the resulting risk that romantic letters would not be written from the heart. The preface to *Chesterfield's* declares, "The fact is a complete letter writer is a complete sham and absurdity. People want to write letters, 'out of their own heads,' and it is impossible to give them 'ready made' letters, which like ready made shirts, shall fit every subject that may require clothing" (8). Not without a sense of humor, *Chesterfield's* illustrates the "absurdity" of copying "'ready made' letters" by representing a scenario in which an "uneducated" rhetor struggles to invent a letter,

> . . . and eighteen cents are expended on that very remarkable work, "The Lady's and Gentleman's Complete Letter Writer, 90th edition." The time comes for another letter; the "Complete Letter Writer" is dragged out from the darkness of the drawer . . . and an hour is spent in the search for a model letter that will just express the writer's feelings and ideas. But, alas! among the three hundred and forty-seven specimens of every style of correspondence, there is not one in which . . . Eliza is reminded that Walter still hopes to meet her, with sentiments unchanged, when she next visits New York. . . . As to the "love letters," the writer thereof has made no provision for Jemima's acceptance of Joseph on condition that he will at once shave off his moustache, and take to all-around collars, and give up punning at the dinner-table. (7)

Lest readers presume these absurd examples are the "sham," *Chesterfield's* offers yet another: "We know a case of a gentleman—at least, a person—who offered his hand to a lady with the help of a letter writer. The letter began, 'Reverend Miss;' how it finished the reader need not be told, but of course the lover was rejected" (8). And lest readers presume the problem in this example is the not-so-gentlemanly person's inadvertent mistake, *Chesterfield's* continues, "Perhaps he should have copied it 'Revered Miss,' but he should not have copied it at all" (8). *Chesterfield's* concludes, "The first step, then, towards attaining the art of letter-writing is, to tear up the 'Complete Letter Writer'" (8).

Chesterfield's still went on to provide countless models, much like any other complete letter writer. But the concerns in *Chesterfield's* echo those of Farrar and Loomis: the advice that romantic letters be written from the heart could be challenged by learners who invented epistolary rhetoric by copying models instead of composing their own from the heart. The heartfelt sincerity of these rhetors was then in question. They might make mistakes when copying—consequential mistakes that closed down the possibility of courtship proceeding to heteronormative marriage. Or, worse yet, these letter writers might be unable to find, even in a complete letter writer, a model fit for what was peculiar to their rhetorical situation. Of course, this sort of completeness would be unnecessary if a wide variety of models were available not for the simple practice of complete copying but for the more complex practice of invention through partial copying in combination with adaptation.[24] Indeed, for particularly inventive composers, models could be adapted in order to invent romantic epistolary rhetoric that further "pervert[ed]" genre conventions and cultural norms—though perhaps not in the ways Farrar had in mind.[25]

Category-Crossing Forms of Address

All three of the already discussed genre conventions were susceptible to queer challenge because of how complete letter-writer manuals provided model romantic letters. In teaching the first genre convention for romantic epistolary address, manuals marked the gender of rhetors and readers such that address was heteronormative, but these same manuals provided at least some resources for composing queerly category-crossing forms of address. Models indicated to learners what was considered appropriate or how manual users should address their romantic epistolary rhetoric on the basis of gender. However, manuals could not guarantee how learners would use the models. Because of how models were presented as resources for invention—not merely as models of writing from the heart but as models with the potential for invention through copying and adaptation—these same models could be copied and adapted in ways that crossed gender categories.

Part of what disposed the generic conventions for romantic epistolary address to gender crossing was the way manuals made the same models available to all learners regardless of gender. There were some manuals, especially conduct and etiquette guides, titled specifically for either men or women. But most complete letter writers, in their bid to be "complete" by providing instruction for all letter writers in all situations, offered the same set of models to both men and women. Complete letter writers even emphasized the usefulness of their models to "both sexes." For example, the preface to *The Complete Art of Polite Correspondence* (1857) states that the "volume is particularly recommended to . . . both sexes" (10). Similarly, *The Complete Letter Writer* (1811) and R. Turner's *Parlour Letter-Writer* (1835) include in their subtitles the following phrasing: *Containing Letters . . . Adapted to the Use of Both Sexes*. Thus complete letter-writer models not only made the same model romantic letters available for use across sex and gender but also hinted at the possibility of uses involving gender-crossing adaptation. In the subtitles just mentioned, for instance, reference to "the Use of Both Sexes" is preceded by the word "Adapted." In terms of romantic epistolary address, learners in same-sex romantic relationships were especially likely to pursue possibilities for using and adapting models regardless of how manuals marked the gender of rhetors and readers.[26] In short, such learners could copy the models made available by manuals but adapt those models by crossing gender categories in order to compose same-sex romantic epistolary address.

Consider how such a hypothetical learner might use a model from *The Complete Letter Writer* (1811). Imagine this learner as a woman in a same-sex, cross-class relationship with another woman from a wealthier family. Much like *Chesterfield's* example of the hypothetical rhetor Jemima, who finds no model for how to accept Joseph "on condition that he will at once shave off his moustache" (7), our imagined learner searches the table of contents for a model of how to address another woman. Though no such model is provided, she finds the letter "From a Gentleman to a young Lady of a superior Fortune" (vi, 102). This model is intended for rhetors who are gentlemen, but because all models are available for use and even adaptation by "both sexes," the hypothetical manual user selects this one from the table of contents. She then uses the model as a resource for inventing her own romantic epistolary rhetoric, copying from the model yet adapting it by crossing gender in order to address "a young lady of superior Fortune." Through this sort of model adaptation, gender-crossing forms of romantic epistolary address could, in Thomas's terms, "detach subjects from gender and sexual subjectivities that then reattach to queer effect" (37).

Some manuals suggested outright, rather than merely hinting at possibilities for, detaching and reattaching with "queer effect." As already discussed, *Chesterfield's* is critical of how most complete letter writers provided models, claiming that "it is impossible to give . . . 'ready made' letters" (8). But the same manual does provide what it calls "skeletons of love letters" (58a). These ready-made skeletons include an introductory paragraph and a closing paragraph to be copied, and rhetors are advised to "fill up between the bones to suit themselves" (58a). While most of the skeletons are written by men, presumably because romantic letter writing comes more naturally for women, "Nevertheless, some of the above skeletons, or parts of them, could be adapted by ladies into letters to their lovers, if they were hard up for ideas" (61a). *Chesterfield's* encourages learners to copy from and adapt models "to suit themselves," including by crossing gendered subject positions for rhetors and readers. While most manuals did not directly encourage such gender crossing, all of them at least provided an extensive array of model romantic letters. These models were available for invention through copying and adaptation, leaving the genre conventions for romantic epistolary address subject to queer challenge through gender-crossing forms of address.

Letter Writing with Urgency and Intensity

Manual instruction also offered at least some invention resources for rhetors interested in romantic relations nonnormative with respect to the second genre convention. Most of the romantic letters included in manuals modeled how to write in keeping with conventions for restraint in the pacing of romantic epistolary exchange according to "straight time." Usually manuals only alluded to but did not include within their pages romantic epistolary rhetoric that was emotionally unrestrained and urgently timed. For instance, while *The Pocket Letter Writer* includes the model "From a lady to a gentleman, in answer to a dishonorable proposal," it also includes "The gentleman's apology" but does not provide a model of the gentleman's dishonorable proposal (93). There were, however, some exceptions.

Later in *The Pocket Letter Writer*'s chapter on romantic epistolary rhetoric, the manual does include a series of three models that more ambiguously teach the genre conventions and cultural norms for the timing of romantic letters and relations: "From a gentleman to a young lady, proposing an elopement," "The lady's answer, consenting," and "The lady's answer refusing." Not surprisingly, the third letter, modeling refusal, gets the final say. In keeping with the predominant manual instruction, the rhetor characterizes the proposal to elope as "repugnant to decorum, prudence, and female delicacy." She insists that, while she feels "equally anxious" for their "union," their "separation will be for a few months only," so they must exercise restraint until "that period so long desired arrives" (103–04).

But the other two letters in this series offer manual users models for how to develop romantic epistolary exchange nonnormative in its urgency and intensity. One of these is a model response in which the rhetor *does* consent to the proposal of elopement. She writes, "Your letter has agitated me greatly; indeed I know not how to conduct myself." But rather than restraining herself and the pace of their relations, she concludes that, while "reason condemns the step you are so anxious for me to take . . . my heart decides in your favor," praying "that nothing unpleasant may attend our rash expedition" (102–03). The other letter included in the series even models how to compose such a "rash" proposal. While the rhetor admits his proposal is of a "hazardous and delicate nature," he implores the reader to respond "without delay," in hopes that "every arrangement shall be made for the journey by to-morrow's sunset" (102–03). He signs the letter, "Yours in anxious expectation" (103). At the very least, manual users copying from these two models would find language for making and accepting proposals to elope quickly. While ultimately leading to the normative *telos* of marriage, eloping did not proceed in keeping with the propriety of "straight time." Epistolary proposals to elope in a rush defied the heteronormative temporality for proceeding cautiously from love, through courtship, to marriage—and thus were, in the manual's terms, "repugnant to decorum." Even where manual users did not copy the language of such proposals directly, the inclusion of these models suggests to learners the possibility of epistolary rhetoric in defiance of genre conventions and cultural norms for the pacing and intensity of romantic relations.

Chesterfield's goes even further in suggesting this possibility, offering manual users resources for composing letters both urgent and intense. In keeping with the predominant manual instruction, where *Chesterfield's* provides the model "From a young Lady, in answer to the proposal of a gentleman who had met her the previous Evening," the manual does not also include the gentleman's "precipitate" proposal (62–63). But *Chesterfield's* does provide one exceptional letter characterized by an unadvised urgency and intensity. Titled "From a young Man, avowing a passion he had entertained for a length of time, and fearful of disclosing it," this model lacks restraint in its intensity of expression. Though the rhetor has entertained his passion "for a length of time," he describes his process as one not of constant dispassionate study but of constant obsession. He writes that he has "so long struggled with [his] feelings"; he "is continually agitated"; he has "been oppressed with a passion that has entirely superseded every other feeling of [his] heart"; and he is "unable to entertain but one idea, one thought, one feeling" (61). This rhetor obviously composes precisely the "outbreak of boyish passion" avoided in the more normatively paced *Chesterfield's* model that I discussed in a previous section (64). As though realizing the extent to which he is not exercising restraint, he writes that he is "throwing aside hesitation," is "alarmed at [his] own boldness" but nonetheless will "lay open [his] whole heart."

Chesterfield's cautions, "we should not recommend this letter for imitation; but people *will* send such letters" (61). In spite of such caution, the manual did provide this model. Again, the letter was marked as a model of what *not* to do. But in the hands of at least some rhetors, the letter could be imitated to do precisely what manuals otherwise taught to avoid. Even in instructing people in normative restraint and temporality, manuals provided models for inventing romantic epistolary rhetoric that threw aside the careful study and caution of "straight time."

Repurposing the Romantic Subgenre

Third and finally, through instruction in genre conventions for rhetorical purpose, complete letter writers taught the romantic subgenre as teleologically oriented to heteronormative marriage. But again, manuals simultaneously rendered this same convention open to queer repurposing. While the categorization of romantic epistolary rhetoric into chapters titled "Love, Courtship, and Marriage" served to emphasize the normative purpose distinctive of the subgenre, other aspects of manuals' extensive use of categories came with queer effects. The categorization of purposes, subgenres, and relationships throughout manuals was beset by slippages that created openings for nonnormative repurposing.

Some of these openings were the queer effects of baggy, catchall categories such as "miscellaneous" and "etc." A number of manuals included an entire catchall chapter with "miscellaneous" in the title, in effect signaling that new model letters had emerged beyond the prior or conventional categories of relationship and subgenre.[27] *How to Write Letters* (1886) states as much directly when offering a definition of "miscellaneous letters." The manual defines miscellaneous letters as "those letters of an accidental or unusual character, to which our complicated relations to society give rise; in short, all letters not elsewhere classified" (Westlake

13). That the "complicated relations to society" that "give rise" to "unusual" letters could include complicated romantic relations is indicated in *Chesterfield's* use of another catchall category, "etc." This catchall is added to the manual's unusual title for a chapter on romantic epistolary rhetoric: "Love, Courtship, Marriage, etc." (53). The open-ended extension of the romantic chapter title more common throughout complete letter writers reveals the inability of conventional categories of relationship and subgenre to ever be complete—as well as the likelihood that actual romantic purposes would exceed manual attempts to categorize them.

Throughout manuals, the use of catchalls such as "etc." and "miscellaneous" suggested that manual users, like textbook makers, might need to break with conventional categories in order to adapt models when inventing "unusual" romantic epistolary rhetoric. This opening to adapt models across subgenre categories could also give way to related adaptations for rhetorical purposes in defiance of the normative *telos* for romantic relations. A model exceptionally susceptible to adaptation through queer repurposing is "Female Ingenuity," a cryptogram presented in at least one edition of *The Fashionable American Letter Writer* (1832).[28] This letter's title is unusual in that, rather than clearly describing a rhetorical situation, the title hints at more ambiguous purposes, of ingenuity. Manual users selecting this model for adaptation would find it particularly useful for pursuing queer romantic purposes.

The model cryptogram is preceded by an explanation that "A young lady, newly married, being obliged to show to her husband all the letters she wrote, sent the following to an intimate friend" (178). Importantly, this is a letter to a friend *about* romantic relations, rather than one written *within* a romantic relation. It is also a letter written by an already married person, rather than for the purposes of pursuing marriage. The model's title and preceding explanation acknowledge explicitly the gendered power dynamics at work within nineteenth-century marriage and, more implicitly, how such dynamics constitute a rhetorical situation in which women might desire ingenious ways of subverting norms. The model is followed by directions for reading cryptogram letters: "The key to the above letter is to read the first and then every alternate line only" (179).[29]

Not decoded, the letter first reads as praise for the rhetor's husband and her life with him. But in following the cryptogram's instructions, readers discover that the letter, if literally read between the lines, complains about the marriage and expresses desire for a former lover. For instance, the letter first seems to say that the rhetor is "blest . . . in the matrimonial state," as her "husband is the most amiable of men," and she has "never found the least reason to / repent the day that joined" them. Once decoded, however, her epistolary rhetoric indicates she does "repent" the marriage. By the first account, her "former gallant lover / is now [her] indulgent husband," whereas in the second decoded account the former lover "is returned," and she grieves that she "might have had / . . . / him" rather than her husband. In the first account, the rhetor is "un- / able to wish that [she] could be more / happy." In the second, she is "un- / . . . / happy."

While this woman writes about and participates in marriage, her epistolary rhetoric suggests purposes that surpass the normative marriage *telos* taught by manual culture. She subverts norms for marriage by composing a letter with a less teleological rhetorical purpose: instead of using the letter to pursue the ends of marriage, she more mischievously navigates genre conventions and cultural norms. This model cryptogram would be instructive not only for married women but for any rhetors whose romantic relations were not entirely in keeping with heteronormativity, whose purposes were not met by the conventional genre of the romantic letter.[30] Taken together, the manual's inclusion of this cryptogram along with "miscellaneous" romantic letters suggests that even the "ends [one] may have" for romantic epistolary rhetoric were subject to the "queer effect" of repurposing across conventional categories of genre and to nonnormative relational ends (C. Miller 165; Thomas 37).

Thus, while complete letter-writer manuals instructed rhetors to write from the heart in keeping with generic conventions, these same manuals also taught rhetorical strategies of invention with "queer effect." Given this instruction in invention through copying and adapting models of language written from others' hearts, manual users may have challenged genre conventions by composing gender-crossing address, exchanging letters with urgency and intensity, and repurposing the romantic subgenre to nonnormative ends. As such, the rhetorical education for romantic engagement through complete letter writers taught conventions for the romantic subgenre of epistolary rhetoric in ways that shaped citizens as heteronormative subjects, yet may have enabled inventive composing in pursuit of same-sex and other queer relations.

Imagining Letter-Writing Manuals as Pedagogical Failures

This analysis of rhetorical education for romantic engagement through letter-writer manuals is marked by an obvious historiographic implication: that feminist histories of manual instruction attend to cultural norms for gender as well as sexuality (along with race, class, and ethnicity). But another possibility also emerges for linking feminist and queer methodologies in order to expand histories of rhetorical education. Specially, I suggest we bring together feminist approaches to critical imagination and queer theories of failure. Doing so may enable historians of rhetoric not only to identify normative genre conventions that were taught where explicit instruction was "successful" but also to imagine queer openings that may have emerged where pedagogies "failed."

Such an approach would extend existing feminist histories of letter-writing manuals as a site of rhetorical education. Again, Jane Donawerth, Nan Johnson, and Deirdre M. Mahoney have teased out the complex ways that manual instruction, on the one hand, constrained (white middle- and upper-class) women's rhetorical participation, limiting it to a private, domestic sphere. On the other hand, this same instruction enabled women's rhetoric, providing a training ground for entry into semipublic and public discourse. In a sense, my analysis of manuals considers a similar pedagogical dynamic—simultaneously constraining and enabling—but with respect to sexuality and romantic engagement. In this way, I counter the exclusion of sexuality from histories of rhetorical education through the normative framing of civic engagement. But, even with this queer methodological move, another challenge remains: the lack of extant evidence for how manuals were used in service of queer rhetorical practices. This challenge facing queer historiography may be addressed through feminist methodologies of critical imagination.[31]

Jacqueline Jones Royster theorized "critical imagination" in her history of African American women's rhetoric and literacy practices (83). In short, critical imagination is a methodology for scholars who seek to develop feminist histories of rhetoric and rhetorical education even where primary archival materials are limited. Grounded in her experiences with productively navigating such limitations, Royster has advocated for "making connections and seeing possibility" based on what "traces" of evidence *are* available (80, 83). She has suggested "finding whatever pieces of the complex puzzle . . . that still exist and then . . . hypothesizing from the evidence, however skeletal it might seem, about what else seems likely to be true" (81).[32] Following Royster, my analysis of complete letter writers draws on a similar form of imaginative reconstruction: with evidence of queer rhetorical practices by nineteenth-century manual users unavailable, my reading of the manuals involves "hypothesizing" about the potential queer effects of their pedagogies, about subversive uses of manuals that seem "likely" given the "traces" or queer openings in the manuals themselves.

Although manual pedagogy was predominantly heteronormative, I critically imagined queer openings with each of the three genre conventions emphasized. First, manual instruction in genre conventions for epistolary address taught heteronormatively gendered, opposite-sex romantic relations. But, given how manuals provided model romantic letters as resources for invention through copying and adaptation, I imaginatively reconstructed that learners may have reinvented the models to compose romantic epistolary address in ways that crossed gender categories. Second, instruction in conventions for the pacing of exchange taught normative restraint in keeping with "straight time." Yet, on the basis of how manuals included cautionary letters consisting of rushed proposals, I critically imagined that learners may have defied normative pacing and restraint by imitating these models of what not to do. Third and finally, manual instruction in conventions for rhetorical purpose taught a normative marriage *telos*. However, in light of the ways some manuals offered examples of letters subverting rather than pursuing normative marriage, such as the model cryptogram, I imaginatively reconstructed how learners may have used cryptogram code to compose still other romantic letters with queer rhetorical purposes.

These queer openings may also be imagined as "failures" of manual pedagogy. I understand failure following Halberstam's *Queer Art of Failure* and Stacey Waite's theorization of this art in relation to pedagogy. For Halberstam, queer failure is not simply about failing to succeed within the terms of heteronormativity, about trying but falling short of some normative goal. Rather, queer failure may be read as an art—an artful resistance to "mastery" through "refusal" and "critique" of the dominant logics used to define success (11). The art of queer failure exposes the failure of heteronormativity itself as one such logic. Drawing out the pedagogical implications of such exposure, Waite has explained that "the refusal or failure . . . exposes the systemic failure of education" ("Andy Teaches Me" 67). "Where there is 'failure,'" as Waite suggested, "we might look to the system that set the scene for the failure in the first place," for "perhaps the failure is a radical critique (whether it knows it or not) of the very system that produced it as a failure" (*Teaching Queer* 58). Where imagining failures to compose epistolary rhetoric in keeping with heteronormative genre conventions, then, I am also imagining the failures of heteronormativity in general and manual pedagogy in particular, both of which "set the scene for the failure in the first place."

It is important to keep in mind that these particular queer failures are critically imagined. As Royster herself emphasized, "the necessity is to acknowledge the limits of knowledge and to be particularly careful about 'claims' to truth, by clarifying the contexts and conditions of our interpretations and by making sure that we do not overreach the bounds of either reason or possibility" (84). Critically imagining how heteronormative manual instruction could have failed in the hands of rhetors composing queer epistolary rhetoric thus requires a twofold carefulness: first, to limit and clarify claims about queer possibilities in keeping with their imaginative nature and, second, to ground those claims in "evidence, even trace evidence" (80). Indeed, as Jean Ferguson Carr, Stephen L. Carr, and Lucille M. Schultz noted in their work on nineteenth-century manuals, "textbooks contain tantalizing traces of expected use and misuse," but "a researcher can never know exactly how a textbook was used" (4). In the case of letter-writing manuals, we do not "know exactly how" they were used (or not) by rhetors composing queer epistolary relations. Still, I urge that we build on the existing studies of letter-writing manuals as sites of rhetorical education by bringing together feminist and queer methodologies for critical imagination and failure. How might we critically imagine still other possibilities for pedagogical, rhetorical, and queer failures within complete letter writers and across nineteenth-century manual culture?

Yet another way to approach this question, even as we lack evidence of exactly how letter-writing manuals were used, is to locate additional "traces" in the epistolary rhetoric of actual people. I turn next to rhetors who we know did participate in same-sex romantic relations and who composed queer epistolary exchange.

CHAPTER 2

"To address you *My Husband*"

Addie Brown and Rebecca Primus's Queer Epistolary Exchange

> My Truest & Only Dear Sister
> What a pleasure it would be to me to address you *My Husband* . . .
>
> Addie Brown to Rebecca Primus (1865)

Same-sex epistolary rhetoric from the past is usually associated with literary and political figures. We might quickly call to mind, for instance, letters between Oscar Wilde and Lord Alfred Douglas, between Emily Dickinson and Susan Gilbert Dickinson, or between Radclyffe Hall and Violet Hunt. Or, if focusing as this book does on the nineteenth-century United States, we might think of epistolary exchange between Abraham Lincoln and Joshua Speed, Walt Whitman and Peter Doyle, and Susan B. Anthony and Anna Dickinson. My study could focus on any of these exchanges or still others suggested by existing histories of sexuality and anthologies of same-sex letters.[1] But well-known same-sex epistolary rhetoric from before the twentieth century is almost always produced by middle- and upper-class white writers, often men, with considerable access to education. In the words of Constance Jones, introducing *The Love of Friends: An Anthology of Gay and Lesbian Letters to Friends and Lovers,* such collections tend to consist largely of letters "selected from the literary realm," by rhetors who "[hail] from the upper classes of the modern Western world" and are "almost entirely white" (8).[2]

My history of rhetorical education and practice turns instead to the epistolary rhetoric of more "everyday" people, by which I mean those not celebrated as public speakers, published writers, or political figures.[3] Here I focus on the same-sex, cross-class romantic exchange composed before, during, and after the

Civil War by two freeborn African American women, Addie Brown and Rebecca Primus. Their epistolary rhetoric is especially significant because, as Eric Darnell Pritchard has asserted, "historical erasure operates as the omission, occlusion, or ignoring of Black LGBTQ people"; evincing this erasure, "very little research in . . . rhetorical studies has been published about LGBTQ people of color" ("Like signposts" 31, 51).[4] With my research focused on the nineteenth century, I emphasize Brown and Primus's queer epistolary practices (as opposed to sexual identities). In Pritchard's terms, these epistolary practices subverted "racialized heteronormativity" through "restorative literacies" (*Fashioning Lives* 26, 33).[5] It was within their epistolary exchange that Brown addressed Primus as "My Truest & Only Dear Sister" but then imagined, "What a pleasure it would be . . . to address you *My Husband*" (Nov. 16, 1865).[6] In this address and throughout their romantic epistolary rhetoric, Brown and Primus queerly composed romantic relations in defiance of cultural norms and the widely taught genre conventions.

Examining Brown and Primus's queer epistolary exchange, I shift attention from *rhetorical education* for romantic engagement through complete letter-writer manuals to *rhetorical practices* of romantic engagement within letters. This move to actual correspondence is important for considering how romantic letters were not only rhetorically learned through genre instruction but also rhetorically crafted in practice. Yet, even as this analysis emphasizes rhetorical practices, it also enriches my account of rhetorical education by showing a wider range of sources from which people learned to participate in romantic relations. While there is no indication Brown and Primus consulted the complete letter-writer manuals already examined, Brown drew on the so-called language of the heart from many other types of texts in order to compose her romantic letters to Primus.

After providing background information about Brown, Primus, and their correspondence, I analyze their queer rhetorical practices with an emphasis on the same three generic conventions—romantic epistolary address, dating, and rhetorical purpose—taught by manuals and considered previously. Brown and Primus learned and used these conventions but challenged the heteronormative gendering, pacing, and *telos* embedded within the genre instruction of complete letter-writer manuals. In crafting romantic epistolary rhetoric addressed to Primus, Brown also drew on the invention strategies paradoxically emphasized by manual instruction in writing "from the heart" by copying and adapting existing texts. Rather than adapting the models in complete letter writers, however, Brown crossed generic lines in order to compose with and about language she found in poetry and the novel. Brown and Primus thus learned the widely taught genre conventions and invention strategies for romantic epistolary rhetoric but queered those conventions and strategies in order to compose their same-sex romantic relations.

Addie Brown and Rebecca Primus's Correspondence

Rebecca Primus was born in 1836 to a middle-class family that was prominent in the African American community of Hartford, Connecticut (F. Griffin 10). Primus's father was a grocery clerk, her mother sometimes took in seamstress work, and they owned their family home. Primus was a schoolteacher. While less is known about Addie Brown's family, she was born in 1841 and spent her early years in Philadelphia. Brown worked primarily as a domestic in multiple locations across New York and Connecticut (10–12). Although it is unclear exactly how Brown and Primus met in Hartford, one possibility is that Brown was a boarder with the Primus family, which helped young black women find work. What is clear, as noted by Farah Jasmine Griffin, is that Brown "was already part of the Primus family circle" by the time her letters to Primus began (18).

The Primus family circle was active within Hartford's religious, educational, and civic organizations. These organizations included two black churches, the Zion Methodist Church and the Talcott Street Congregational Church, where abolitionist meetings were held and the activist pastor James Pennington served as minister. Also significant within Hartford's African American community were schools where Pennington as well as Ann Plato were teachers and social and civic organizations such as the Prince Hall Masonic Lodge and Hartford Freedmen's Aid Society (12–13). Both members of this community, Brown and Primus were "women who loved each other romantically" but "who were no less committed (in fact, were more committed than most) to the struggle for black freedom and progress" (7). Being from a family prominent in the community, Primus especially "worshipped in, was educated in, and was employed by black institutions with an explicit political focus—that of black freedom and uplift" (12). Educated as a schoolteacher, Primus went south to Royal Oak, Maryland, where she helped the Hartford Freedmen's Aid Society start a school for formerly enslaved African Americans following the Civil War.[7]

Brown, in contrast, had little access to formal education, but she aggressively pursued opportunities for self-education. As Griffin wrote in her edited collection of Brown and Primus's correspondence, Brown's "letters reveal the lively . . . voice of a woman who keeps up with current events and seems to read more books than does her more educated friend. As time passes, Addie's . . . writing improves, and she takes advantage of every opportunity to improve herself and her station in life" (79). Brown articulated her views on education in a letter to Primus that references Harriet Beecher Stowe's *Uncle Tom's Cabin*. In this letter Brown admiringly described meeting someone who "is very much of a Lady very much accomplished" (June 20, 1866). Brown recounted how the "Lady," after being away from home to work as a bookkeeper, tried to return, but "the Miss. River was frozen and she had to cross it." The lady doubted she could cross, until she imagined "how grand it would be to handed it down from generation to generation that she had to walk on the *ice* and also thought of Eliza in Uncle Tim [*sic*] Cabin." Commenting on the lady's story, Brown wrote, "It beautiful to hear her relate it her language is superb. I often think when people has a chance to have a Education why will they throw it away they have lost golden opportunities." Brown did not intend to "throw . . . away" any chances or opportunities for self-education through reading and letter writing.

To examine Brown and Primus's epistolary rhetoric, including portions of their letters not contained in Griffin's necessarily condensed collection, I conducted primary archival research at the Connecticut Historical Society in Hartford. Brown's romantic letters to Primus began in 1859. Most were written while the women were separated by work, whether because Brown had left Hartford to find employment as a domestic or because Primus moved to teach in the school she helped start. The letters ceased in 1868, after Brown married Joseph Tines. Brown died shortly after, in 1870; Primus then married Charles Thomas at some point between 1872 and 1874 (F. Griffin 235; White, "Rebecca Primus" 281). She saved her letters from Brown for more than sixty years, until her own death in 1932 (White, "Rebecca Primus" 284).

Unfortunately, as is often the case, only Brown's half of the romantic exchange is extant. However, as Griffin has explained, along with Karen Hansen and Barbara Beeching, it is possible to infer Primus's participation. What allows such inference is that Brown generally answered Primus's letters by repeating back an understanding of what Primus had written previously and then composing a response. In addition, the envelopes that held Brown's letters were saved, with some of Primus's writing on the outside of them. Prior studies have paid little attention to these envelopes, perhaps because they were separated from the letters during early archival processing.[8] Letters from Primus to her family are also available. I cite these letters and Primus's notations on envelopes where relevant to my analysis of her and Brown's romantic epistolary exchange.

Also of note with respect to the primary materials is the matter of spelling, punctuation, and transcription. While Brown's spelling and punctuation reveal her limited access to formal schooling, it is important to keep in mind that conventions for spelling and punctuation were less standardized in the nineteenth century. In my transcriptions of the letters, I have retained spelling, punctuation, and capitalization as they appear in the originals. Except where otherwise noted, I have also retained the original emphasis, using italics in place of underlining. If the original language remains unclear, I have bracketed my best estimations or question marks. Where language is scribbled out, I have used the overstrike function. My choice to transcribe in keeping with the original letters does mean that Brown's may be difficult to read at times, particularly because she rarely used punctuation in the early correspondence. I made this choice mainly out of respect for what Brown learned and accomplished rhetorically in spite of her relative lack of access to formal education. I also made this choice in order to be transparent about my own uncertainties in attempting to understand certain portions of her letters. That said, readers who prefer edited letters can find many of them in Griffin's excellent collection, *Beloved Sisters and Loving Friends.*

My own analysis of Brown and Primus's romantic letters is the first within the fields of rhetoric, communication, and composition. But the women's rich and extensive correspondence has garnered the attention of historians, including those interested in sexuality and nineteenth-century romantic friendship between women.[9] Most relevant to my research is how Griffin and Hansen have interpreted the letters in order to characterize the nature of Brown and Primus's relationship, emphasizing how it was erotic as well as romantic.[10] Griffin, who considered Brown and Primus's commitments to "both each other and black liberation," offered that, "If we are to believe Addie's letters, her relationship with Rebecca was not simply an affectionate 'friendship' or sisterhood. Several of Addie's letters have fairly explicit references to erotic interactions between herself and Rebecca" (5–6).[11]

Like Griffin, Hansen has highlighted these explicit references to erotic interactions.[12] She has intervened in scholarly debates about romantic friendship by challenging the romantic friendship thesis: that women involved in romantic friendships, using the language of romantic love to express strong feelings, were not engaged in erotic or sexual relationships. Hansen argued instead that, while "Addie and Rebecca had a romantic friendship . . . they also indulged in an erotic sensuality" ("'No *Kisses*'" 186). One of the moments in the letters that led Hansen to thus interpret their relationship is "an explicit discussion of a sexual encounter between Addie and a white woman" (180). In that discussion, Brown "revealed a sexual practice" that Hansen termed "bosom sex" (185–86). Brown wrote that she did not allow the white woman she slept with full access to her breasts, and Brown's later letters seem to respond to Primus's jealous reactions and inquiries (186). Across the letters, "'Bosom talk' appears everywhere," with Brown referencing bosoms in association with physical longing and sensuality (187). As Hansen detailed, Brown "expressed her longing for Rebecca by evoking the image of Rebecca's bosom," "often spoke of exchanging caresses, kisses, and hugs, and of sharing a bed," "repeatedly compared her feelings toward Primus to those between women and men," and "delighted in the fantasy of marriage to Rebecca" (186–87). Read alongside the primary letters, Hansen's analysis is convincing in its conclusion that Brown and Primus's relationship was "an explicitly erotic—as distinct from romantic—friendship" (184).

While I agree with Hansen's and Griffin's interpretation of Brown and Primus's correspondence, I suggest another approach to reading their romantic epistolary rhetoric. I have already introduced the interpretive difficulty that faces historians of sexuality and nineteenth-century romantic friendship: the difficulty of ascertaining on the basis of letters (and diaries) whether a given writer not only made use of romantic language but also engaged in same-sex erotic and sexual relations. Here, rather than offer another reading of Brown and Primus's correspondence that characterizes the nature of their romantic relations by trying to determine their erotic practices and what they did *outside* the letters, I instead focus on their rhetorical practices and what they did *within* the letters themselves. As a historian of rhetoric, I pursue an approach to reading romantic letters not as evidence of past identities or relations but as learned and crafted rhetorical practices. I ask how romantic epistolary rhetoric was learned and crafted even by women such as Brown and Primus, whose same-sex romantic relations were not modeled in the genre instruction of complete letter-writer manuals.

Queering Genre Conventions within Same-Sex Epistolary Rhetoric

As discussed in my analysis of complete letter-writer manuals, the instruction they provided in conventions for the romantic letter genre embedded a heteronormative conception of romantic relations (which also presumed normative whiteness and constrained cross-class relations). Manuals taught romantic epistolary address as heteronormatively gendered, taught exchange as restrained in pace and intensity, and taught rhetorical purpose as oriented to a marriage *telos*. But this same instruction in genre conventions was susceptible to queer subversions, effects, and failures. While I previously identified *potential* epistolary subversions by hypothetical learners, I now analyze how Brown and Primus *actually* queered genre conventions within their epistolary rhetoric. As African American women in a cross-class romantic relationship, Brown and Primus learned and used the generic conventions, yet queered them by addressing each other across normative categories of gender and relationship, pursuing their romantic exchange with urgency and intensity, and repurposing romantic epistolary rhetoric to nonnormative erotic and even political ends.

Romantic Address across Categories of Gender and Relationship

To some extent, Brown and Primus learned and used the genre conventions for epistolary address as taught by complete letter-writer manuals. In addressing Primus, Brown began her letters with a left-aligned salutation line, positioned just below the right-aligned date and above the body of the letter. Also in keeping with conventions for address, Brown often used the words "My" and "Dear" within the salutation line. But Brown and Primus obviously defied conventions for specifically romantic forms of address. Whereas manuals taught romantic epistolary address as marked by gender difference, Brown composed romantic epistolary rhetoric addressed to another woman. Primus's notations on envelopes of when she received and responded to Brown's letters show that Primus affirmed that same-sex romantic address with her response. More interesting is how, in the absence of generic conventions for how exactly one woman was to address another in a romantic letter, Brown and Primus negotiated alternative forms of address that crossed both the categories of gender and the categories of relationship and subgenre emphasized by manuals.

Salutation lines for Brown's romantic epistolary rhetoric include the following category-crossing terms of address: "my dearly adopted sister," "my ever dear friend," "my dear & dearest Rebecca," "my darling friend," "my loving friend," "my beloved Rebecca," "my dearest & most affec[tionate] friend," "my only dear & loving friend." These terms of address suggest a same-sex relation that is familial (these are sisters, even adopted sisters), *and* that is friendship (these are friends), *and* that is romantic (these sister-like friends are not only dear but also dearest; darling, loved, beloved, affectionate; only, most, and ever).[13] These terms certainly queer the normative gendering of romantic epistolary address. The terms of address also cross the very categories of relationship that manuals used in separating chapters on the subgenres of familial and friendship letters from chapters on the subgenre of romantic letters.

Brown and Primus wrestled with generic conventions for address through further negotiation of these terms within the bodies of their letters. Consider, for instance, their negotiation of the epistolary address "sister." In an 1862 letter, Brown seemingly responded to Primus's request to be addressed as "my *sister*": "now My Dearest here is nexe question you ask a favor and that is this too *call* you my *sister* and then you ask me if it will be agreeable O My Darling Darling you know it would it has been my wish for sometime I dare not ask My Dear I cannot find words to express my feeling toward you is all I can say I will address you as such" (Mar. 1862). Although she "cannot find words to express [her] feeling toward" Primus, Brown not only found it "agreeable" but also insisted it was her own "wish" that she "address" Primus as "sister." Later, just before concluding the letter, Brown in turn asked Primus, "my Dear will you in your nexe address me by my new title . . . don't forget." Keeping the agreement, Brown addressed Primus as "sister"—not "friend"—in the salutation lines of subsequent letters.

Still, conversation continued as Brown and Primus struggled with the terms of address for their relationship and what those terms might mean. Even in the 1862 letter, Brown stated that she "cannot find words to express" her feelings, suggesting the term "sister" did not quite do it. Then, four years later, Brown assured Primus, "you have been to me more then any living soul has been or ever will be you have been more to me then a *friend* or *Sister*" (Apr. 10, 1866). Brown began the next line with the address "My Idol Sister," a variation of which she used in another letter but never in a salutation line (June 25, 1861). Yet, in closing the letter, Brown lamented, "I wish that I could express my feelings to you" and signed it, "Sister Addie" (Apr. 10, 1866). Again, Brown agreed to use the address "sister" within the salutation line and sometimes even the signature line, but within the body of her letters she negotiated with Primus over the meaning of that address. Within these negotiations, Brown made grand romantic claims about Primus being "more then any living soul has been or ever will be," insisting that Primus was "more" than a sister, "more" than a friend. At the same time, Brown asserted that the terms of address available within their negotiations did not "express" her feelings.

Brown fantasized about another term of address that might better express her feelings: husband. While Brown's salutation in the letter from which I have drawn this chapter's epigraph is "My Truest & Only Dear Sister," she began the body of her letter with "What a pleasure it would be to me to address you *My Husband*" (Nov. 16, 1865). "Husband" was certainly an address in defiance of the genre conventions for letters between women. It defied heteronormative genre conventions by crossing categories of gender, relationship, and subgenre. A woman writer addressed a woman reader not only romantically but with the term "husband"—and, at the same time, with the term "sister." That said, Brown did not entirely defy genre conventions. Instead, she seemed hyperaware that the address "husband," whatever she might write about it within the body of her letter, did not belong in the salutation line. Brown did not use the term there and, where she did, she also uses the conditional tense ("What a pleasure it *would* be"). Brown kept her agreement not only with the conventions of epistolary rhetoric but also with Primus, by continuing with the salutation "sister." Still, keeping "husband" out of the salutation line did not prevent Brown from fantasizing about it and its associated "pleasure," from sharing that fantasy with Primus. This line is more a shared fantasy than a request, but Brown continued to negotiate the genre conventions for address, the terms she would use with Primus, and even what those terms might—or "would," under different cultural conditions—mean. While Brown and Primus learned the conventions for epistolary address, they used and negotiated terms of address in ways that crossed the categories of gender and relationship taught by manuals.

Epistolary Exchange with Urgency and Intensity

Brown and Primus similarly learned genre conventions for dating epistolary rhetoric but subverted cultural norms for pacing and restraint within romantic epistolary exchange. In the most basic sense, Brown and Primus did date their letters in keeping with formal conventions. In Brown's romantic letters to Primus—as well as in Primus's letters to her family—the women preceded their left-aligned salutation with a right-aligned date, where they provided the location from which they wrote, followed by the date. The first of Brown's saved letters, for example, begins with "Waterbury Aug. 2 1859." But, in teaching this basic convention for dating letters, complete letter-writer manuals also embedded cultural norms for a nineteenth-century version of "straight time," for normatively timing romantic epistolary exchange through the exercise of restraint with respect to the pacing and intensity of courtship (Halberstam, *Queer Time*). With the heteronormative *telos* of marriage unavailable to their same-sex relationship, the temporality of Brown and Primus's epistolary rhetoric obviously operated outside the "straight time" of courtship. Yet they also defied the widely taught temporality in other ways, by composing their romantic exchange with urgency and intensity.

Paradoxically in Primus's case, her lack of restraint is evident precisely because she kept such disciplined track of the timing of her epistolary rhetoric. Although Primus's letters to Brown are unavailable, the saved envelopes from Brown's letters include Primus's notations, in which she tracked the dates when she received and responded to letters. The back of a typical envelope, for instance, includes a notation like the following: "Rec July 3rd / 1861 / Ans July 8th / 1861." This careful attention to timing is matched by an exercise of discipline in her epistolary exchange with family. While away from Hartford and teaching in Royal Oak, Primus maintained a regular practice of writing to family once a week. In the opening lines of a letter addressed to "My dear Parents & Sister," Primus expressed her awareness of conventions for letter pacing by explaining that she was "writing your weeklie—I style it 'The Home Weeklie'" (Apr. 27, 1868). Primus apparently maintained this regular schedule of writing to her family. In another letter to them, she began, "This quiet Sabbath P.M. I seat myself with pen in hand to write my 'Home Weeklie'" (Nov. 29, 1868). In fact, it was cause for explanation when Primus did not stick to her disciplined schedule for writing. She explained elsewhere, for example, "I have been obliged to postpone writing your weekly until now on acct. of being from home" (Apr. 4, 1868).

In contrast with her home weeklies to family, Primus was less restrained in the timing of her romantic letters to Brown. On the one hand, some of Brown's epistolary rhetoric does suggest there was an expectation that the women would exchange regularly timed letters, perhaps a letter per week. Brown even began one letter with an explanation much like Primus's to her family. Brown wrote, "My reason for not sending my weekly missive last week was on account of sickness" (Jan. 19, 1868). On the other hand, the body of correspondence makes clear that neither woman exercised the normative restraint taught by manuals. While aware of the possibility for an evenly paced epistolary exchange, both wrote more frequently than once a week during the periods when they were separated geographically. In Primus's case, her notations on envelopes indicate that she frequently "Ans[wered]" letters from Brown within one to four days, thus writing more than just once per week.

Even this frequency was not marked by consistency. Suggesting Primus's inconsistency, Brown began a letter by acknowledging with delight that Primus had written sooner than expected. Brown exclaimed, "To my surprise you send me a ans sooner then I expected how delighted I was even those around me could see that I was. . . . I work with much lighter heart then I have all this week" (Nov. 16, 1865). In another letter, Brown questioned Primus about not writing as expected: "What shall I attribute to your silence to? You are not punishing me for not writing last week are you?" (Jan. 14, 1867). Of course, Brown's first question quickly led to a second, which indicates that she too did not write when expected. These questions suggest both an awareness of genre conventions for letter pacing and a practice of pacing letters somewhat inconsistently, with the timing of their letters, like the terms of their address, being negotiated through their romantic epistolary exchange.

Brown exercised even less restraint than Primus, writing to her with frequency and sometimes urgency. Brown often wrote another letter to Primus even before there had been enough time for Primus to answer the prior letter, even before the notes on envelopes suggest Primus had answered. At times Brown wrote as much as once a day or more than once in the same day. Relatively early in their correspondence, for example, Brown mailed Primus letters dated September 25, September 28, September 29, and October 2, 1861. On September 28, Brown wrote not once but twice, first in the "morning" and then again at "midnight—twelve o clock precisely." In the first entry, Brown wrote, "I think its about time that I heard from you I have been looking very patincely for a letter and have not received any as yet." By the second entry, it seems Brown had received a "kind and Affec letter," but her early remarks "about time" and "looking very patincely" raise questions about just how patiently she looked for that letter. Brown wrote with frequency (five letters in seven days) and urgency ("its about time"). While Brown and Primus generally dated their letters according to generic convention, their romantic epistolary rhetoric was not in keeping with the measured and studied restraint recommended by manuals. Operating outside the "straight time" of courtship in pursuit of heteronormative marriage, their epistolary rhetoric queered norms for the temporality and intensity of romantic relations.

Repurposing to Erotic and Political Ends

Brown and Primus most defied the cultural norms embedded in the genre instruction of manuals through the rhetorical purpose of their romantic letters. Manuals taught that romantic letters served a generic purpose within a courtship process that was teleologically oriented to heteronormative marriage. But, like the exceptional cryptogram writer represented in manuals and considered previously, Brown and Primus composed epistolary rhetoric with more subversive purposes. Although they did later marry men, both women navigated their rhetorical situation by writing for purposes not limited to the generically conventional marriage *telos*.

In spite of how Brown and Primus otherwise adapted conventions, cultural constraints were such that they simply could not marry each other.[14] Brown wrote a good deal about marriage not being an option with Primus. I have already quoted the letter in which Brown fantasized about "What a pleasure it would be to me to address you *My Husband*," but she realized her would-be address could not be (Nov. 16, 1865). In another letter, Brown proclaimed romantic love for Primus but paused over the question of what her claims might actually "come to" given that Primus was a "Girl" and not "a man": "no *kisses* is like yours. . . . You are the first Girl that I ever *love* . . . you are the *last* one. . . . I mean just what I say . . . if you was a man what would things come to" (Aug. 30, 1859). Elsewhere, Brown relayed that Primus's mother "said I thought as much of you if you was a gentleman she also said if either one of us was a gent we would marry" (Jan. 21, 1866). Across their correspondence, Brown recognized that their letters could not pursue heteronormative marriage. One of Brown and Primus's purposes for writing romantic letters, then, was to acknowledge and find ways of coping with the constraints that prevented them from pursuing the generic ends of marriage with each other.

Navigating these constraints involved coming to understand (and then to persuade Primus of) the economic reasons to marry a man. Relatively early in their correspondence, Brown wrote to Primus about a suitor, "Mr. Lee," explaining, "I act so indifferently that he dont know what to make of me. . . . I like him as a Friend and nothing more then that. . . . I cannot reciprocate his love" (May 24, 1861). Still, Brown conceded, "but Dear Rebecca if I should ever see a good chance I will take it for I'm tired roving around this unfriendly world." Brown realized that the institution of marriage might provide relative economic stability, particularly for an African American woman whose employment as a domestic involved being "tired" from working nearly nonstop and "roving around" from one state and job situation to the next. Brown's "good chance" did come, after years of being courted by another suitor, Joseph Tines. But her letters to Primus represented that courtship as anything but romantic. Most of Brown's statements about Tines were lukewarm at best, and she unfavorably compared her feelings for him to those she had for Primus. When Brown began to write of him more fondly, even the letter most overtly expressing "love" for Tines was ambivalent. While Brown wrote, "I had the pleasure of seeing Mr. Tines twice last week," she clarified, "I shall miss him very much *if your not here* I should not care very much he seems to be rather doubtful of my love for him I do love him *but not fasinated and never will*" (Oct. 25, 1866, my emphasis). Almost a year after expressing these feelings, Brown complained that her employer did not pay her fully or fairly and announced her coming elopement (Oct. 15, 1867).[15]

While reflecting the material conditions in which Brown lived, her approach to marriage also developed through her romantic epistolary rhetoric. Consider, for instance, a letter in which she attempted to persuade Primus to view marriage differently. At a time when work had taken Brown to New York, she wrote, "My loved one I want to ask you one question that is will you not look at my marrying in a different light then you do . . . perhaps see you about three time in a year I'm sometime happy more time unhappy I will get my money regular for two or three week and then irregular what would you rather see me do have one that truly *love* me that would give me a happy home and or give him up and remain in this home . . . Rebecca if I could live with you or even be with you parts of the day I would never marry" (Feb. 23, 1862). Through ongoing conversation with Primus about marriage, Brown developed her economic reasoning for marrying. Brown insisted she would "never marry" if she could "live with" Primus "or even be with" Primus more often. But they were separated by work, and Brown neither saw Primus nor got paid regularly. Primus was Brown's "loved one," but with no option to marry each other, Brown preferred to marry a man who "would give . . . a happy home" rather than stay in her current work and living situation as a domestic.[16]

Amid the constraints that made marriage with each other impossible, Brown and Primus defied the conventional purpose for romantic epistolary rhetoric by writing about nonnormative erotic relations with others. They wrote not only about relations with the men who later became their husbands but also about relations with other women that were not teleologically oriented toward marriage. In an exchange while Brown was working at a private boarding school, she made frequent mention of her flirtatious interactions with other workers, at times writing in response to Primus's inquiries. Brown informed Primus that the workers "visit" each other—"two of them English—one of them I call her my female lover"—and, a week later, that "the girls are very friendly towards me . . . sometime just one of them wants to sleep with me perhaps I will give my consent some of these nights I am not very fond of White I can assure you" (Oct. 20, 27, 1867).[17]

In Brown's later references to those nights, she wrote of what Hansen termed "bosom sex" (186). Brown responded to Primus's concern "that is my bosom that captivated the girl that made her want to sleep with me" with the assurance that "had my back towards her all night and my night dress was button up so she could not get to my bosom" (Nov. 17, 1867). Brown further assured Primus that "I shall try to keep you favorite one always for you" but then provoked with "should in my excitement forget you will pardon me *I know*." In a later letter, she insisted, "I thought I told you about the girl sleeping with me," evading the question of "whether I enjoyed it or not" and even back peddling with "I don't know what kind of an excitement I refer to but I presume I know at the time" (Dec.

8, 1867). Certainly Brown's purposes included flirtatiously provoking jealousy. What I mean to emphasize, though, is how she and Primus discussed yet another nonnormative relation, a cross-race erotic interaction between two working-class women, an interaction certainly not teleologically oriented to marriage (or its classed and racialized iterations emphasized by manuals). This discussion simultaneously composed Brown and Primus's own nonnormative relation: it perhaps fueled their ongoing exchange; it definitely was part of what they wrote about and so what rhetorically constituted their relationship through letters. In writing about relations with others, they—like the cryptogram writer—repurposed the letter genre to nonnormative ends.

Brown and Primus also defied conventions for rhetorical purpose by using their romantic letters to comment on political life. Not surprisingly, given the gendered norms for interactions between women and men, manuals did not model conventions for incorporating political discussion within romantic epistolary rhetoric. Such discussion was simply absent from the models, which represented the rhetorical situations of romantic and political life as distinct. But Brown and Primus wrote more in keeping with the patterns in African American women's rhetoric identified by Shirley Wilson Logan, Elaine Richardson, and Jacqueline Jones Royster. As Royster's research on nineteenth-century African American women's rhetoric has made clear, they were "fully aware of the material conditions of their lives and equally aware of the public discourses swirling around them"; they wrote "within an environment of activism, advocacy, and action," "a context of resistance" (110). Similarly situated and aware, Brown and Primus invented epistolary rhetoric that not surprisingly involved discussions of political action and resistance to racism. While Primus's romantic letters to Brown are not extant, Primus discussed racial politics in virtually every letter addressed to her family while she was away teaching at the freedmen's school in Royal Oak. For Brown's part, even in her romantic epistolary rhetoric, she commented on electoral and racial politics.

Brown developed an increasing interest in politics over the course of her romantic correspondence with Primus, especially after the Civil War and as Reconstruction supposedly began. Brown's interest in politics extended to figures elected to public office—even though African Americans were denied the right to vote in Hartford until 1876 (F. Griffin 90). Depending on the figure in question, Brown expressed both glee and disdain. Upon learning that "in Boston the Republican have nominated a colored man for the legislature no one but Mr. Charles B. Mitchell," Brown wrote that she was "delighted our color will be a people get a few more states like Mass." (Nov. 4, 1866). Upon hearing that "the President Johnson expect to be in Hartford the 26th," she wrote that she "wish some of them [his *friends*] present him with a ball through his head" (June 23, 1867). Brown's commentary on political figures was not separate, however, from her romantic purposes. In the same letter, and even in the lines directly following her wish for Johnson, she expressed a more conventional romantic longing, wishing for Primus to return from Royal Oak to Hartford so they might see each other: "how long will it be before I can have the pleasure of seeing you . . . do not Rebecca consent to teach another month O do come home won't you" (June 23, 1867).

Brown's epistolary rhetoric also served purposes simultaneously romantic and political; she wrote to Primus about public debates, lectures, and publications explicitly about racial politics. In one letter, Brown reported, "Colonel Trimble of Tennessee is going to lecture at Talcott street Church on Wednesday evening the subject is the capacity of colored men." She looked forward to his lecture: "I think I shall go for I would like to hear him" (Feb. 24, 1867). In the next letter, Brown offered her lengthiest account of a lecture. In part, she wrote, "Col Trimble his subject was, Colored Mans Capacity, he spoke very well . . . he also spoke of [Reverend Henry Highland] Garnett, [Frederick] Douglass and other distinguish men the day would come when states would allow every man vote he also said that he was going back to Tennessee and take two blackest men one on each arm and go up to the ballot box" (Mar. 3, 1867).

Brown's account of Trimble's lecture about racial politics and the vote coexisted with her more romantic sentiments. In the same letter, for example, Brown wrote of how she would like to send her "very nice" breakfast to Primus, promising that when they were together next, "I shall make some . . . for you and only you" (Mar. 3, 1867). Brown also wrote that Primus's letters "always affords me much pleasure . . . and I sometime feels that you are near," and she mentioned that "I had a singular dream about you." Through letters like this one, Brown continued her romantic epistolary exchange with Primus while also exchanging information and commentary about racial politics. Although legally barred from political participation in the form of voting, and although instruction in the genre conventions for romantic epistolary rhetoric seemed to bar all political discussion, Brown repurposed the genre in order to share with Primus her sentiments about not only their romantic relationship but also electoral and racial politics. Brown thus challenged manuals' separation of romantic purposes from political life.

Brown and Primus's rhetorical practices exemplify how at least some rhetors creatively queered genre conventions in defiance of cultural norms. Their epistolary rhetoric demonstrates a familiarity with genre conventions, which they certainly used. But they negotiated forms of epistolary address that crossed the categories of gender, relationship, and subgenre taught by manuals. The pace and intensity of their romantic epistolary exchange was more urgent and less restrained than advised. And they repurposed the romantic letter genre to compose their same-sex relationship, write about erotic relations with other women, and comment on racial politics—none of which was modeled by manuals.

RHETORICAL STRATEGIES OF INVENTION FOR ADAPTING THE LANGUAGE OF THE HEART

In addition to learning but queerly subverting the genre conventions taught by manuals, Brown and Primus practiced rhetorical strategies of invention remarkably parallel to those taught by manuals. Complete letter writers characterized romantic epistolary rhetoric as a matter of simply expressing sincere feelings by writing from the heart, yet paradoxically taught strategies for invention through copying and adapting model letters written from others' hearts. Like the hypothetical learners imagined in my analysis of manuals, Brown and Primus were in a prime position to not merely copy but queerly adapt models, in large part because manuals did not include models of same-sex romantic letters. While I have found no evidence that Brown and Primus consulted the model letters circulated within complete letter-writer manuals, their correspondence suggests Brown did practice the rhetorical strategies of invention taught by manuals. But rather than copying model letters, she crossed generic lines to copy and adapt language from poetry and the novel.[18] Brown invented romantic letters to Primus in two ways: by composing *with* the language of the heart as copied from poetry and by composing *about* the language of the heart as copied from the novel.[19] In both cases, Brown adapted the language of others' hearts, making it her own by putting it in the service of her same-sex romantic epistolary rhetoric.

Composing with Language of the Heart from Poetry

When inventing romantic epistolary rhetoric by copying and adapting language from poetry, Brown neither used quotation marks nor attributed her sources. Still, it is clear that Brown did copy, even where the earlier sources cannot be located, because of a marked change in style.[20] Most of Brown's letters are written in a conversational style, by which I mean that her seemingly stream-of-conscious language is in keeping with the commonplace manual instruction to write as though speaking on paper. Where Brown copied from poetry, in contrast, her style shifted quite drastically, with the copied language utilizing repetition, rhythm, and scene in ways familiar from poetic verse. But where Brown copied the language of the heart directly from poetry, she did not passively adapt to the language or its sentiments.[21] Instead, she took ownership of the copied poetry by adapting it to invent her same-sex romantic epistolary rhetoric.

Brown most often copied language from others' poetry in order to open her romantic letters to Primus. Consider, for instance, the following opening to what is an eight-page letter. After dating and addressing her letter, Brown began with language likely copied from poetry. Then, several lines down, I have noted where Brown made the shift in style characteristic of her copying from poetry.²²

> New York Nov 14 1861
> My Ever Dear Friend
> yes when twilight comes starlings [?] us with all its gentle influences when the purple and gold have melted quite out of the sky when clouds of bright amber splashed with crimson have sunk deep into a rosy bed and the day-god ~~have~~ himself has you down into that far off lake beyond the world and only above there seems to hang out still silent canopy of deeply darkly blue it tis then I ~~think~~ am in this deepest ~~of~~ thought of you you only yes tis then I think of joys which can never be mine tears streams down my cheeks and some flow down the channel back into my heart. [stylistic shift here] one day last week I felt sad I did not rec your letter and I thought perhaps mine had shared the same fate as the other but on Monday between [?] o clock that sadness was remove I could not express the joys in perrusing you very loving & interesting Epistle but still there was one or two things made me feel bad

I describe the copied language with which Brown began the body of this letter as poetic in part because of the repetition of "when," which creates rhythm and rhymes with the primary romantic sentiment: "it tis then" that the speaker thinks of the addressed—and, as Brown made this language her own, that she thought of Primus. Brown's shift, from the copied language she began with to her more typical conversational language, is especially evident in subsequent lines. Brown wrote, "tears streams down my cheeks and some flow down the channel back into my heart," and she used the only periods on this page of the letter. Then, in stark contrast, she wrote, "one day last week I felt sad" and "one or two things made me feel bad." Brown thus used copied language to get started with composing her romantic epistolary rhetoric addressed to Primus.

Brown took ownership of the copied language by adapting it to express romantic sentiments she likely shared and then transitioning to still other sentiments. In the letter, Brown seemed to use the copied poetry to convey what she probably meant: it was nighttime when she thought of Primus, but with bittersweet tears because Primus would never be hers in the way she would like. Moreover, Brown transitioned from the copied "joys which can never be mine" to her own "joys in perrusing" Primus's "very loving & interesting Epistle." Similarly, Brown transitioned from the sadness in the copied language to another sadness, about not receiving a letter from Primus when desired. Finally, she transitioned again to what caused her to "feel bad." Brown adapted the copied language not merely to imitate clichéd expressions of romantic feeling but to begin her letters and then express a more complex range of feeling.

With this letter, it is also important to note the dual way Brown's epistolary rhetoric was both romantic—as in "of or relating to romantic love"—and Romantic—as in "of or relating to Romanticism." The letter is romantic in its contemplation of and expression of longing for a love object; speaking of an "object," the letter is also romantic in its version of love as possessive ("mine") and narrowly focused on one ("you only you"). At the same time, the letter is Romantic in its crafting of a scene of beauty, simultaneously natural and aesthetic, as the occasion for contemplating love and inspiring composition; speaking of inspiration, phrasing such as "deeply darkly blue" is reminiscent of language particular to the Romantic poets Lord Byron and Robert Southey ("Darkly, deeply, beautifully blue" in Byron, "Blue, darkly, deeply, beautifully blue" in Southey). Crossing categories of gender, race, and class, Brown made Byron's and Southey's Romantic language her own in order to invent epistolary rhetoric that shared her romantic sentiments of joy, longing for Primus, and grief at her absence.

Another way Brown took ownership of copied poetry was by combining it with direct epistolary address. Brown reframed the language she copied from poetry by interspersing it with salutation-like forms of epistolary address beginning with "dear" and "my." In another letter, for example, Brown followed her salutation, "My Ever Darling Primus," with a contemplation of the moon that was definitely copied (Mar. 16, 1862). Most of the language Brown used here can be found in "Reveries by Night," which was published in the literary periodical *The New-York Mirror* (1831) and, later, in Theodore Sedgwick Fay's *Dreams and Reveries of a Quiet Man* (1832).[23] Brown deleted from Fay's text an early phrase and several sentences and even an entire paragraph from later in the piece. In one of the places where she cut Fay's language, she interjected with yet another epistolary address, only then to proceed further with copied language that came later in Fay's essay. Brown wrote, "the moon tonight is so exquisite in its picturesque effects—so magical and subduing every thing that is touched by it is etherealized and elevated and softened beautiful object are invested with higher beauty grandeur rises to sublimity and sublimity oppresses the mind with heavy weight of admiration. *Dear friend* how perfectly still how hushed is all around but for . . ." (Mar. 16, 1862). Brown finished this last sentence and train of thought differently than Fay did. Then, after a few more lines about the moon, she again used direct address, this time quite conversationally: "well my Darling I suppose you think enough of [expatiate?] about the moon." Aside from Brown calling Primus "Darling," this portion of the letter is not especially romantic.[24] What I mean to highlight, though, is how Brown made copied text her own by reframing it with the epistolary address of "my Darling" and "Dear friend."

A final way that Brown's use of language from poetry amounts to invention through active adapting rather than passive copying is that she selected which words, lines, and stanzas to redeploy for her own same-sex romantic purposes.[25]

In another letter from that same month, Brown elected to insert just one copied line, which was both preceded and followed by her more typical style. Following conversational sentences about a party, she wrote, "wish I could see you when billows roll and waves around me rise one thought of *thee* will clear the darkest skies My Dearest to day I rec you very kind & Affectionate Epistle" (Mar. 1862). The more poetic phrasing here is a version of "When the billows roll and waves around me rise, / One thought of thee will clear the darkest of skies." These lines appear in a later edition of *Hill's Manual of Social and Business Forms* (1883) as one among many poetic "Selections for the Autograph Album" (141). Of course Brown did not have access to this edition of *Hill's*, published after her death. But in keeping with the tradition of poems collected in autograph albums, these same lines were almost certainly compiled elsewhere before they appeared in *Hill's*.[26] Regardless of where Brown encountered the lines, my point is that she selected these specific lines, rather than others just before or after them, and she elected where to place the lines in relation to the rest of her letter. Brown also redeployed the lines in service of her own rhetorical purposes. Once adapted for her romantic letter to Primus, the lines amplified both Brown's prior expressed longing, a desire unfulfilled—"I wish I could see you"—and her next expressed pleasure, a desire that was fulfilled—Primus's "very kind & Affectionate Epistle" might not "clear the darkest skies," but it did leave Brown "in good spirit" and "gave [her] a great deal of pleasure" (Mar. 1862). Here and elsewhere, Brown copied the language of the heart from poetry written primarily by white men, but she took ownership of that copied language when inventing her romantic epistolary rhetoric addressed to Primus.[27]

Composing about Language of the Heart from the Novel

Brown's rhetorical strategies of invention included not only composing *with* the language of the heart from poetry but also composing *about* the language of the heart from the novel. Most interesting is Brown's writing on Grace Aguilar's domestic novel, *Women's Friendship* (1850), about a relationship between the middle-class Florence and the aristocrat Lady Ida. Whereas Brown copied from poetry without attributing her sources, she cited this novel. In her first letter to Primus about the novel, Brown prefaced the language she copied with a direct reference to the novel's title and author. She wrote, "O my Darling I read a book called women friendship it was a [splendid?] book I wish I could sent it to you for to read . . . the author of it is Grace Aguilar" (Jan. 30, 1862). Brown further marked her practice of copying with "I will give you little idea of it." In this way, she distinguished between Aguilar's language and her own. As with her copying from poetry, however, Brown drew text from Aguilar's novel in order to invent romantic letters to Primus. Brown not only relayed the novel's story to Primus but adapted that story by reframing it with direct epistolary address in order to prompt an ongoing exchange with Primus about friendship, marriage, and the nature of their own same-sex romantic relationship.

On the one hand, Brown quite predictably copied from *Women's Friendship* to share with Primus a version of the novel's story. In Brown's first letter about the novel, the text she copied amounts to a total of three and a half pages of her eight-page letter (Jan. 30, 1862). She began her retelling by copying directly from the opening of the novel. Here Florence's mother offers a "warning address" about her "warm attachment" to Lady Ida when, "on the receipt of a note" from Ida, Florence becomes "animated" with "its rapid perusal," "bound[ing] toward her mother with an exclamation of irrepressible joy" (Aguilar 1). The mother warns that "friendship even more than love demands equality of station" (1). Later in Brown's letter, she began to copy more selectively from portions of the novel, especially chapters 2 and 7, and she combined this copied language with her own summary of the novel's plot (10, 39–40). Brown described how Florence is continually cautioned against expecting anything other than disappointment from her relationship with Ida, because they will be separated for a time by distance, when Ida is away from England in Italy, as well as because Ida will marry. Part of what Brown copied is Ida's insistence that "I may still be Florence's friend," and Brown emphasized Ida's promise to be there for Florence in case of any difficulty (Jan. 30, 1862). Through a combination of copying and summarizing, Brown thus retold the novel's story, sharing it with Primus.

On the other hand, Brown did more than simply retell the novel's story. She reframed this retelling through her insertion of epistolary address, in order to make explicit connections between herself and the middle-class Florence, between Primus and the aristocrat Ida, and between the two pairs' relationships and feelings. In copying language from the novel's opening, for example, Brown first interrupted with, "my Darling I'm writing this miscellaneous I know you will understand it." Here she directly addressed Primus with the salutation-like "my Darling," while also signaling that Primus's understanding of what was copied from the novel depended on the larger context of their ongoing romantic epistolary exchange. In another interruption to the language copied from *Women's Friendship*, Brown claimed, "Florence and Lady Ida became warm friends Florence love her as I do you." In this case Brown was more direct about how Primus might take the "little idea" Brown "will give" of the novel: she intended for the story of Florence and Ida's friendship to speak to the ongoing narrative of her and Primus's relationship. Interrupting copied language with the direct epistolary address of "my Darling," Brown initiated an exchange with Primus about relationships in general and their romantic relationship in particular.

Even without Primus's written responses, it is clear from a later letter that Brown's rhetorical strategy of invention affected just such an exchange about friendship and love. In spite of Brown's earlier insistence—that "I know you will understand it"—it turns out her writing about *Women's Friendship* was anything but clear to Primus. Instead, Brown's epistolary rhetoric prompted a back-and-forth questioning about these women's own friendship. Three weeks later, after two other letters and an "unexpected visit," the exchange continued:

> you say that you have suffered for the last few months yes I now do credit your words and never again will you suffer if I can help it then you ask me if I believe that you love me or did I ever believe you did yes I did think you love me and truly think you do now you ask my forgiveness for the pain that you have cause me my Darling my Sweet Friend you have my forgiveness my Darling you friendship is ever been pure to me Rebecca when I spoke of that book I did not mean in that light that you think you did but some day I may be more capable of making you understand what I had reference too no Rebecca you never did anything [? ly] to me no anything else that way my only beloved friend I will not agree with you in this point you say I need never name the tie which exist between us Friendship this term is not [agreeable?] to you and you even say that you are not worthy of it call it any thing else but this O My Darling is that you no no never well call it any thing else as long as *God* is my witness it pure and true Friendship and you are worthy of it and more so never again pen such thought if *love* me. (Feb. 23, 1862)

With Brown's references to what both "the book" and Primus "say," this letter evidences an exchange prompted by Brown's writing about *Women's Friendship*. In conversation with each other and the novel, Brown and Primus traded expressions of suffering, apologies, and assurances. Brown refused to agree with Primus on at least some points. They explored questions about their relationship: Was it "pure"? Was it "true"? Was it best called "friendship"? What makes one "worthy" of pure and true friendship? What thoughts may an African American woman "pen" to another within a romantic letter?

Had Brown turned to the model letters in letter-writing manuals, she would not have found a "name" specific to her love for and relationship with Primus. But Brown instead crossed generic lines (as well as those of race and class), drawing on the language of the heart and form of friendship modeled in the novel. She both copied language from *Women's Friendship* and wrote about the novel, in order to invent her romantic letters to Primus. In addition to sharing with Primus the story of the novel, Brown reframed that story with direct epistolary address, developing an ongoing exchange about friendship, love, and marriage. Brown also took ownership of the language of the heart as copied from poetry by reframing that poetic language with direct epistolary address, actively selecting specific lines to copy, and using the copied language to initiate her romantic letters and develop expressions of romantic sentiments. Brown practiced rhetorical strategies of invention that, while not necessarily learned from letter-writing manuals, relied on adapting language copied from others' hearts.

In the absence of specific references to complete letter writers or language obviously copied from the manuals, it is impossible to know with certainty whether Brown and Primus consulted that popular form of rhetorical education for romantic engagement. But it is clear that these African American women learned and adapted the rhetorical strategies of invention as well as the genre conventions widely taught by manuals and the broader culture. While manuals taught readers to invent romantic epistolary rhetoric by copying the language of the heart from model letters, Brown drew instead on the novel and poetry, adapting the language she copied in order to compose her same-sex relationship with Primus. And, whereas manuals taught a heteronormative conception of romantic relations as defined by gender difference, paced with restraint, and oriented to a marriage *telos,* Brown and Primus developed queer rhetorical practices for romantic engagement. These women queered conventions for epistolary address by addressing each other; composed an epistolary exchange that exceeded conventions for the urgency and intensity of romantic relations; and, unable to marry each other, addressed and exchanged letters for the rhetorical purposes of pursuing nonnormative romantic and erotic relations with both each other and others. Brown also repurposed epistolary rhetoric to not only romantic but also civic ends by writing about racial politics within her romantic letters to Primus.

Reading Romantic Letters as Learned and Crafted Epistolary Rhetoric

This analysis of Brown and Primus's romantic engagement through queer epistolary rhetoric reinforces my prior discussion of manual culture's "queer failures" (Halberstam, *Queer Art*). Brown and Primus's actual queer subversions of normative genre conventions are akin to those critically imagined failures of heteronormative rhetorical education through manuals. Yet this rhetorically oriented approach to Brown and Primus's correspondence also holds more interdisciplinary implications for how letters are read within histories of sexuality in general and nineteenth-century romantic friendship in particular.

Histories of sexuality rely fundamentally on letters as records of past romantic relationships. In the case of romantic letters between women, historians "debate how to interpret" the letters, as Carroll Smith-Rosenberg explained, but still they "constitute one of women's principal sources of information about women's . . . feelings for one another" ("Diaries and Letters" 234, 236).[28] There is no way around this methodological reliance. Indeed, I want to emphasize, my own research would have been impossible were it not for existing histories, particularly those by Farah Jasmine Griffin and Karen Hansen. But in focusing on sexuality and romantic relations without attention to rhetorical teaching and learning, some histories inadvertently reinforce the commonplace conception of romantic letters as what Patrick Paul Garlinger called "authentic . . . evidence" (ix).[29] Such histories treat romantic letters (and diaries) as unstudied expressions of heartfelt feeling and thus as evidence of extratextual romantic practices and even sexual identities within a given period.[30] I suggest instead that letters be read as epistolary rhetoric—as rhetorically learned and crafted texts—as evidence of rhetorical instruction in generic conventions. Such an approach allows histories of romantic friendship between women to consider new questions that go beyond what are now two familiar debates.

The first familiar debate concerns whether "women's letters . . . suggest sexual involvement" or "passions [that] were platonic" (Smith-Rosenberg, "Diaries and Letters" 236). Hansen addressed this debate in her study of Brown and Primus's epistolary exchange. While acknowledging that they "left no evidence of genital contact," Hansen argued that, "Rather than simply a romantic outpouring of sentiment, the passion between Addie and Rebecca that suffuses the letters expressed a self-consciously sexual relationship" (183). This argument rested on a reading of a series of letters in which Brown described what Hansen characterized as the "sexual practice" of "bosom sex"—"providing access to . . . breasts"—with Primus as well as another "female lover," an English woman (186).[31] On the basis of this reading, Hansen maintained, again, that Brown and Primus's relationship was "an explicitly erotic—as distinct from romantic—friendship" (184). Griffin concurred that, "If we are to believe Addie's letters, her relationship with Rebecca was not simply an affectionate 'friendship.' . . . Several of Addie's letters have fairly explicit references to erotic interactions between herself and Rebecca" (6). In hedging with "If we are to believe Addie's letters," Griffin made clear the limits of letters as evidence offering a conclusive picture of what happened between Brown and Primus. Hansen, too, in elaborating on how she reached her conclusions about "bosom sex," underscored the interpretive complexities of reading letters as evidence of past relations. Still, both scholars read the correspondence partly to ascertain or at least speculate about extradiscursive erotic and sexual relations.

My analysis of romantic letters alongside manual instruction suggests how we might read romantic correspondence like Brown and Primus's in another way: as rhetorically learned and crafted. There is room to further contextualize romantic epistolary rhetoric, in other words, in relation to the genre conventions that were taught within the culture. In my analysis of the same series of letters, I asked not what Brown's writing about "bosom sex" suggested regarding her sexual activities and relations with Primus and other women. Instead, I focused on how Brown as a learner navigated the widely taught genre conventions for romantic epistolary rhetoric, considering the significance of her electing to write to Primus about erotic interactions with another woman. Nineteenth-century complete letter-writer manuals taught that the normative purpose for romantic epistolary rhetoric was to pursue marriage, and model letters did not take up the subject of erotic and sexual practices. While there is no evidence Brown used complete letter writers, she composed her romantic letters to Primus within a rhetorical situation culturally subject to the same generic conventions so widely taught by popular manuals. Yet Brown rhetorically crafted her letters in defiance of those conventions. She wrote letters that did not pursue the heteronormative *telos* of marriage, writing instead about erotic relations with women other than Primus. So, whether or not the extant correspondence can answer the question of how these women engaged in extratextual sexual practices, what the letters do make clear is how Brown crafted her epistolary rhetoric in queer defiance of genre conventions and cultural norms.

A second familiar "controversy" within scholarship on romantic friendship concerns "the degree to which society unproblematically accepted the intense emotional relationships between women" (Hansen 179–80). Addressing this point of controversy, Hansen elaborated on her interpretation of a letter in which Brown offered "a chronicle of a heated debate between Addie, Rebecca's mother and a disapproving neighbor" (180).[32] Situating this letter within the broader correspondence, Hansen acknowledged that Brown and Primus's relationship "was highly visible and deeply enmeshed in the domestic networks of Hartford's African-American community" but argued that the relationship was recognized as competing with the attentions of male suitors and accepted by community and kin only to the extent it did not "interfere with relations with men" (178, 189, 200). On this point Griffin registered disagreement. Writing about the same "heated debate," Griffin instead asserted that, "Rebecca's family and friends recognize the closeness of the relationship . . . and seem to treat Addie's emotional response . . . as a girlhood crush" (84). "In this respect," Griffin noted, her "interpretation differs from that of Karen Hansen, who argues that the community knew of the nature of Addie and Rebecca's relationship and supported it, but nonetheless encouraged both women to eventually turn their affection to men" (290 n. 2). Here too, both Griffin and Hansen recognized that Brown and Primus's letters are not straightforward evidence but are open to interpretation. In noting that Hansen's "interpretation differs," Griffin highlighted how the reading of the letters is indeed a matter of interpretation (290). Hansen also reminded readers that "other interpretations are possible. . . . Understanding sexual relationships between women in the nineteenth century will always be a challenge, because of the centrality of texts as historical evidence . . . and their multiplicity of meanings" (200).

On this second point of debate about social acceptance, there is again another way to respond to the "challenge" of interpreting romantic letters. Instead of reading Brown and Primus's correspondence in order to "understand . . . sexual relationships," I read the letters to understand rhetorical education and practices for romantic engagement. I read the "texts as historical evidence" of *textual* practices. While my prior consideration of the letter Hansen referenced was brief, I focused not on the familiar question of what Brown's account of Primus's mother's comments might indicate regarding community acceptance. Instead, I read this letter as suggestive of how Brown and Primus adapted the genre conventions for rhetorical purpose taught by letter-writing manuals. I noted that, in electing to write that Primus's mother "said I thought as much of you if you was a gentleman she also said if either one of us was a gent we would marry," Brown crafted epistolary rhetoric that defied genre conventions for pursuing heteronormative marriage (Jan. 21, 1866). In this and other letters, she wrote to acknowledge and cope with the generic and cultural constraints that prohibited her from pursuing marriage with Primus simply because she "was [not] a gentleman."

In these brief comparisons of how Hansen, Griffin, and I read Brown's letters, I do not disagree with their interpretations. Nor do I underestimate the original scholarly contributions of Hansen's and Griffin's research. I understand their research to be groundbreaking, especially because prior studies of same-sex romantic friendships between women had focused on white women (Hansen 179, 183). Understandably, in making such necessary scholarly interventions, Hansen and Griffin continue to read Brown and Primus's correspondence as evidence that might shed light on the familiar points of debate about sexual involvement and social acceptance. In suggesting, alternately, that we read romantic letters as evidence of how learners rhetorically crafted them in relation to widely taught genre conventions, I also do not mean to frame my offering as a preferred methodological approach. However, because histories of same-sex romantic relations between women seem to return again and again to the same questions, I do urge taking up new approaches. I invite historians of sexuality, romantic friendship, and rhetoric to join in considering how we might complicate interpretations of romantic letters through greater attention to the ways they are evidence of rhetorical instruction and practice as much as they are of romantic feelings and relations.

Of course, Brown and Primus were not alone as learners whose queer epistolary rhetoric challenged heteronormative rhetorical education and generic boundaries with important historiographic implications. Nor was Brown alone in composing epistolary rhetoric that, as previously discussed, traversed boundaries between intimate and political discourse. Instead, Brown joined a tradition of nineteenth-century writers who used their so-called private and personal letters to develop explicitly political commentary and critiques of public life.[33] In characterizing this epistolary phenomenon, William Merrill Decker echoes

Lauren Berlant and Michael Warner, reminding us that "what we identify as the private life is a conventionalized and hence public construction" (6). I turn next to another writer—one quite differently situated in terms of gender, sexuality, race, class, and educational background—whose queer epistolary rhetoric also traversed the domains of private and public life, of romantic and civic rhetoric.

CHAPTER 3

"Somehow or other, queer in the extreme"

Albert Dodd's Civic Training and Genre-Queer Practices

> This verse though, by the way, to me doth seem /
> somehow or other, queer in the extreme.
>
> Albert Dodd, "Epistolary" (1836)

Like Addie Brown and Rebecca Primus's romantic epistolary exchange, Albert Dodd's rhetorical practices defied the widely taught genre conventions and cultural norms for composing romantic letters and relations. The dominant manual instruction emphasized models in which a learner like Dodd would have addressed a woman and exchanged cautiously timed letters directed toward the heteronormative *telos* of marriage. In contrast, his diary reports he composed romantic epistolary rhetoric addressed to multiple women as well as men, often with urgency and impatience and at no point oriented to the goal of marriage. Thus his rhetorical practices were queer, like Addie Brown and Rebecca Primus's, in keeping with the first definition offered in my introductory chapter. Yet his practices were also "somehow or another, queer in the extreme" in a second way, insofar as he not only subverted genre conventions and cultural norms for romantic epistolary rhetoric but also transgressed normative distinctions between and among other genres related to the letter (Apr. 1836).

Although Dodd's romantic letters are not extant, he wrote about his romantic epistolary practices within a commonplace book turned diary as well as a poetry album.[1] In understanding this broader network of multigenre practices as epistolary rhetoric, I am informed by Suzanne B. Spring's research on early nineteenth-century student writing that crosses multiple genres but operates according to an "epistolary logic," insofar as "address and exchange are central aspects" ("'Seemingly Uncouth Forms'" 633, 638). Dodd developed his multigenre epistolary rhetoric while a college student, first at Washington (now Trinity) College and then at Yale College (now University). I frame Dodd's extant writing as both multigenre and epistolary: as taking the form of multiple genres other than the letter, yet functioning according to an epistolary logic of address to and exchange with readers. Accounting for Dodd's multigenre epistolary practices widens my scope to include rhetorical practices for romantic engagement through a variety of genres. In addition, examining Dodd's education and practices alongside Brown and Primus's enables consideration of a diverse range of learners. Brown, Primus, and Dodd can be understood as diverse by gender, sexuality, race, class, and educational background. While Brown avidly pursued opportunities for self-education, for instance, there is no indication she had access to formal schooling in rhetoric, much less to a classically modeled rhetorical education for civic engagement. This was precisely the sort of education available to Dodd as a privileged, upper-class white man.[2]

After characterizing his epistolary rhetoric composed while a college student, I analyze how Dodd repurposed his rhetorical education for civic engagement to romantic ends. Dodd's rhetorical education at Washington and Yale was classically oriented to civic participation through training in public oratory about political questions. Not surprisingly, this education prepared him for a career in law and politics. But Dodd also repurposed this education, transferring his learned rhetorical awareness to develop multigenre epistolary rhetoric for participation in romantic relations. These practices were "genre-queer," to use Kazim Ali's term, not merely because Dodd engaged epistolary logics while composing across multiple genres. Such multigenre epistolary practices were not uncommon in the writing of nineteenth-century students. Rather, Dodd's practices were genre-queer because of how he transferred his learning from civic to romantic domains, transgressed generic lines with a critical awareness that recognized generic distinctions but refused their boundaries, and, perhaps most important, did both in order to compose romantic relations that subverted the norms and conventions taught during the postal age.[3]

Albert Dodd's Multigenre Epistolary Rhetoric

Albert Dodd shared with Addie Brown and Rebecca Primus a close relationship to Hartford, Connecticut. Twenty-three years before the first of Brown's extant letters to Primus, sent from Waterbury to Hartford, Dodd inscribed the opening pages of his commonplace book and poetry album "Albert Dodd / Washington College / Hartford, Conn." (July 26; Jan. 1836). Like Primus, Dodd was from Hartford. He was born in 1818.[4] But, like Brown, he died young. In 1844 he drowned while crossing the Mackinaw River on horseback.[5] Although Dodd never married, Jonathan Katz has suggested that Dodd may have been romantically involved with his law partner, Jesse W. Fell (31).[6] Dodd's obituary indicates that Jesse was present at a meeting called when Dodd died. Six months later, Jesse married for the first time, at the "advanced age of thirty-seven" (Katz 31).

Dodd's obituary also references his studies at Washington and Yale, celebrating that "He was a finished classical scholar, well informed in general literature." It was while a student at Washington that Dodd started writing in his commonplace book turned diary and in his album of poetry. The commonplace book suggests Dodd began his studies at Washington in 1834 (July 31, 1836). Dodd was later suspended from Washington following what Peter Gay has called "some disagreeable imbroglios with college authorities" (206)—or what Dodd himself termed the "Junior Rebellion" (Feb. 5, 1837). In 1837, after a nearly three-month silence between diary entries, Dodd wrote, "I have left Washington C. now, doubtful forever" (Feb. 2, 1837). He explained, "The causes which led the Faculty to punish me were mostly erroneous, but I own that I deserved what was inflicted, only, of the many dark deeds which were committed, they did not happen to hit upon the right ones, which by I should suffer." The next day, Dodd continued, "Having expiated the reckless course of the last term by suspension I returned to College again, fully determined to behave tranquilly . . . nor make any more trouble" (Feb. 3, 1837). Determination was not enough, apparently, because another day later Dodd referred to "The affair which has now resulted in my second . . . suspension from College" (Feb. 4, 1837). In these same entries, Dodd also implied that one of the young men he was interested in romantically, John Heath, may have played some role in the suspension. But the precise "causes," "affair," or "rebellion" that led to Dodd's suspension from Washington are unclear.

Dodd quickly resumed his studies at Yale. While the suspension "made a fuss at home" and "was the cause of . . . partial estrangement, on the part of John Heath, from me," Dodd insisted, "I do not and did not care much for the suspension" (Feb. 2, 3, 1837). Nor did the suspension impede his educational advancement. Less than two weeks after first writing about the suspension, Dodd turned to plans to resume his studies at Yale. He wrote, "Here I am at home spending day after day and week after week in idlene[ss], when I ought to be 'up and doing.' If I expect to enter at Yale the next term, I have got much yet to do to gain an easy admission" (Feb. 14, 1837).[7] While Dodd had "much yet to do" before his admission to Yale, this work was accompanied by the play of fantasy. Dodd fantasized about being a student at Yale with another of the young men who interested him romantically: "If he would only go to Yale now, and I too, how I should like it!" (Feb. 26, 1837). Just a few months later, Dodd reported that at least the latter half of his fantasy had come true. He located himself in New

Haven, noting, "Shall apply to be examined tomorrow," and two days later "got through my examination and am a Junior at . . . Yale" (May 28, 30, 1837). Inside the front cover of his diary, Dodd entered a second inscription: "Albert Dodd / Yale University / New Haven, Conn." (July 11, 1837).[8] He successfully graduated with the class of 1838 (*Catalogue* 13).

I conducted research on Dodd in the Yale University Library's Manuscripts and Archives, which holds the Albert Dodd Papers.[9] The papers include Dodd's commonplace book turned diary, his poetry album, and a few letters to family members from his post-Yale years. These materials are rich in their accounts of Dodd's educational and romantic life while a student at both Yale and Washington. Unfortunately his romantic letters were not saved. However, Dodd did write about his romantic epistolary rhetoric within his diary. Like much nineteenth-century writing about same-sex romantic relations, Dodd's diary is marked by intriguing absences and moments of self-censorship. There are places where he did not name "things" but instead referred to them with dashes or abbreviations. For example, in an entry about "things that trouble me particularly," Dodd worried over "that —— which has long troubled me; and also ——. . . . Besides there is M. O. —— I dare not write even here these things —— which it is my prayer may soon be settled" (Feb. 5, 1837).[10] There are also places where Dodd or someone else cut pages from the diary. In one of these instances, Dodd pondered his affections for a man and a woman: "it seems the nature of my affection . . . was really the same. . . . Yet one was for a female, the other for"—and it is precisely here that pages are cut from the diary (Feb. 7, 1837). Still, in many other portions of the diary, Dodd's writing about his romantic relations and epistolary rhetoric remains available for study.

My analysis of Dodd's romantic epistolary practices and rhetorical education is the first in the fields of rhetoric, communication, and composition. Yet, like that of Brown and Primus, Dodd's writing has elicited attention from historians of sexuality and nineteenth-century romantic friendship. Katz and Gay, as well as E. Anthony Rotundo, have examined Dodd's diary in order to account for how his same-sex relations with men constituted friendships romantic and even erotic in nature.[11] Gay, for instance, highlighted a diary entry in which Dodd directly contemplated whether his feelings for Heath suggested more than friendship. Dodd wrote, "It is not friendship merely which I feel for him, or it is friendship of the strongest kind. It is a heart-felt, a manly, a pure, deep, and fervent love" (Feb. 4, 1837).[12] Along similar lines, Rotundo pointed to diary entries in which Dodd admired Anthony Halsey's physical appearance and described spending the night together, embracing and kissing (7).[13] Dodd wrote, "Often too [Halsey] shared my pillow—or I his, and then how sweet to sleep with him, to hold his beloved form in my embrace, to have his arms about my neck, to imprint upon his face sweet kisses!" (Mar. 27, 1837).[14] Katz considered these and other diary entries and, seeming to echo Karen Hansen on the relationship between Brown and Primus, concluded, "The intensity of Albert's feelings exceeded romantic friendship by including an erotic element" (32).

While Dodd pursued romantic and erotic relations with men, these relations occurred alongside those with women. Dodd used the phrase "Dear, beloved trio" to refer to not only Heath and Halsey but also Julia Beers. In one of many diary reflections on his affections for both women and men, Dodd wrote, "L-o-v-e, love; what is love? I can't describe it. All I know is that there are three persons in this world whom I have loved, and those are, Julia, John, & Anthony. Dear, beloved trio" (Mar. 24, 1837). While Dodd may have "loved" just "three persons" up to that point, he would go on to meet and write about romantic relations with Elizabeth Morgan and Jabez Smith.[15] As Rotundo explained, "Albert's romantic life . . . mixed male and female love objects," such that "rapturous musings about John Heath mingled freely with love poems to a woman named Julia, and the journal entries which glowed with his passion for Anthony Halsey filled the same volumes as those which expressed his yearning for a beloved young lady named Elizabeth" (8). Katz similarly acknowledged that Dodd experienced "strong attraction to men as well as women" (32).[16]

My work is obviously informed by these histories of sexuality and romantic friendship. But, like in my analysis of Brown and Primus's romantic epistolary rhetoric, I again take a different approach. As a historian of rhetoric, I focus on Dodd's rhetorical training and development of genre-queer epistolary rhetoric for composing romantic relations. I thus examine his seemingly private writing about his romantic epistolary rhetoric alongside his school-sponsored writing and accounts of educational experiences. Rather than reading his commonplace book, diary, and poetry album as evidence of the nature of his romantic and erotic feelings, I read the texts as multigenre epistolary rhetoric that was learned and crafted.

To understand how Dodd developed his multigenre epistolary practices, I identify potential relationships between what he learned at Washington and Yale and how he crafted his genre-queer romantic epistolary rhetoric. I study institutional records of instruction at Yale, consulting primary sources including annual catalogues as well as student and professor lecture notes, to piece together the specific features of Dodd's classically modeled rhetorical education. I also examine Dodd's diary account of his educational experiences at Yale and Washington. As Shirley Wilson Logan has emphasized, diaries are important to examine within histories of rhetorical education because learners both write about their "formal instruction" and "record . . . their self-education projects" (30). In this way, diaries may function as "evidence of enacted rhetorical education" (118).

CLASSICALLY MODELED RHETORICAL EDUCATION FOR CIVIC ENGAGEMENT

Albert Dodd's rhetorical education was, on the one hand, classically oriented for civic engagement, designed to prepare privileged men for participation as citizens and leaders. I consider this feature of Dodd's training first because it is the one most widely emphasized within existing histories of rhetorical education, and he did go on to an expected career in law and politics. On the other hand, Dodd repurposed this training for civic engagement to romantic ends. His repurposing was likely enabled by two other features of his classically broad education: he studied not only treatises and oratory by Greek and Roman rhetors but also Greek and Latin literature; his practice in public oratory involved speaking as well as writing, in that he wrote a great deal as he prepared for debates and exhibitions about political questions. The breadth of Dodd's rhetorical training across a range of different genres and purposes is significant because, as I later show, this breadth enabled him to transfer his learning from civic to romantic realms in order to develop genre-queer epistolary rhetoric.

Orientation to Civic Participation

Dodd's classically modeled rhetorical training was in keeping with Yale's reputation. As Robert Connors recounts, then-president Jeremiah Day's "Yale Plan was the touchstone of conservative classical college curricula in the nineteenth century" ("Day, Henry Noble" 161). According to John C. Brereton, the Yale report of 1828 favored classical education in general and classically modeled rhetorical education in particular (5–6).[17] Especially early in the century, when Dodd studied at Yale, its rhetorical training may have come closer to following a classical model than any other institution in the U.S. collegiate system.[18]

First and foremost, Dodd's rhetorical education was classically modeled in its orientation to civic engagement. Such education had long trained privileged young men for civic participation via the senate, pulpit, or bar. These potential arenas for civic participation were taken up directly as a debate topic assigned by Rev. Chauncey A. Goodrich, the professor of rhetoric and oratory at Yale from 1817 to 1839 (Hoshor). Alongside other educational and political topics, he prompted students to debate "Which affords the greatest field for Oratory: the Pulpit or the Bar?" (Wightman).[19] Regardless of which side Dodd might have taken when debating this question in college, he later put his own rhetorical education in the service of civic engagement through the bar—as well as the beginnings of a career in politics.

Following his graduation from Yale, Dodd "pursued his legal studies with Hon. Mr. Ellsworth, and was admitted a few years since as an attorney at the Hartford county bar" ("Obituary"). "Determining to settle in the growing West,"

Dodd moved to St. Louis, Missouri, and then to Bloomington, Illinois, where "he opened a law office." According to *Biographical Notes of Graduates of Yale College,* Dodd "prospered in his profession" there (Dexter 288). Dodd reported the same in a letter from Bloomington to his brother Edward. Dodd wrote, "in the legal line I can safely say I am doing very well" (Mar. 13, 1844).

Also in Bloomington, Dodd "took an active part in politics; and had promising prospects before him" (*Biographical Record* 53). In the same letter to Edward, Dodd went on: "As to my political debut it is not yet made, and I content myself with talking in favor of Van Buren, free trade &c., against Clay, a tariff &c. A number of my friends want me to run for the Legislature, and I should get the nomination" (Mar. 13, 1844). Dodd expressed some hesitation, having "hardly been [in Bloomington] long enough to push forward," but resolved, "I am not at all concerned that I can do something in that line in the course of time." Dodd's lack of concern was warranted: "On the very day of his death, he was nominated by a convention which assembled at Bloomington, as a candidate for the State Legislature" ("Obituary"). Dodd's classically modeled rhetorical education prepared him for civic participation in law and politics. His obituary thus characterized him as not only "a finished classical scholar" and "citizen" but also as "an attorney" and "candidate for the State Legislature."

Broad Study of "Rhetorical" and "Literary" Genres

Part of how Dodd's rhetorical education prepared him for this civic participation was through study of orators and rhetorical theorists concerned with legal and political affairs. But in addition to being classically oriented to civic engagement, his rhetorical education was also classically broad in its coverage of a range of genres. While he studied classical Greek and Roman rhetorical treatises, he did so alongside Greek and Latin literature. In other words, his familiarity with multiple genres included both those that are clearly "rhetorical" and those that are, in present-day terms, "literary."

Certainly Dodd's classically modeled rhetorical education paid considerable attention to classical oratory and rhetorical theory. Dodd studied Isocrates, Plato, and Quintilian. Most studied, though, were the Greek orator Demosthenes and the Roman orator Cicero, both statesmen whose rhetorical practice and theory were concerned largely with law and politics.[20] According to Yale's annual *Catalogue* from the academic year Dodd was admitted, "recitations in the books here specified" included, in the second part of the sophomore year, "Cicero's Brutus" and "Select Orations of Demosthenes, begun"; in the third part of the sophomore year, "Select Orations of Demosthenes, finished" and "Cicero de Oratore, begun"; and, in the first part of junior year, "Cicero de Oratore, finished" (27–28).[21] As the *Catalogue* indicated, Dodd would have been examined on this reading even though he entered Yale as a junior (25); his diary entries confirm he did take an examination in order to enter Yale as a junior (May 28, 30, 1837). In addition to this reading for the examination and junior year, "A course of Lectures on the oration of Demosthenes for the crown, [was] delivered to members of the Senior Class" (*Catalogue* 28). Lecture notes by Professor Goodrich also suggest Dodd was trained in the oratory and rhetorical theory of Demosthenes and Cicero (Goodrich, "Family Papers").[22] In keeping with Goodrich's notes, those taken by another of his students, though predating Dodd, also reference Demosthenes (Wightman).[23]

Nor was such training in classical rhetoric limited to Dodd's time at Yale. In the "Preface" to the commonplace book he began while a student at Washington, he referenced Lord Chesterfield, who in one letter of advice to his son recommended, "pray read *Cicero, de Oratore,* the best book in the world to finish [an orator]" (July 29, 1836; Chesterfield 134). Just as Dodd's study of classical oratory and rhetorical theory predated his time at Yale, it stayed with him following graduation. In his own letter of advice to his brother Julius, Dodd wrote a postscript that included "Cicero's oratory" in a list of "good books to study" (Apr. 12, 1842).[24] Dodd was thoroughly learned in classical rhetorical theory and oratory, especially that of Cicero and Demosthenes.

Yet, with important implications for how he repurposed his rhetorical training to romantic ends, Dodd's study of Greek and Roman political speeches and rhetorical theory was not distinct from Greek and Latin language and literature. At Yale, entering freshman were examined on not only Cicero but also "Virgil, Sallust, the Greek Testament, Dalzel's Collectanea Graeca Minora . . . Andrews and Stodard's Latin Grammar, Goodrich's Greek Grammar, Latin Prosody, Writing Latin" (*Catalogue* 25). In addition to "a Professor of Rhetoric and Oratory," the faculty included "a Professor of the Latin Language and Literature" and "a Professor of the Greek Language and Literature" (26). Required texts from across the years of instruction included "Folsom's Livy," "Adam's Roman Antiquities," "Xenophon's Anabasis," "Horace," "Homer's Iliad," "The Captivi of Plautus," "Tacitus," "Select Tragedies, viz. the Prometheus of Aeschylus; Antigone and Electra of Sophocles; Alcestis of Euripides" (27).

Dodd's own writing specified the literary sources he encountered during his studies.[25] While he was at Yale, his poetry album cited the *Greek Anthology* as a source for lyric poems and epigrams. These include several attributed to the lyric poet Anacreon. Far from being rhetorically oriented to civic life, most of the poems included are about wine. For example, one translation begins as follows before turning to wine: "Why teach me the laws / And rhetorician's rules, / And all the profitless / Learning of the schools" (Apr. 1838). Another entry in the poetry album is an epigram about wine and love: "Wine, and the baths, and love of ladies / Leads one quickest down to Hades" (Dec. 1838). During Dodd's years at Washington, he also entered lyric poems in his album. His album includes a "Translation from the Aeneid / Book fifth, line 835," an epic by the Roman poet Virgil (Feb. 1834). Importantly, Virgil's *Aeneid*, unlike the other poems mentioned, is concerned with politics. While including the tragic love story of Aeneas and Dido, the poem's emphasis is on the Roman empire, political conflict, and war. Dodd's poetry album also contains three translations of odes and epistle verses from another Augustan-era lyric poet, Horace: "Translations from Horace / Book 2nd, Ode 16th / To Grosphus," and "Translations from Horace / Book 4th Ode 7th / To Torquatus" (Apr. 1836). Dodd's poetry album indicates that his study of classical literature attended to epigrams and lyric poems taking the form of the epic, ode, and epistle. His classically modeled education exposed him to a wide range of texts, including those associated with both rhetoric and poetry. Not surprisingly, then, when Dodd wrote his letter of advice to Julius, his recommended list of "good books to study" included not only "Cicero's oratory" but also "Virgil" (Apr. 12, 1841). Also not surprisingly, as Dodd developed multigenre rhetorical practices for participating in romantic life, these practices were both epistolary and poetic.

Practice with Oratory and Writing

A final feature of Dodd's classically modeled rhetorical education was that it prepared students for civic participation through significant practice in oratory. Rather than simply reading and studying classical rhetorical theory and speech transcripts, students trained as orators themselves. Through this training, Dodd gained practice with public speaking on questions of political import. Here too Dodd's rhetorical education was broad, in that training in oratory was accompanied by significant practice with writing.

At Yale, Dodd's rhetorical education emphasized declamations, debates, and exhibitions as forms of training for public speaking. The *Catalogue* explained, "The Senior and Junior Classes have forensic Disputations once or twice a week, before their instructors. There are very frequent exercises in Declamation before the Tutors, before the Professor of Oratory, and before the Faculty and Students in the Chapel" (28). The importance of this training in public speaking was further underscored by awards "for declamation in public" (29). Dodd also gained practice with public speaking before becoming a student at Yale. During his period of suspension from Washington, an exhibition preoccupied him nearly as much as his romantic life. In fact, in a diary entry about his affections for women and men, he pondered, "I don't know what; it may be this Exhibition which most occupies my mind at present" (Feb. 7, 1837). While the rest of this diary entry lends little credence to the possibility that the exhibition most occupied Dodd's mind, there is no doubt that he thought and wrote of it often, variously referring to it as "W. C. P. Exhibition" and "the Panthenon [*sic*] Exhibition" (Feb. 5, 13; Mar. 19; Apr. 8, 1837). Perhaps because of his suspension, one entry mentions needing to get "a final permit of the Faculty" in order to "speak at" the exhibition (Mar. 19, 1837). In another, Dodd reported that he went "to College to attend Society," and he went on to describe a "debate," which eventually turned to "the question of putting off the exhibition," suggesting that his participation was related to membership in a debating society at Washington (Mar. 4, 1837). In multiple entries, Dodd recorded that he had gone "to College" to prepare for the exhibition and intended to complete the exhibition before turning his attention to other activities, including studying for the Yale entrance examination (Feb. 5, 7, 13; Mar. 4; Apr. 2, 1837).

Exhibitions, debates, and declamations at Washington and Yale served as practice in public speaking because they took place before audiences. Again, as Yale's *Catalogue* states, declamations were "in public," and students frequently spoke before the professor of oratory, before other instructors, tutors, and faculty, and before fellow students (28–29). Dodd's diary confirms that he spoke before audiences. After the Washington exhibition, he concluded that his speaking "went off well considering. The room was full, with an audience very select. On the whole, I believe the audience was quite pleased" (Apr. 8, 1837). Of course, no matter how "select" the audience was, this exhibition functioned as training for speaking publicly before an audience.

Such rhetorical training prepared Dodd for speaking publicly on questions of civic import. Certainly he encountered political speeches. For instance, on the same day he recorded his final preparations for the Washington exhibition, he remembered, "Last Wednesday went up to the City Hall to listen to Daniel Webster's speech" (Apr. 2, 1837). Dodd himself also spoke on and debated political questions. The debate topics Professor Goodrich assigned at Yale are suggested by the papers of another student of rhetoric. With few exceptions, almost all of the topics had to do with education or politics (Wightman). Debates on education included, for instance, "Ought the higher branches to be included in the education of ladies?" and "Which is the most beneficial a public or private education?" Examples of more overtly political topics were "Which is entitled to the most honor—Columbus for discovering the new world—or Washington for preserving our Country?"; "Ought the United States to take possession of Cuba?"; and "Ought free blacks in our country to be allowed the right of suffrage?" Dodd presumably debated a similar range of educational and political topics, including questions about what the country's government and laws should do or support.

While Dodd's rhetorical education at Yale and Washington offered practice in public speaking through participation in exhibitions, declamations, and debates, it is important to keep in mind the role of writing. A shift from public speaking to more private writing is often cited as a feature of the mid-nineteenth-century decline in classically informed rhetorical education. "Yet plenty of writing took place," Brereton has cautioned, even in eighteenth-century colleges. He cited

Yale in 1766 as one example, in that students submitted writing to an instructor before delivering it orally (4). Dodd's writing during his time at Yale confirms that assigned debates were something that, at least initially, he had "to write." In one diary entry, for example, Dodd explained, "I have got a debate to write on the question 'Ought government to support a class of men exclusively devoted to literary pursuit?'" (June 18, 1837). With no hesitation about his position, Dodd added, "I espouse the negative." Less than a month later, he exclaimed, "O dear me, I have got to write a Debate for tomorrow! A job!" (July 11, 1837).

Also according to Dodd's diary, much writing was involved in his preparations for the Washington exhibition. In one entry, after remarking that he had "done more [writing] in the past month or two," he described in detail what exactly he had written: "Besides letters and this diary, I have scribbled a poem of 200 lines, for the Panthenon Exhibition, together with one or two smaller pieces in the rhyming line on various occasions. Then I finished a philosophical Colloquy which Gillett [probably another student] began, though I did more than three fourths of the whole, for the same exhibition, and now I have finished my comedy of about 45 pages letter paper. On the whole the goose quill has lately become more habituated to my hand, and writing has seemed to come more readily than in a long time before" (Feb. 14, 1837). By Dodd's own account, preparing for an exhibition involved much writing, including writing across a range of genres. The exhibition functioned as training for public speaking in particular, as well as for writing "more readily" in general.

As I have detailed, Dodd's rhetorical education was classically modeled: it was oriented to civic engagement through law and politics, included study of classical oratory and rhetorical theory, and provided training in public speaking on political questions. At the same time, his rhetorical education was classically broad: he studied Greek and Roman rhetoric alongside Greek and Latin language and literature and practiced oratory alongside writing. So even as his rhetorical education emphasized public discourse for participation in civic life, this education was broad in its exposure to multiple genres—for rhetoric and poetry, oratory and writing—with a range of purposes.

It was likely this exposure to and practice with multiple genres and purposes that enabled Dodd to repurpose his rhetorical education through "transfer" from civic to romantic domains. Studies of transfer emphasize that clear, one-to-one transfer of skills from one situation to another is difficult to capture in research and unlikely to occur within student writing (Brent, "Crossing Boundaries" 562).[26] But what does transfer are "dispositions" or "'habits of mind,'" such as "rhetorical thinking" (Bereiter ctd. in Brent, "Crossing Boundaries" 563). The disposition that facilitates transfer involves "general rhetorical knowledge," "wide-ranging and flexible" rhetorical thinking, and "rhetorical awareness" (Brent, "Transfer, Transformation, and Rhetorical Knowledge" 411;

"Crossing Boundaries" 565). Dodd developed such flexible rhetorical thinking and awareness through his classically modeled and broad rhetorical training, and he transferred this awareness from civic to romantic domains of rhetorical participation.[27]

Genre-Queer Practices for Romantic Engagement

Dodd repurposed his broad training to develop four queer rhetorical practices for participating in romantic relations. Having encountered examples of same-sex attraction and homoerotic relations in classical texts, he wrote about them as a strategy for composing rhetorics to compare and deliberate about his nonnormative romantic epistolary relations with men and women. He also transferred his flexible rhetorical awareness in order to make a generic shift from composing a school-sponsored commonplace book to writing a diary. This generic shift enabled further rhetorical invention, as he wrote about romantic epistolary exchanges and even practiced direct epistolary address within his diary. Finally, he experimented in the diary as well as a poetry album with forms of romantic address and exchange that were simultaneously epistolary and poetic. He developed these multigenre practices with awareness of his moves between generic categories. Such moves are "genre-queer" in that, even as Dodd recognized generic distinctions, he resisted the normative boundaries that might limit practices of and related to epistolary rhetoric (Ali 36). It is in these ways that his multigenre epistolary rhetoric was "somehow or other, queer in the extreme" (Apr. 1836).

Composing Self-Rhetorics on Literary Representations of Same-Sex Erotic Relations

My analysis of the relationship between Dodd's classically modeled rhetorical education and his queer practices begins in a predictable place, with his writing about representations of same-sex erotic relations. The homoerotic undercurrents throughout classical education, rhetoric, and literature are well established.[28] It comes as no surprise, then, that Dodd read, translated, and wrote about texts that include representations of same-sex relations. Recall, for instance, some of his references discussed already. Depending on the specific texts Dodd had in mind when making these references, he may have found homoerotic representations in works as varied as those by Demosthenes and Virgil as well as the *Greek Anthology*.[29] Most relevant to Dodd's romantic epistolary rhetoric addressed to young men and women, however, was his writing about the Greek myth of Zeus and Ganymede. This myth first appeared in Greek literature in Homer's *Iliad,* which was required reading for Yale students (*Catalogue* 27). By "the beginning of the thirteenth century," Byrne Fone has explained, Ganymede "had become the eponymous symbol for homosexual love," and "later readers generally interpreted the story to be a founding myth of male love" (16, 107).

Dodd's reference to this myth of male love appears in "The disgrace of Hebe & preferment of Ganymede," a rhymed verse in his poetry album (Dec. 1837).[30] In Dodd's verse, Jove "had a dinner / . . . all of the gods, male and female, present were," and "The radiant Hebe, all blooming in beauty, / Was flying about, performing her duty / As cupbearer." Although "accustomed was she to the business . . . she hit / her foot against Mercury's wand." As she "fell," "her robes" opened, and "those parts were exhibited / To show which by modesty's law is prohibited." Jove, "vex'd at this breach of decorum . . . sent her away in disgrace," and "Ganymede he sent for, to serve in her place. / Which station forever he afterword had, / Though to cut Hebe out so in fact was too bad." In this rendition of the myth of Zeus and Ganymede, Dodd located a story about the replacement of Hebe by Ganymede, about her "disgrace" and his "preferment."

It is noteworthy that this myth even offers an example of same-sex erotic relations, which certainly were not modeled within nineteenth-century letter-writing manuals. Of greater significance, though, is how Dodd may have drawn on the story about the "preferment of Ganymede" over Hebe in order to understand his own affections for men and women. The story in Dodd's verse not only references the early myth but also bears thematic resemblance to *Hebe and Ganymede,* a poem from the Middle Ages that "is an example of an extensive debate literature that argued the merits of desire for boys and that for women" (Fone 107).[31] In Dodd's diary, he certainly debated with himself about the relationship between his affections for young men and for young women.

In characterizing Dodd's writing as a debate with himself, I have in mind Kimberly Harrison's concept of "self-rhetorics."[32] Self-rhetorics include "self-persuasion," which is "evidenced and carried out by the self-talk" used in diaries, yet "aim[ed] toward rhetorical performance" (*Rhetoric of Rebel Women* 15–16).[33] In this way, diarists may act as what Chaïm Perelman and Lucie Olbrechts-Tyteca have called "self-deliberators": those who "serve as their own audiences, arguing for a particular understanding of their experiences in the same way that they might with another person" (ctd. in Logan 34). Self-rhetorics include such self-deliberation but, again, are "directed" not only "to the internal audience of the self" but also "to external audiences," insofar as writers use the diary addressed to the self to prepare for addresses to others (7). In Dodd's case, he composed self-rhetorics in his diary to deliberate over how to understand his feelings for men and women as well as to prepare for the performances of his rhetorical self within epistolary rhetoric directed outward to audiences.

Dodd's deliberations drew on basic rhetorical strategies of comparison and definition. For example, in the diary entry that is most widely cited by historians, he had written, "it seems the nature of my affection for A. H. and J. F. H. was really the same as that which I had for Julia. Yet one was for a female, the other for . . ." (Feb. 7, 1837). Here someone cut pages from the diary, but, as Katz has noted, "Obviously, 'a male' completed the thought. . . . Albert was struck by the similarity of his 'affection' for men and for women" (28). Dodd did point to the similarity—"it seems the nature of my affection . . . was really the same"—but what seems to have "struck" him, I would say, is that such affection was the same even though "one was for a female, the other for. . . ."[34] In another entry comparing further his feelings for men and women, Dodd asked, "what is love?" He responded with the already mentioned declaration of his "Dear, beloved trio"—Heath, Halsey, and Beers—the "three persons in this world whom I have loved" (Mar. 24, 1837). Just days before, however, Dodd had described his love for Halsey as greater than that for Heath. Dodd wrote that Halsey "lately seems to have occupied my thoughts more than J. H. and I feel as if I loved him more ardently and intensely than John. I do perhaps; but both are very dear to me" (Mar. 21, 1837). In this moment of ranking, Beers received no mention. Rather than defining what love is, Dodd admitted that he could not "describe it" and wrote instead to compare his feelings.

It is in light of how he debated his affections and even the possibility of preferring Halsey to the other members of the beloved trio that Dodd's entry of "The disgrace of Hebe & preferment of Ganymede" takes on rhetorical significance. As Katz has explained, "Considering Albert's cutting out Julia for John, Anthony, and Jabez, the poem shows him employing ancient Greek myth, and the iconic, man-loving Ganymede to help him comprehend his own shifting, ambivalent attractions" (31). Dodd "began to use his knowledge of ancient affectionate and sexual life to come to terms with his own," Katz continued, and this was "a common strategy of . . . upper-class, college-educated white men" during the early nineteenth century. I similarly understand Dodd's engagement with classical texts and their representations of same-sex affection. He referenced the Greek myth of Zeus and Ganymede, which suggests possibilities for same-sex relations that, occurring alongside relations with women, show some preference for men.[35] In this way, Dodd repurposed his classically modeled rhetorical education to romantic ends. Having studied a broad range of classical texts, he encountered homoerotic representations of same-sex relations. He engaged with these representations in order to compose self-rhetorics, through which he compared his feelings for the men and women to whom he addressed romantic epistolary rhetoric.

Shifting Genres from Commonplace Book to Diary

In addition to representations of same-sex relations, Dodd's classically modeled rhetorical education exposed him to rhetorical practices in multiple genres for a range of purposes. In the second practice I consider, Dodd transferred his learned genre awareness and disposition to "rhetorical thinking" in order to transgress boundaries among the commonplace book, diary, and romantic epistolary rhetoric (Brent, "Crossing Boundaries" 563). Dodd purposefully shifted from composing a school-sponsored commonplace book to a semiprivate diary. This change in genre was significant because, as I consider next, the shift enabled Dodd's writing about romantic epistolary rhetoric.

Dodd was encouraged to keep a commonplace book as part of his education. In keeping with how this book has been categorized by Yale archivists, historians of sexuality and romantic friendship treat the book simply as a diary. Yet Dodd's initial intention to compose not a diary but a commonplace book is clearly marked. One of the pages just inside the front cover is inscribed, "My / Original / Common Place Book." As Dodd outlined in his "Preface" to the commonplace book, a professor at Washington suggested the practice of commonplacing, which Dodd eventually took up as a project of self-education in order to improve his writing: "It has seemed to me, reflecting oft and deeply on the necessity of acquiring a proficiency in composition, that the end would be best attained by spending a small portion of each day, if possible, in writing down my thoughts, *currente calamo*, freely and at random, on any subject which may arise in my mind. This plan was recommended to our Class by Proff. H. some time ago, and though, until now, by me rejected, yet it is not too late now to attempt to profit by the suggestion" (July 29, 1836).

Commonplace books such as Dodd's played an important role in Western rhetorical education that may be traced from Aristotle to Quintilian and throughout medieval, Renaissance, and Enlightenment education. As Susan Miller has described, commonplace books were first conceived of as "repositories for rhetoric's common topics" (22). Especially by the nineteenth century, though, commonplace books included not only "the copied quotations that first defined their purpose" but also "notes, self- and school-sponsored essays, journals, correspondence, speeches, legal documents, school exercises, and many other familiar forms" (35). Commonplace books functioned as a practice space to prepare students for discursive participation in more public forums.[36]

In keeping with this rhetorical tradition, Dodd's commonplace book consists primarily of what seem like self- and school-sponsored essays. In spite of his stated aim to compose *currente calamo,* offhand and without premeditation, he "confined himself" in early entries "in the somewhat stilted way of someone following formulas" (Gay 206). There are five dated entries following Dodd's "Preface" and prior to his generic shift.[37] In all, he maintained his commonplace book for just over three months, with one of the entries about his inattention to the book. Then, after complete inattention over the course of almost four months, Dodd made his generic shift from the commonplace book to a diary.

Whereas Dodd started his commonplace book at the suggestion of a professor, it was reading the diary of one of his romantic interests, Heath, that "gave [Dodd] the notion" to turn the book into a diary (Feb. 2, 1837).[38] This generic shift, like his initial purpose, is clearly marked. After the last commonplace book entry, he drew a line, left the rest of the page blank, and entered a new inscription: "Diary." Such a shift within the same book was not uncommon. Citing Dodd's diary as one example, Ronald Zboray and Mary Saracino Zboray have traced the complex ways people "recognized [the] distinct form and purpose" of different genres, yet "in practice . . . often merged formats, so that a diary, for example, could easily morph into a scrapbook, or a scrapbook into a commonplace book" ("Is It a Diary?" 106, 102). As Zboray and Zboray asserted, "the very moment these documents shift form or genre is often ripe with significance" (103). The moment of Dodd's generic shift was indeed significant to his genre-queer epistolary rhetoric.

Dodd's generic shift from a commonplace book to a diary was significant because, in writing meta-commentary about the shift, he demonstrated the sort of "rhetorical thinking" and awareness of genre that he had learned—a rhetorical awareness that guided his subsequent multigenre epistolary practices. In addition to marking his shift from commonplace book to diary with blank pages and distinct genre-based titles, he described the shift in the first entry following the new title page. With characteristic self-admonishment for laziness, Dodd began, "The plan which I had laid out for this book, in my preface, seems not to have been followed very closely or faithfully and the reason is sheer neglect and laziness on my part. I am perfectly ashamed of myself, for the last date here is months ago. I might have filled this by the present time if I had done as I ought, and I will strive after this—but I won't make any rash promises; it will be better to scribble along when convenient, and, by the way, it appears to me that it might be better that this volume should rather partake of the nature of a Diary, than to be followed out exactly after the manner which I first proposed to myself" (Feb. 2, 1837). Dodd's account, in spite of his use of the passive voice, shows him making a purposeful decision about switching from a commonplace book to a diary. He acknowledged the possibility of returning to his earlier proposal with greater determination and discipline. But rather than promising to do so, he decided to "scribble along when convenient." He recognized that his decision constituted a shift in genre: away from the commonplace book he "proposed" in his "Preface," toward "a Diary."

In writing meta-commentary about his decision to make this shift, Dodd demonstrated the sort of flexible and rhetorically oriented genre awareness developed through his classically broad training in a range of genres. He also demonstrated his learned rhetorical awareness of how a shift in genre involves a shift in purposes for writing. This same awareness would guide Dodd's subsequent practices. Rather than shifting from the commonplace book to the diary in a way that maintained clear distinctions between those two genres, his move to compose a diary gave way to still other genre-queer practices.

Inventing Romantic Epistolary Address and
Exchange through Diary Writing

Dodd's third genre-queer practice involved writing in his diary about romantic epistolary address and exchange. To some extent, he wrote *about* romantic epistolary rhetoric in keeping with the conventional purpose of the diary genre: "to record daily events" (Zboray and Zboray, "Is It a Diary?" 102).[39] For instance, he reported on trips to the post office, letters sent, and letters received (June 16, 1837). He wrote about romantic epistolary exchanges with Beers, Halsey, Heath, Morgan, and Smith. Particularly in the case of this romantic epistolary rhetoric, Dodd described delight at those letters received and anxiously awaited others. In the span of just one month, he wrote, "Yesterday I received a welcome letter from John H. which I have been anxiously looking for. . . . Why don't my dear Tony answer my letter? I do long to hear from him again"; then, "Expect letters from . . . Heath . . . & Halsey. Why don't they write!"; and finally, "got a letter from Anthony, a very long and interesting one. . . . What a good fine hearted dear fellow Anthony is! I love him beyond all expression" (Mar. 21; Apr. 16, 17, 1837). Here Dodd's use of the diary to record the sending and receiving letters was generically conventional. Yet this record is indispensable in the absence of extant romantic correspondence, because it identifies with whom Dodd exchanged his romantic letters. Dodd's record is also suggestive of how his romantic epistolary rhetoric defied generic conventions by addressing multiple suitors, women and men, at the same time.

More inventive than Dodd's diary writing *about* letter writing, though, was his genre-queer practice of using the diary to *do,* or enact, romantic epistolary rhetoric. His diary functioned as a site of rhetorical invention in that he used it to develop and enact romantic epistolary practices of address.[40] Operating according to an epistolary logic, he experimented with composing direct epistolary address in his diary in order to address Heath in ways he reported not daring to through actual letters. Dodd's diary suggests that, while he was open about the intensity of his feelings when writing to Halsey and Smith, his letters to Heath were more guarded. Consider, for instance, the diary entry in which Dodd explored his love for Heath, contemplating how it "is not friendship merely. . . . It is a heart-felt, a manly, a pure, deep, and fervent love" (Feb. 4, 1837). Dodd hoped he would see Heath again and then shifted to direct address: "shall I never see him again? O that I could! 'John, dear John, I love you, indeed I love you. But you are not here, you cannot hear me confess this too [*sic*] you, a confession which perhaps you would care not for.'" Dodd did more than write about his love for Heath; he declared this love by using the rhetorical figure of apostrophe to compose second-person address with the salutation-like "dear." Dodd further distinguished this romantic epistolary address from the rest of the diary entry by using quotation marks. He also wrote with rhetorical awareness of Heath's inability to "hear" his epistolary confession of feelings, because it was made within the genre of the diary.

In the rest of this diary entry, Dodd returned to an account of events and described further his feelings for Heath, referring to Heath in the third person. In the final sentence, Dodd hoped "that we may meet again" but concluded, "in the meantime, we can write to each other and thus renew that intercourse which has been so inconspicuously broken off." It is not just that Heath could not "hear" Dodd's confession, for Heath would not read it either. While Dodd wrote to Heath, he did not use epistolary address to declare his romantic feelings within letters he intended to exchange with Heath. Instead, he used his diary to practice the epistolary address he would not compose in actual letters. His awareness here of the relationship between different genres and their audiences was learned through his formal rhetorical education and further developed through his diary writing about romantic epistolary rhetoric.

Nor was this use of the diary to compose epistolary address an isolated instance. In another entry, Dodd reflected on "the beloved form" of Heath, imagining him "in my presence" (Feb. 19, 1837). Shifting to direct address, Dodd asked, "Shall I never see you again dear John?" He lamented that, when they were in Heath's room together, talking "freely," "I ought to have told him of my deep and burning affection for him. . . . John I love you much, do you love me?" Of course Dodd expected no answer because he wrote aware that, regardless of how he might address Heath through the genre of the diary, he did not and would not do so through conversation or letters: "I never did tell John this, and perhaps it is all for the best; but John, here, in my private volume, whose pages shall be surveyed by no eyes, here in the receptacle of my passing thoughts, here do I repeat my secret avowal of deep, devoted attachment; my friend, companion . . . sole inhabitant of my heart" (Feb. 19, 1837). While Dodd did not expect Heath to read the direct address and declarations of love, he used apostrophe and the multigenre practice of composing epistolary address within a private diary in order to say to Heath what he could not bring himself to say otherwise. But, however clear Dodd's awareness was about the diary as a "private" genre for making "secret" avowals, the limits of the diary's guaranteed privacy are also clear. Here two more pages were cut from the diary (though not necessarily by Dodd), and the remaining pages are publicly available to present-day researchers. Still, in his genre-queer practice, Dodd composed romantic epistolary address to Heath not within letters but within what he intended to be a private diary.

It is possible Dodd also used the diary to practice and prepare for romantic epistolary address that *did* find its way into letters. He certainly used the diary to address other romantic interests, such as Halsey, with whom Dodd seems to have been more open about his feelings. In the entry about his "Dear, beloved trio,"

Dodd declared his "love" for Halsey in the third person. Dodd then turned to a second-person, epistolary-like address, with "Tony, How I long to see you, to embrace you, to press you to my bosom, my own dear Tony!" (Mar. 24, 1837). A few days later, Dodd again turned from writing *about* to writing *to* Halsey: "Dear, dearest Anthony! Thou are mine own friend, my most beloved of all! To see thee again! What rapture it would be, thou sweet, lovely, dear, beloved, beautiful, adored Anthony!" (Mar. 27, 1837). Of course, this extant romantic address is in Dodd's diary, but in this case the diary may have functioned much like a school-sponsored commonplace book, as a practice ground for more "public" writing, for composing address in actual epistolary rhetoric. In the same entry, Dodd referred to his ongoing epistolary exchange with Halsey: "I must write to him soon in answer to his last letter." Moreover, in Dodd's diary writing about Halsey, unlike that about Heath, there is no indication Dodd held back in expressing his feelings. This romantic epistolary address that he composed in his commonplace book turned diary may have found its way into his answer to Halsey's letter.

Dodd's genre-queer practice of composing romantic epistolary address within a diary emerged from his school-sponsored commonplace book. He started with the commonplace book genre, typical to classically modeled rhetorical training and recommended within his formal education. Then, informed by his learned rhetorical awareness of genre, purpose, and audience, he transferred this training to make an intentional shift from a commonplace book to a diary. Having made this shift, he operated according to an "epistolary logic," using the diary to write about romantic epistolary rhetoric and even to enact romantic epistolary address (Spring, "'Seemingly Uncouth Forms'" 638).

Mixing Epistolary and Poetic Address and Exchange

Dodd also enacted romantic epistolary rhetoric through poetic forms. Enabled by his broad training in a range of genres, he developed a fourth genre-queer practice of composing romantic epistolary address and exchange that crossed the generic lines that separated letters, poetry, and epistle verse.[41] The genres Dodd encountered through his classically broad education included lyric poetry in the form of the ode, as previously discussed, as well as the epistle verse. Epistle verses are, quite simply, poems of direct address that read as letters. The two most influential strands within the Western epistle verse tradition are those following Ovid, more known for verses that take up questions of romance and love, and Horace, for those that take up questions of morality and philosophy (France 516–21). Descriptions in Yale's *Catalogue* suggest that Dodd studied the epistle verses of Horace, who was listed as required reading throughout the curriculum (27). The influence of Horace is also evident in Dodd's poetry album (Apr. 1836).[42] Yet, even as evidence suggests he studied Horace rather than Ovid, Dodd drew on what he learned about epistle verse to compose specifically romantic address.

In addition to writing in his diary about composing romantic epistolary rhetoric, Dodd recounted addressing and exchanging what he called the "poetique." French for the adjectives "poetic" and "poetical," the term "poetique" was used by Dodd as a noun, seemingly to mean writing with a close relationship to the romantic letter genre. He claimed on multiple occasions to write a poetique to the young men he was interested in romantically.[43] In one of these diary entries, Dodd mentioned the poetique alongside other genres he encountered and practiced through his classically modeled rhetorical education. After remarking that he had a "debate" to write, Dodd continued, "I have also to write a 'poetique' to John Heath, besides numerous other epistles" (June 18, 1837). When Dodd later reported on having written the poetique, he seemed to make a greater distinction between it and other epistolary rhetoric: "I have got a letter from Jabe Smith. Have written a 'poetique' to J. Heath, a letter home for money, and one to the Tailor for a coat before the fourth of July" [June 27, 1837]. Dodd represented the poetique as a form of writing that, even if not the same as a letter, operated according to an "epistolary logic": he addressed the poetique to other men and exchanged it with them as one would a romantic letter (Spring, "'Seemingly Uncouth Forms'" 638).

Dodd's poetry album includes romantic poems also framed by an epistolary logic of address. In keeping with the epistle verse tradition, poems such as "To Elizabeth" are titled with a direct address (June 1838).[44] Others, though not titled with direct address, address Dodd's romantic interests by name. Within one of many entries simply titled "Stanzas," the speaker begins, "To Love!" (June 1835). But the poem soon addresses the woman of Dodd's "Dear, beloved trio," Beers, with language characteristic of his diary entries about love: "to be beloved, / what rapture to the soul it gives! / . . . / sincerely, deeply, ardently, with pure affection . . . / . . . / Yes Julia I do love thee." In the concluding stanza, Dodd wrote, "I adore thee; I confess / the sincere feelings of my heart," even "though my words my thoughts express" not "with Sapphic art" (June 1835). In poems like these, Dodd declared his feelings in ways that blurred generic lines between poetic and epistolary address. The poems betrayed his awareness of both generic overlap and generic distinction. He saw a relationship between the letter and poetry, but he recognized that his own "words," his attempt at romantic address both epistolary and poetic, was not exactly "Sapphic art" (June 1835).

Somewhat ironically given Dodd's reference to Sappho, the celebrated Greek poet of same-sex love, his extant poems that are framed by an epistolary logic generally appear to have addressed women readers. But these poems are queer in other ways, in that they transgress generic boundaries between epistolary rhetoric and poetry. Most queer is the poem "Epistolary," which Dodd himself characterized as "queer in the extreme" (Apr. 1836). Like the "Stanzas," "Epistolary" is framed by an epistolary logic of address, not through direct address in the title but internally; Dodd began its ninth stanza, "And dearest Julia." Beyond this epistolary address, and in spite of its normatively opposite-sex construction, the poem is indeed queer. In this poem, rather than simply writing in keeping with the epistle verse tradition, Dodd used meta-commentary and the rhetorical figure of digression to call attention to what he found "queer"—and what I characterize as "genre-queer"—about his multigenre practice.

Dodd's learned and transferable genre awareness is evident throughout this poem, as he highlighted the generic tensions in what he called an "epistolary rhyme": tensions between the conventions for epistolary rhetoric and those for rhyming verse. His title for the poem, "Epistolary," obviously emphasizes epistolary rhetoric, whereas the writing itself is located within his poetry album and, consisting of twelve numbered stanzas of eight lines each, clearly takes the form of a poem. He began in keeping with the conventions for letters, by locating himself in time and place, and then, in the next line, made a move characteristic of the piece, by calling attention to what he had just done: "At Greenvale, Hartford, in Connecticut, / This nineteenth day, of April . . . eight- / teen hundred thirty six . . . / . . . / . . . is the date. / Both as to . . . time / And place, of this epistolary rhyme." Also characteristically, Dodd's meta-commentary included a digressive parenthetical. He interrupted the provision of location and date, noting that he wanted "(a rhyme . . . in that third line, but / . . . cannot find a good one)." This parenthetical underscores the requirements of epistolary rhetoric—location and date—and those of poetic verse—rhyming lines.

Dodd used the figure of digression to highlight tensions regarding other conventions for content, representing the requirements of verse as interrupting those of the letter. He began the second stanza, "But stop: that verse, before I farther go, / If you have no particular objection, / Requires as it doth seem to me, although / 'Tis right enough, a little circumspection." After offering this circumspection, he explicitly called it a "digression." In the ninth stanza, he returned from his poetic digression to direct address, writing, "And dearest Julia now I turn to thee, / Since this long preface I am safely through." Dodd devoted the rest of the poem to content conventional for romantic letters. The speaker asks Beers how she is, what news she has, and how her family, cat, and dog are. As the piece begins to close, Dodd promised to write again "another day," and he requested, "in the mean time I do hope and pray / that I from you a letter may receive, / relief to my anxiety to give."

Finally, Dodd did close with another direct epistolary address and even a form of signature: "Julia, now farewell! / . . . / . . . / . . . / . . . / . . . / . . . I now have got / unto the end . . . / . . . I am ever yours, A. D." Yet again, Dodd used meta-commentary to emphasize the strangeness of his generic experiment. It is after declaring he has come to "the end" but before the signature that he interrupted with "which seemeth odd to me." And it is just before this final stanza that he remarked, "This verse though, by the way, to me doth seem / somehow or other, queer in the extreme." Throughout this romantic epistolary rhyme, Dodd drew on the epistle verse traditions he had encountered through his classically broad education in rhetoric and literature.[45] With a flexible rhetorical knowledge from broad educational experiences with a range of genres, he transferred what he had learned in order to compose multigenre romantic address to Beers that was queerly epistolary and poetic—that was genre-queer in its refusal to become "stuck in a sense of separation between genres, as in gender binaries" (Ali 36).

All four of Dodd's genre-queer practices repurposed his rhetorical education. This formal training prepared him for civic engagement in keeping with classically modelled rhetorical education as well as nineteenth-century expectations for privileged white men. Although he met these expectations by pursuing a career in law and politics, he queered cultural norms in other ways. His diary suggests that his romantic epistolary rhetoric was queer in its defiance of the genre conventions widely taught by nineteenth-century manual culture. Moreover, his multigenre epistolary practices queerly transgressed generic lines. Dodd's commonplace book, diary, and poetry album were not only multigenre but genre-queer: he crossed generic lines with a rhetorical awareness that refused closure for generic distinctions, and he did so to compose nonnormative romantic relations with men and women. In transferring what he had learned at Washington and Yale, Dodd also crossed normative lines between romantic and civic life: he transferred what he had learned through his rhetorical education for civic engagement to develop his rhetorical practices for romantic engagement.

Rhetorically Situating Letters within Networks of Related Genres

This analysis of Albert Dodds's rhetorical education and genre-queer practices, like that of Addie Brown and Rebecca Primus's romantic epistolary rhetoric, holds implications for interdisciplinary histories of sexuality. In addition to the proposition that we read romantic letters as crafted and learned epistolary rhetoric, my queer history of rhetorical education suggests another way to nuance interpretations of letters, through greater attention to their significance within networks of other related genres. The need for such attention is clear within scholarly interpretations of Dodd's multigenre epistolary practices. Like histories of nineteenth-century romantic friendship between women, histories of romantic friendship between men examine their letters to consider whether their romantic relations involved erotic and sexual contact, as well as to determine the degree to which the relations were accepted socially. These same two questions were pursued by Peter Gay, Jonathan Katz, and E. Anthony Rotundo as they drew on Dodd's diary, commonplace book, poetry album, and familial letters as evidence of his romantic feelings and relations.[46] But here I consider Dodd's multigenre epistolary rhetoric in relation to a third point of interpretive debate—whether romantic relations between men were limited to youth.

Rotundo has argued that what distinguished romantic friendships between men, otherwise similar to those between women, was confinement to one phase of life, the period of youth between boyhood and manhood. In a study of multiple friendships between young men, Rotundo characterized youth as a key feature of relationships that, by definition, served "the needs of young men at a perilous time of transition" (21). But in the case of Dodd, Rotundo came to this conclusion on the basis of his interpretation of Dodd's diary and letters and without consideration of the rhetorical complexities of related genres. Here I examine how Rotundo, along with Gay and Katz, has read Dodd's writing as evidence of whether his romantic relations with men continued after graduation from Yale. I show how their approaches to interpreting Dodd's writing may be complicated by reading it as rhetorically situated in relation to multiple genres.

Rotundo's assertion that Dodd's romantic relations with men were limited to his youth is based on a comparison between Dodd's diary writing about his romantic relations with men while a college student and his few extant letters to family members during his postcollege years. Contrasting Dodd's diary and letters, Rotundo asserted that Dodd's "correspondence grew impersonal and showed no indication of the romantic passions he had experienced just a few years before" (17). This interpretation fits with Rotundo's broader observation across instances of romantic friendship between men, that such relationships were confined to youth. Yet Rotundo's conclusion seems to rely on a reading of secondary rather than primary materials. Instead of citing the primary materials as examined through archival research, he accounted for them through citation of Gay's research (7, 23 n. 26). Gay speculated that Dodd's participation in romantic relations with men may have ceased following his graduation from Yale in 1838. According to Gay, "It seems probable . . . —we cannot be sure—that [Dodd's] masculinity triumphed over his homosexual appetites" (211). To support this hypothesis, Gay drew on Dodd's epistolary rhetoric addressed to family following graduation. Just three letters are available: one to his brother Julius in 1841, one to his mother in 1843, and another to his brother Edward in 1844. As Gay rightly noted, Dodd wrote nothing of his romantic life in these letters, and his advice to Edward emphasized control and emotional "self-mastery" (211).[47] It is by contrasting this epistolary rhetoric with Dodd's diary that Gay supports his proposal, that Dodd's masculinity "triumphed over" his homosexual desires, "just as his programmatic even temper overcame his intermittent depressions" (211).

In speculating that Dodd later overcame the "homosexual appetites" of his college years and especially in basing this suggestion on a comparison between Dodd's diary and his later letters, Gay showed less rhetorical awareness of genre than Dodd himself learned through his formal rhetorical education at Washington and Yale. In Gay's triumph hypothesis—as well as Rotundo's repetition of it—both historians seem to have ignored the differences and relationships between the genres of the diary and the letter, as well as between the subgenres of the romantic letter and the familial letter. Certainly we can expect that Dodd would write much more about his romantic life in a diary than he would in epistolary rhetoric addressed to family members. And certainly we can expect that Dodd's letters to family, especially his letter of advice to a brother, would demonstrate greater emotional control than is evident in his relatively private diary, particularly given that the letter is dated more than five years after the last diary entry (Mar. 13, 1844; Oct. 14, 1837). In other words, Dodd's letters did not "grow impersonal" about his romantic life; all of his extant letters to family *were* more impersonal than his diary on that particular subject. While Dodd probably experienced growth between 1837 and 1844 in any number of ways, the most significant differences between his diary and his letters to family are *generic* differences. These generic differences across the primary materials available do not disprove Gay's hypothesis. But nor do they support any claim that Dodd may have "triumphed" over his romantic and erotic attractions to men.

Katz's very different interpretation of the primary materials underscores that the question of whether Dodd's romantic relations with men were confined to his youth is a matter of speculation, which cannot be resolved through readings of his extant writing. In contrast with Gay, Katz wrote, "That Albert perhaps found the reciprocal love he sought is hinted at in his later history" (31). Katz recited the familiar account of Dodd's post-Yale years but added that Dodd "became a law partner of the bachelor Jesse W. Fell" (31). Here Katz cited his sources from extended research about Fell, claiming that, the year Dodd died, Fell "personally carried Albert's private papers (including, apparently, his diary) to Albert's father in the East" (31, 354–45 n. 11).[48] Katz's suggestion about what "perhaps" transpired between Dodd and Fell makes clear, particularly in contrast with the hypothesis of Gay and Rotundo, how inconclusive the primary materials are with respect to Dodd's postcollege romantic relations.

While I raise questions about Gay's and Rotundo's interpretations of Dodd's extant epistolary rhetoric, I want to emphasize that my own research would have been impossible were it not for their and Katz's prior work. Nor is it my intention to offer an alternative argument about whether Dodd's romantic relations with men were confined to his youth. Rather, I mean to show how interpreting Dodd's multigenre epistolary rhetoric may be approached differently. Specifically, I urge that we rhetorically situate letters within a broader network of genres and subgenres. Dodd developed rhetorical awareness of genre through his formal education at Washington and Yale, and he drew on this awareness in developing multigenre and genre-queer practices for composing romantic epistolary rhetoric. As historians interpret his writing, attention must be paid to his learned rhetorical awareness and to the complexity of his practices between and across different genres and subgenres. In this way, both rhetorical studies of genre and histories of rhetorical education have much to offer histories of romance and sexuality through rhetorically attuned frameworks for further historicizing the texts of intimate life. How might we read such texts within the context of not only genre-specific instruction but also networks of other related genres?

The multigenre epistolary rhetoric left behind by Dodd offers a rare glimpse into his rhetorical thinking and generic practices across civic and romantic domains. Even as his formal rhetorical education for civic engagement seemed to enable his epistolary practices for romantic engagement, Dodd repurposed this training to queer ends, defying normative genre conventions for epistolary rhetoric as well as the normative objectives of civic instruction. In this sense, his rhetorical practices, like those of Addie Brown and Rebecca Primus, may be read as a "queer art of failure" (Halberstam, *Queer Art*). I gesture next toward still other implications of queer failure for future histories of rhetorical education for romantic engagement.

Conclusion

Toward Queer Failure

> Failure is something queers do and have
> always done exceptionally well.
>
> Jack Halberstam (2011)

The now familiar story of Eliza's love letters concluded predictably with a conventional happy ending. That is to say, the story's ending was in keeping with the teleological orientation taught by the heteronormative rhetorical education of her time. Although her fiancée, Horace, had broken their engagement after reading her early romantic letters, over time she learned to compose epistolary rhetoric that rendered the break in their relationship temporary. Eliza and Horace reunited through romantic letters and pursued the normative purpose for the genre. To put it another way, Eliza overcame her initial rhetorical, pedagogical, and relational "failures." She was "successful" in learning to write generically conventional love letters and in achieving the heteronormative progression promised by nineteenth-century letter-writing manuals: "love, courtship, and marriage."

Understood according to this heteronormative logic of success, my history of epistolary instruction and practice is a history of pedagogical and relational failure. Complete letter writers instructed everyday people in how to achieve the happy endings of stories like Eliza's. The manuals taught genre conventions for address, pacing, and purpose, while also embedding a conception of romantic relations as heteronormatively gendered, temporally "straight," and teleologically oriented to marriage. But this heteronormative instruction failed insofar as it was marked by openings that could be seized with queer effects by learners in nonnormative romantic relations. Addie Brown, Rebecca Primus, and Albert Dodd were such learners, all failing in their queer rhetorical practices. While Brown and Primus learned genre conventions widely taught by manuals, the women queered those conventions through same-sex epistolary address and exchange that refused mastery of both straight time and its normative *telos*. Dodd's rhetorical practices also failed, insofar as he subverted the normative focus on civic engagement within his classically modeled college-level training, instead transferring what he had learned to develop genre-queer epistolary practices for romantic engagement.

But to name these failures is no slight to Brown, Primus, and Dodd's rhetorical ingenuity. Quite the contrary. To turn toward failure is to place their rhetorical practices, however generically unconventional for the period, within a longer story—a history not limited to the happy endings of letter writers such as the fictional Eliza—a history that underscores the failures of both heteronormative rhetorical education and heteronormative historiographic practices. This history is a story in which failure is, as Jack Halberstam has asserted, "something queers do and have always done exceptionally well" (*Queer Art* 3). Characterizing failure as a practice one might do "exceptionally well" of course challenges normative ideas about success and failure, and this is precisely the point where failure functions as cultural "critique" (11). As Stacey Waite has emphasized in her work on queer failure and pedagogy, attention to failure does not disregard the inventive ways that learners navigate cultural norms, generic conventions, and rhetorical constraints. Rather, this sort of critical attention underscores how larger cultural forms and educational systems "set the scene for the failure in the first place," how they "produced it as a failure" (*Teaching Queer* 58).[1]

I advocate, as this book comes to a close, that our "queer movement" within histories of rhetoric and sexuality gather further momentum through movement toward such failure (Morris, "Archival Queer" 147). In a first sense, this type of queer movement involves studying the rhetorical practices of still other learners like Brown, Primus, and Dodd—learners who failed by the heteronormative standards within their given historical contexts and, in so doing, revealed the failures of heteronormative rhetorical education. Research on additional sites of rhetorical education for romantic engagement and a broader range of queer rhetorical practices would not only expand histories of rhetoric but also hold historiographic implications for interdisciplinary histories of sexuality in terms of how the texts of intimate life are interpreted. As my analysis of Brown and Primus's epistolary rhetoric concluded, historians may take up a rhetorical and pedagogical stance that nuances approaches to same-sex romantic letters within histories of so-called romantic friendship. Specifically, histories of sexuality might move beyond familiar debates about romantic friendship by reading romantic letters as epistolary rhetoric that is learned and crafted. Moreover, as my analysis of Dodd's genre-queer epistolary practices showed, there is room for historians of sexuality to rhetorically situate letters in relation to a broader range of genres. Here historians of rhetoric, in moving toward queer failure through further study of queer rhetorical practices, have the potential to contribute in meaningful ways beyond rhetorical studies.

But, in a second sense, moving toward failure means confronting the failure of historiography itself where queer rhetorical practices like Brown, Primus, and Dodd's have gone understudied in the fields of rhetoric, communication, and composition. Specifically, this queer movement exposes the failure of citizenship and civic life as normative historiographic frames in rhetoric. With respect to histories of rhetorical education, it underscores the failure of histories oriented exclusively to civic engagement to account for queer practices in the nineteenth century.

The reasons to engage in queer movement toward failure are not limited, however, to becoming more inclusive of queer rhetorics within histories of rhetorical education. As Karma Chávez has argued, moving beyond the "long standing investment in the normative function of citizenship" within rhetorical studies is not merely a matter of confronting, yet again, our "history of exclusions" ("Beyond Inclusion" 163–164). Instead, she wrote, "it is imperative that we break from that history, not in order that Rhetoric may become a more inclusive discipline but so that it may become something entirely different: a discipline constituted through non-normative, non-citizen, non-Western perspectives and ways of knowing and being" (164). Such a break amounts, in Halberstam's terms, to failure as resistance to "mastery" through "critique" and "refusal," insofar as successfully mastering rhetoric's historiographic norms means focusing on a narrowly conceived civic domain as though it were separate from that of romantic, private, or intimate life (11).[2]

In histories of rhetorical education, queer failure as a critical break from the normative focus on civic engagement involves movement toward a discipline simultaneously constituted through nonnormative historiographic ways of knowing and attentive to queer ways of being rhetorical. While my own queer history of rhetorical education has maintained a focus on Western practices from the nineteenth-century United States, I invite scholars across rhetoric, communication, and composition to join in developing histories of rhetorical education for romantic engagement within other cultural locations and historical periods—not simply to be more inclusive but also to encourage new kinds of historiographic failure that will allow rhetoric to be constituted in nonnormative ways.

We may resist mastery of what Chávez called the "citizenship narrative" in rhetoric and move toward historiographic failure through attention to rhetorical education for romantic engagement well before and after the postal age (163). While I opened with Eliza's distinctly nineteenth-century story, we can just as easily imagine a present-day Eliza. Expected to reply to Horace's romantic epistolary address and wanting to avert potential failure, Eliza enters into her

Google search box "how to write a love letter." The search returns advice articles from wikiHow, BuzzFeed, the *Atlantic,* and Hallmark. One of the first tips she encounters is, "1. Don't worry that love letters are a thing of the past."[3] In spite of such reassurance from articles about romantic epistolary rhetoric, however, it is more realistic to imagine that our twenty-first-century Eliza, or Liz, receives her romantic messages via text, Facebook, Snapchat, Tinder, or any of the many other dating sites and apps. So Liz instead Googles "online dating how to." This Liz also finds advice on rhetorical practices for composing romantic relations from wikiHow and the *Atlantic,* as well as Lifehack and the *New Yorker.*[4] These are just a few of many examples from only the first page of search results, and, as Liz reads on, she finds more articles as well as advertisements for books and apps that promise to assist with everything from the so-called lost art of love letters to romantic communication in a digital age.

Our hypothetical Liz also finds that, although rhetorical and pedagogical practices for romantic communication have evolved considerably, certain problems and possibilities seem to persist across historical and technological specificities. In the digital as much as the postal age, everyday people such as Liz are faced with questions about developing language practices for romantic engagement. How, for instance, does one learn language practices for rhetorically participating in romantic relations, and where can models be found? How do learners successfully balance inventing their practices in keeping with such instruction and also writing "from the heart"? And, when desires and relations are queer within the context of contemporaneous conventions, how do people fail "exceptionally well" by learning to compose nonnormative relations from the models, genres, and practices available to them?

In exploring these questions through archival research on romantic epistolary rhetoric in the nineteenth-century United States, I found it was taught and learned through the overt genre instruction of popular letter-writing manuals, from examples found in cultural texts such as poetry and the novel, and even via transfer from formal college-level rhetorical training for civic engagement. Diverse learners drew on the genre conventions and rhetorical awareness widely modeled and taught, and yet, in writing "from the heart" to compose epistolary rhetoric for queer romantic relations, they necessarily subverted cultural norms and transgressed generic and educational boundaries. The instruction and practices under study here show that rhetorical education invents both civic and romantic life. In teaching generically conventional practices for romantic relations, rhetorical education for romantic engagement shaped U.S. citizen subjects as heteronormative romantic subjects. At the same time, this rhetorical education was subject to queer failure and reinvention: learners creatively crafted queer and genre-queer practices for composing nonnormative epistolary rhetoric that failed by the standards of normative instruction.

Even as my concept of rhetorical education for romantic engagement has emerged from archival investigation of romantic epistolary rhetoric, it also suggests further opportunities for historiographic practices that move beyond civic engagement and toward queer failure. Whereas my study of the postal age has taken the romantic letter genre as its touchstone, rhetorical training in other genres and modes will be more salient in studies focused on different historical periods and cultural locations. I have formulated my definition of rhetorical education with the goal that it be relevant for such studies. Again, I define rhetorical education for romantic engagement as *the teaching and learning of language practices for composing romantic relations.* Crucial to the potential relevance of this concept is my use of the broad (perhaps even vague) phrase "language practices." While "language" maintains some interest in the role of alphabetic language, "practices" are not limited to romantic epistolary rhetoric or even to alphabetic writing. Instead, depending on the context under study, scholarship may consider rhetorical instruction and practices that are written and spoken, digital and multimodal.

Histories of Western rhetorical education for romantic engagement could examine, for instance, the ways classical rhetorical training through oral dialogue and declamation exercises prepared young men for rhetorical participation in specific forms of same-sex erotic relations. As noted in my analysis of Dodd's encounters with representations of homoerotic relations within classical rhetoric and literature, eroticized same-sex relations between men (and with boys) were a fairly standard feature of classical rhetorical education. In Isocrates as well as Plato, such relations were seen as pedagogically productive for learning through oral dialogues about rhetoric. Moreover, as Erik Gunderson's work suggests, rhetorical exercises through the genre of declamation amounted to another important form of rhetorical training with potential connections to same-sex relations between Roman men. While Gunderson's scholarship is more concerned with rhetorical (and psychoanalytic) theory, future historical research could examine rhetorical education for romantic engagement in this context. Such research could move toward queer failure in both senses, the pedagogical and rhetorical as well as the historiographic. First, this research may ask, how did training in rhetoric teach cultural norms for privileged young men's participation in same-sex erotic relations, pedagogical and otherwise, as well as opposite-sex romantic relations and marriage? And where did such training fail, as evinced through queer rhetorical practices? Second, and just as important, how may historiography attentive to such practices fail by the standards of the citizenship narrative within rhetoric, thus queering even those histories that focus on the most disciplinarily normative contexts of Ancient Greece and Rome?

Of course, movements toward queer failure within histories of Western rhetorical education need not be limited to these contexts. Another potential starting point for historical research on periods prior to the nineteenth century is suggested by Catherine Bates's history of courtly rhetoric in Elizabethan language and literature. Bates has considered modern as well as prior meanings of courtship, analyzing literary representations of "both 'courtship' in the sense of wooing or making love to another person, and 'courtship' in the sense of being a courtier, of suing for favour, of behaving as courtiers should behave" (1). Whereas Bates offered what is primarily a study of literary and linguistic history, another history more focused on rhetorical education for romantic engagement could investigate questions like these: how were English people taught rhetorical practices for participating in courtly love during the Elizabethan era? How did this instruction fail by producing queer practices? And how may a historiographic focus on the different types of courtship rhetoric—that of both the wooer and the courtier—fail in terms of normative distinctions between romantic and civic domains?

Future studies of rhetorical education for romantic engagement may move toward queer failure through consideration of not only historical but also present-day instances of teaching and learning. There is almost no end to the popular pedagogical texts that now teach language practices for rhetorically participating in romantic relations. These pedagogical texts include a large number of twenty-first-century manuals. While taking book form, such manuals move beyond strictly alphabetic language; they teach the rhetoric of romantic engagement via multiple genres and modes, addressing language practices that are verbal, embodied, visual, and digital.

One intriguing and disturbing example is Robert Greene's popular "primer," *The Art of Seduction*.[5] Greene's book approaches seduction precisely in the way that Plato warned against in his condemnation of rhetoric and that nineteenth-century letter-writing manuals also cautioned learners to avoid. Instructing readers about the social power of seduction, Greene has identified types of seducers and "victims," and he taught "cunning" strategies and "tactics" for how seducers make an "art" of persuading and manipulating their victims (xx–xxv). Interestingly, Greene drew most of his types from literary figures of the past, so that the "rake" and the "coquette" of the eighteenth and nineteenth century persist in this twenty-first-century instruction (17–28, 67–78). While perpetuating cultural norms for gender, sexuality, and power in ways that raise obvious ethical dilemmas, Greene's book is ripe for a study of rhetorical education for romantic engagement that accounts for its popular pedagogy rather than simply discounting it as manipulative and sexist. Such a study could move toward queer failure in both senses. First, how does Greene's instruction in composing romantic relations through the art of seduction fail by the standards of contemporary norms for ethical and "healthy" relationships? And how are his own seductive pedagogical aims subject to failure, to appropriation toward queer and feminist ends? In the second sense of queer failure, how may the examination of manuals like Greene's fail in terms of historiography's normative orientation to civic engagement by taking up questions of power and seduction that so fully saturate political and intimate life?[6]

Other studies of present-day rhetorical education for romantic engagement that move toward queer failure may consider books that teach language practices not limited to the alphabetic. In addition to how-to articles like those our hypothetical Liz found, available books range from *The Rules for Online Dating: Capturing the Heart of Mr. Right in Cyberspace* to *Love @ First Click: The Ultimate Guide to Online Dating*, from *The Intelligent Woman's Guide to Online Dating* to *Online Dating for Dummies*.[7] These books offer advice on representing oneself through visual and digital rhetoric as well as participating in the various forms of exchange afforded by dating websites, messaging platforms, apps, and other forms of digital communication. Such guides could be examined to look at questions such as these: how does their instruction teach shifting cultural norms as well as new modes for rhetorical participation in romantic relations? And what openings for queer failure emerge with digital forms of rhetoric for romantic engagement?

To fully understand the complexity of present-day rhetorical education for romantic engagement, future studies will need to compare books like these to other manuals offering less normative instruction. While the majority of popular books generally presume heterosexual relations, other manuals focus on same-sex relations. Manuals such as *Man Talk: The Gay Couple's Communication Guide* teach readers how to use language within romantic relations between men; books on gay and lesbian relationships more broadly, such as *Permanent Partners: Building Gay and Lesbian Relationships That Last,* include advice chapters focused on language practices, especially in oral communication.[8] These books raise questions about how instruction in language practices for same-sex relations may also embed culturally normative or "homonormative" conceptions of those relations as oriented to long-term (even "permanent") coupling.[9] In present-day contexts, what are perhaps more queer are manuals that teach language practices for participating in relationships that, regardless of the genders of those involved, are oriented not to the couple but to various nonmonogamous configurations. Guides such as *Redefining Our Relationships: Guidelines for Responsible Open Relationships* and *The Ethical Slut: A Guide to Infinite Sexual Possibilities* include extensive instruction in how to communicate about emotions, jealousy, and boundaries within nonmonogamous relations.[10] Studies that examine such guides alongside the more heteronormative ones may ask questions like these: how do these books teach different language practices and cultural norms, both conventional and queer? How do the guides focused on same-sex and nonmonogamous relations encourage queer failure, functioning as a refusal and critique of heteronormative and homonormative cultures in the United States?

Future studies of rhetorical education for romantic engagement should also move toward queer failure while turning to a broader range of cultural contexts, not limited to Western and colonial rhetorics, as the work of Chávez along with that of Qwo-Li Driskill, Wendy Hesford, Carol Lipson and Roberta Binkley, and Malea Powell would advise in various ways. There is a need to interrogate the relevance of Western concepts of romantic and erotic love within global and indigenous contexts. Scholars may explore how such concepts do and do not travel (in relation to more material flows) with imperialist, colonizing, and/or queer effects.

Potential research sites for such exploration are suggested by interdisciplinary studies, such as Laura Ahearn's *Invitations to Love: Literacy, Love Letters, and Social Change in Nepal* and Nicole Constable's *Romance on a Global Stage: Pen Pals, Virtual Ethnography, and "Mail Order" Marriages*. Constable, for example, has considered multiple modes of correspondence among Filipinas, Chinese women, and U.S. men within the context of globalization. These correspondents wrote to one another in pursuit of marriage, with hundreds of Internet dating and "mail order" companies involved in the process of exchange. While Constable's ethnographic study focused on the experiences of the women and men involved, a study of rhetorical education for romantic engagement could examine websites associated with Internet dating businesses that offer instruction in rhetorical practices for transnational online dating across significant geographic and cultural distance. What heteronormative conventions are emphasized within this instruction in language practices for composing cross-cultural relations? How is this same instruction marked by queer failure with respect to various culturally specific notions of relational success?

Investigation of contexts beyond the West could further queer movement toward failure as a critique of rhetoric's normative citizenship narrative. Like Western concepts of romantic and erotic love, our very notions of "citizenship" and "civic" would need to be interrogated, as suggested by Chávez as well as by Amy Wan. Here scholars may consider how sites of rhetorical education for romantic engagement shape citizens, noncitizens, global citizens, and even citizens as global consumers. As Constable's study indicated, many present-day pedagogical texts—especially those published and sold online—circulate globally. How do these texts teach language practices that encourage particular forms of state-sponsored romantic relations? At the same time, how does their instruction fail in terms of culturally varied concepts of success for romantic, marital, familial, kinship, and/or community relations? How might such instruction, circulating globally and teaching genres and modes for romantic communication across cultural lines, put further pressure on the very idea of "civic" rhetoric as necessarily tied to citizenship or nation?

My concluding account of possible starting points for future studies is by no means exhaustive—just as our hypothetical Liz's first page of search results was not. Countless other websites, manuals, and past pedagogical practices could be studied. But what I hope this account intimates is the wide-ranging potential for subsequent scholarship to use, extend, appropriate, complicate, and revise my concept of rhetorical education. Reconceptualizing rhetorical education as oriented to not only civic but also romantic engagement, I invite scholars to examine the teaching and learning of language practices for composing romantic relations across different cultural contexts, historical periods, and, by extension, genres and modes of romantic rhetoric. While this book has taken up questions raised by the story of Eliza's romantic epistolary rhetoric, the new questions I raise by way of conclusion are intended to prompt research that is simultaneously romantic and civic—rhetorical, pedagogical, and queer—with relevance for histories of rhetoric and sexuality as well as our own present-day relations.

May we, in pursuing such research and moving toward queer failure, answer Charles Morris's call to "produce rhetorical histories . . . that will warrant and arm our queer scholarship, pedagogy, and activism" ("Archival Queer" 147). And may our histories arm pedagogy and activism that seizes "opportunities," as Jonathan Alexander and David Wallace encourage, to engage learners in "challenging discussions about how the most seemingly personal parts of our lives are densely and intimately wrapped up in larger sociocultural and political narratives that organize desire and condition how we think of ourselves" (W302–03).[11] In these ways and many others, may we think of our queer histories of rhetorical education as holding the potential to both learn from and teach the stories of everyday people like Liz, Eliza, Horace, and Belinda; Addie Brown and Rebecca Primus; and Albert Dodd, John Heath, Julia Beers, Anthony Halsey, Jabez Smith, and Elizabeth Morgan.

Notes

Prologue

1. The name for Godey's "changed . . . numerous times during its tenure" (Mahoney 415 n. 12). The story "Eliza Farnham; or, The Love Letters" consists of two parts: "Part the First" (217–20) and "Part the Second" (245–50). Published under the name "Miss Leslie," the story has been attributed to the conduct writer Eliza Leslie, whose manual *Miss Leslie's Behaviour Book* (1839) includes a chapter on letter writing. *Selections from Eliza Leslie* reprints the story (81–114). For discussion of Leslie's conduct writing as well as *Godey's*, see Peary.

Introduction

1. The emphasis is in the original here and throughout, except where otherwise noted.

2. Ronald has challenged this common representation of classical rhetoric.

3. Enoch made this point as well (6).

4. See also Bacon and McClish; Bordelon; Gold and Hobbs; McClish; Rothermel ("Sphere of Noble Action"); Royster; Stock; Stuckey; Wetzel. On the persistence of citizenship as a key concept within present-day pedagogy, see Wan.

5. While these lists are by no means exhaustive, other queer rhetorics scholarship that is historical or pedagogical in orientation includes Alexander and Gibson; Alexander and Rhodes; Alexander and Wallace; Branstetter; Brookey; Carstarphen; Cavallaro; Cloud; Cram; Gibson, Marinara, and Meem; Gross and Alexander; Lipari; Monson and Rhodes; Narayan; Sloop, "Lucy Lobdell's Queer Circumstances"; VanHaitsma; Watts. Cox and Faris's bibliography accounts further for a range of queer rhetorics scholarship across communication and composition.

6. Queer scholarship within rhetorical studies also explores the relationship between publicity and privacy (Chavéz, "Beyond Inclusion"; Cloud; Lipari; Morris, "Introduction"). In insisting on the public nature of privacy, queer theorists and rhetoricians continue a long tradition within feminist activism and interdisciplinary feminist scholarship of studying the ways notions of "private" and "public" restrict women's power, sexuality, and movement (Elshtain; Fraser; C. Griffin; Johnson, *Gender and Rhetorical Space*).

Simplistic divisions between "public" and "private" are challenged within literary, cultural, and social histories of the letter as well (Decker; Favret; Gilroy and Verhoeven; Hewitt).

7. The distribution of civil rights via marriage is a central issue in queer politics. Much queer scholarship is critical of liberal assimilationist political projects that attempt to secure rights largely on behalf of middle-class and white citizens of the United States in ways that, within late capitalism, recuperate liberal political theory and its emphasis on individualism, privacy, and choice. These political projects work at the expense of many people within and beyond the current borders of the United States. As Eng has stated, "queer liberalism's claims to state-sanctioned rights, recognitions, and privileges implicitly reinforce a normative politics, not just of family and kinship, but of U.S. citizenship" (28). Yet it is often the case that, as Eng admitted, borrowing the language of Spivak, "we 'cannot not want'" the rights and recognitions that these political projects promise (25).

8. In Berlant and Warner's terms, the "official national culture" of the United States has been constructed as heterosexual on the basis of ideas about privacy that "cloak its sexualization of national membership" (547). They have called this construction "national heterosexuality," explaining that it "is the mechanism by which a core national culture can be imagined as a sanitized . . . space of pure citizenship" (549). In contrast with how this national culture is imagined, "intimacy is itself publicly mediated" (553). On nationality and sexuality, also see Berlant, *Queen of America;* Cvetkovich; Parker, Russo, Sommer, and Yaeger; Radhakrishnan.

9. Other critical perspectives regarding concepts of citizenship within rhetorical studies include Rufo and Atchison; Wan.

10. Scholarship on constitutive rhetoric includes Anderson; Charland; Clark; Jasinski; C. Olson. Olson has outlined the "two overlapped but distinct traditions" of constitutive rhetoric, noting how they build on the work of Burke as well as Althusser (86–87).

11. It would be a mistake, in other words, to merely shift attention away from civic engagement, toward romantic engagement, as though the two were distinct. As Cloud has argued, it is problematic to "valorize" practices deemed "private" without simultaneously attending to their "relevance" for what gets defined as "public" and "political" (26).

12. For an overview of rhetorical genre theory, see Bawarshi and Reiff.

13. Here I paraphrase Berlant and Warner, who defined heteronormativity as "the institutions, structures of understanding, and practical orientations that make heterosexuality seem not only coherent—that is, organized as a sexuality—but also privileged" (548 n. 2; ctd. in Morris, "Introduction" 16 n. 17).

14. Moreover, contemporary practices associated with LGBTQ life within late capitalism may be "homonormative" (Conrad; Dinshaw et al.; Duggan; Eng; Muñoz; Stryker). As Hoang explained, in conversation with Halberstam, "There is also a homonormative time line. We pity those who come out late in life, do not find a long-term partner before they lose their looks, or continue to hit the bars when they are the bartender's father's age. We create our own temporal normativity outside the heteronormative family" (Dinshaw et al. 183–84).

15. Alexander and Rhodes have defined queer rhetoric as "self-conscious and critical engagement with normative discourses of sexuality in the public sphere that exposes their

naturalization and torques them to create different or counter-discourses, giving voice and agency to multiple and complex sexual experiences" ("Queer Rhetoric" n. pag.; see also *Sexual Rhetorics*). On the distinction between queer practice and identity within queer theory and especially historiography, see Butler ("Critically Queer"; *Gender Trouble*); Chauncey; Foucault; Halperin (*How to Do the History*); Hansen ("'No Kisses'"); Katz; Rotundo ("Romantic Friendship").

16. On another related genre not considered here—the "crush note," usually exchanged at women's schools and colleges—see Horowitz; Inness.

17. For other formulations of genre in relation to queer lives and practices, see Gardiner; Karkulehto; Lazar. Of particular note in rhetoric and communication is Rand's theorization of form and queerness in relation to agency.

18. When developing his concept of "genre-queer," Ali cited Wilchins's discussion of normative gender systems and binaries, which draws on Butler's theory of gender performativity (Ali 29; Wilchins 27–28). See also Butler, "Imitation and Gender Insubordination"; "Genrequeer"; Hawkins; Nestle, Wilchins, and Howell.

19. Nor do I mean to imply that writers engaged in queer rhetorical practices hold a monopoly on inventive challenges to generic categories. Indeed, as Singer and Walker have insisted, "We organize our textbooks and courses into tidy generic categories, but literary genres are notoriously difficult to theorize or define. We think of genres as fixed and clearly bounded when in fact transgression is the norm . . . we would argue that there is no such thing as non-hybrid genre" (3).

20. See Donawerth; Gage; Johnson; Mahoney; Poster and Mitchell; Schultz; Spring; Trasciatti.

21. Garlinger explained further that "the letter functions as an open closet—or, at least, a door to the closet—to recuperate, at moments ahistorically, queer subjectivities from the past" (189 n. 1). In other words, "The letter replicates the tropological dynamics of the closet as a space that contains intimate thoughts and secret desires, hidden behind the protective veil of an envelope" (x). However, "This is not to suggest that letters are more authentic or sincere [than autobiography], but rather that notions of authenticity and sincerity are fundamentally different for letter writing" (xvii). See also Faderman, *To Believe in Women;* Jones.

22. It is easy to call to mind the most flagrant instances: someone locates letters that "prove" a person was gay, or in a same-sex romantic friendship, or in a romantic friendship that was not sexual. For example, controversies over how Eleanor Roosevelt and Abraham Lincoln are remembered turn in part on alterative interpretations of their letters (Cloud; Morris, "My Old Kentucky Homo").

23. In the metaphoric sense, the rhetoric of courtship is for identification within communication that requires "transcending . . . social estrangement" between different social classes (Burke 208). In the literal sense, the rhetoric of courtship is for transcending estrangement within the process of romantic courting. This estrangement may include the "mystery" involved in any courtship, though Burke focused especially on the social mystery between "different kinds of beings," including differently sexed or gendered beings, who court each other (208–09). For scholarship on Burke's metaphoric rhetoric of

courtship, see Clair and Anderson; Heath; Kraemer. On Burke's literal rhetoric of courtship, see Derrin; Nelson; Scruggs; Sedinger; Thames; Zwagerman.

24. Here I have in mind Plato's *Phaedrus* and *Gorgias*. Kelley focused on *Phaedrus* and *Symposium*, concluding that "The ratio developing out of both dialogues is this: Love is to seduction as Truth is to rhetoric. Rhetoric is the semblance of wisdom as seduction is the semblance of love" (79). In Ballif's account of Western rhetoric's dismissal of sophistry and women, she has offered a poststructuralist seduction away from distinctions between truth and deception. See also Blythin; Brockriede; Erickson and Thomson; Tiles; Weaver.

25. Bates's literary history clarifies how the meaning of the verb "to court" is culturally and historically specific. Older meanings included the courtship of "being at court," "being a courtier," "suing for favor," and "behaving as courtiers should behave." The more "modern meaning of courtship—'wooing someone'"—emerged in the sixteenth century and has come to include "the interactive behavior and ritual between two people who are emotionally and romantically engaged" (1, 6). For scholarship that engages with Bates's conception of the rhetoric of courtship, see Lee; Runge; Sedinger.

26. As Zwagerman has explained, "courtship, in the rhetorical, Burkean sense, need not be manipulative" (147).

27. In this respect, my methodology is inspired by Buchanan's study of delivery: she considered both how delivery was taught through the rhetorical education of elocutionary manuals and how delivery was enacted through the rhetorical practices of specific speakers.

28. In addition to the cultural historians and rhetorical theorists cited throughout, Barthes and Derrida have theorized epistolary writing, especially in terms of presence and absence as well as the instability of gender and sexuality. See Ballif (92); Davidson (9); Decker (14); Favret (13, 18, 20); Garlinger (xl); Gilroy and Verhoeven (7); Kauffman (xli, 317); Love (32).

29. Gaul and Harris and Schultz have also discussed postal reform. For additional information about the U.S. Post Office, see Decker; Fuller; Henkin; John.

30. See Halloran; Halloran and Clark. Other complicating accounts of these nineteenth-century shifts include Bordelon ("'Resolved'"); Brereton; Connors (*Composition-Rhetoric*); Crowley; DePalma; Horner; Johnson (*Nineteenth-Century Rhetoric*); Kitzhaber; Legg; Mendenhall; Ricker ("'Ars Stripped of Praxis'"); Whitburn.

31. For more on the place of letter writing within the history of Western rhetoric, see Bannet; S. Carr; Murphy; Poster; Poster and Mitchell; M. Richardson; Sullivan.

32. On increased access to higher education, see Brereton; Carr, Carr, and Schultz; Connors (*Composition-Rhetoric*); Gold; Kates; Kitzhaber.

33. See also Schultz (123).

34. On women's theories of conversation as a rhetorical practice, see Donawerth (*Conversational Rhetoric*).

35. As Favret, along with Gilroy and Verhoeven, have shown, this fiction of the letter was instantiated by literary critics constructing a relatively limited archive that consisted mainly of eighteenth-century English and French epistolary novels—ones primarily written by men and about women heroines, such as in *Clarissa, Pamela, Julie,* and *Evelina*. More recent scholarship has constructed a broader archive inclusive of other kinds

of epistolary novels, literature, and actual letters that represent both women and men composing epistolary rhetoric. Scholars thus have come to more complex conclusions, exploding the presumptive association between women and letters and revealing it to be a fiction. In the field of rhetoric and composition, S. Miller has also challenged the association between women and letters that saturates scholarship on the nineteenth century.

36. See also Chauncey; Halperin (*How to Do the History*); Katz; Rotundo ("Romantic Friendship").

37. See Sedgwick; Somerville.

38. For continued citations of Faderman and Smith-Rosenberg's early work, see Rotundo ("Romantic Friendship"); Seidman. The earlier accounts have been complicated by Smith-Rosenberg herself ("Discourses of Sexuality and Subjectivity"), as well as Comment ("'When it ceases'"); Diggs; Sedgwick; Somerville; Vicinus (*Intimate Friends;* "'They Wonder'"); Wood.

39. Halberstam also made this argument ("Perverse Presentism").

40. See, for example, Cloud; Diggs; Faderman (*Surpassing the Love of Men*); Morris ("My Old Kentucky Homo"); Smith-Rosenberg ("Diaries and Letters"; "Female World").

41. Examples of what Diggs pointed out can be found in Faderman (*Surpassing the Love of Men* 18–19, 250–51, 414).

42. See Lystra; Rothman.

Chapter 1: "The language of the heart"

1. Letters were frequently published in periodicals, and, regardless of the intended purpose of such publication, it provided readers with sample letters from which to learn. In addition, my research has uncovered hundreds of nineteenth-century periodical articles about letter writing. For analysis of periodicals that taught letter writing, see Johnson (*Gender and Rhetorical Space*); Mahoney.

2. Mahoney has noted that women learned to write letters through "even the sensational literature of the period" (411). This relationship between letters, literature, epistolary fiction, and cultural pedagogy has been extensively analyzed by literary critics and historians (Altman; Bray; Cook; Favret; Gilroy and Verhoeven; Hewitt; Kauffman; Zaczek). Nineteenth-century letter-writing manuals also pointed to the learning of epistolary rhetoric from fiction (Chesterfield's 55–56; *Fashionable American Letter Writer* 167).

3. One example is Montague's letters and epistle verses, which were collected and reprinted in nineteenth-century New York and Philadelphia. Articles on letter writing that represented Montague as the genius of female letter writing in the English language—and thus a pedagogical model—were published by a range of periodicals ("Art. XXII"; "Letter Writing" (a); "Letter-Writing" (b); "Odds and Ends"; "On Letters and Letter-Writers"; "Reviews"; "Woman's Genius").

4. The treatise that most influenced letter-writing instruction as a feature of college-level rhetorical education is Blair's *Lectures on Rhetoric and Belles Lettres*. The popularity of Blair's rhetoric played a role in the inclusion of letter writing within nineteenth-century textbooks designed for classroom use. Some composition textbooks focused entirely on letter writing, such as Loomis's *Practical Letter Writing* (1897). More commonly, textbooks

included sections on letter writing; an example is Newman's *A Practical System of Rhetoric* (1836). This textbook was incredibly popular—by one account "first published in 1827 and in its twentieth printing by 1846" (Berlin 36), by another "the most widely used rhetoric written in America between 1820 and 1860, going through at least sixty 'editions' or printings" (Connors, *Composition-Rhetoric* 220). In Gage's survey of almost two hundred composition textbooks, 52 percent included letter-writing instruction (201). Gage concluded that it was "a considerable and consistent feature of composition instruction throughout the period, though clearly a dispensable one" (201).

5. See also Cavallaro; Enoch; VanHaitsma ("Romantic Correspondence").

6. Other histories of Western letter-writing instruction include Bruce; Chartier, Dauphin, and Boureau; Murphy.

7. These definitions can be found in Bannet (44, 277); Blair (346); Masten (378). Paraphrased versions of Blair's definition also appear in manuals throughout the nineteenth century (*Business and Social Correspondence* 60; Hardie 1; Loomis 7). Manuals that copied other lines from Blair include *How to Write Letters* (Westlake 12–14) and *The Useful Letter Writer* (x–xi, xxi–xxii).

8. The manual contents I cite throughout my analysis are characteristic of the broader sample, except where otherwise indicated. Many model letters were compiled and reprinted across manuals, as was common within nineteenth-century textbook production (Bannet; S. Carr; Nietz). *The Fashionable [American] Letter Writer* was especially popular up to and at midcentury. According to Johnson, it was "first published in 1818" and "went through twenty-seven editions into 1860," making it "The most successful American letter-writing manual for over half a century" (*Gender and Rhetorical Space* 189 n. 5). Another manual I cite frequently, *Chesterfield's*, was "modestly successful . . . at midcentury" and "went through three editions between 1857 and 1860" (189 n. 5). J. Carr has cautioned, however, that it is difficult to pinpoint the popularity of nineteenth-century manuals and textbooks: "The numbers of textbook copies sold in the nineteenth century is always an elusive bit of 'knowledge.' Scholars propose a figure, based on extrapolations from known editions and school populations, publishers' blurbs, or early bibliographic records" (228 n. 48). Yet, as Carr demonstrated through examples of specific books, the sales figures proposed on the basis of such extrapolation vary widely, as do claims about popularity.

9. It is problematic to use the term "American" in reference only to people living in (or citizens of) what is now the United States, because such usage ignores people throughout the Americas in ways complicit with colonialism. Where I use the term, I do so to underscore how letter-writing manuals from the nineteenth century presented their pedagogy as distinctively "American."

10. *The Useful Letter Writer* distinguishes between letters "From a young Tradesman" and those "From a young Gentleman" (v). Similarly, *The American Lady's and Gentleman's Modern Letter Writer* [185] distinguishes between multiple romantic letters from "A Gentleman" and one letter from "A Man Servant to the Object of His Affections," which clearly teaches class-specific ways of maintaining and cultivating same-class romantic relationships (43–44).

11. Conquergood made a similar point in his work on eighteenth- and nineteenth-century elocutionary manuals, which he understands as teaching elocution "redefined as the performativity of whiteness naturalized" (325).

12. While Johnson realized "the crucial function of the courtship letter," it was beyond the scope of her study to emphasize instruction in this subgenre and its gendering of romantic relations (*Gender and Rhetorical Space* 96). Thus her most extended attention to romantic epistolary rhetoric came in an endnote, where she acknowledged that manuals typically included instruction in appropriate ways for unmarried women and men to address each other (188). Similarly, Mahoney mentioned a manual focused on teaching "love-letters," but only in passing (414). Bannet and Trasciatti did briefly consider nineteenth-century manual instruction in romantic letter writing (198+; 85–88), and S. Miller discussed learning through the practice of romantic letter writing (201–06).

13. Whereas my study focuses on historically specific genre instruction, Davidson has considered what she framed as timeless about the romantic letter. Explaining that it "is a genre with its own set of rules and conventions," she asserted, "The variations in the formula that have taken place across centuries and continents and even, surprisingly, across the great divide of the sexes are relatively minor when compared to the features of the love letter that persist relatively unchanged" (8–9). For discussion of specifically nineteenth-century "heterosexual love letters," see Albertine (141).

14. See Halttunen; Hewitt; Zaczek.

15. This series was copied and adapted from Gregory's *A Father's Legacy to His Daughters*, which was published in London (1774) and reprinted in the United States (1834). The series also appeared in other complete letter writers, including *The Complete Letter Writer* (1811), *The Pocket Letter Writer* (1840), and *The New Parlor Letter Writer* [1853]. *The New Parlor Letter Writer* is named on its inside title page as such and is catalogued by the library as *The New Parlor Letter Writing*. But the manual is titled *The Complete Letter Writer* on its outside cover. While there are differences between *The Complete Letter Writer* and *The New Parlor Letter Writer*, there are also pages that are exactly alike (such as 68–77; 78–84). In these ways, the models in complete letter writers were not only subject to copying but copied themselves (S. Carr).

16. Some manuals were more explicit. *Letter-Writing Simplified* insists that "All letters should be dated" (12). *Frost's* explains that "Every letter or note should be carefully dated. . . . The date of the letter comprises the city or town, state and country in some instances, day of the month, month and year" (Shields 29).

17. On this point from Halberstam, see also Dunn ("(Queer) Family Time" 137).

18. While offering a third alternative, Dunn has characterized two general ways that scholars approach queer temporality: as a negative, critical rejection of "reproductive futurism," following the work of Edelman, or as an affirmation of productively queer alternatives to normative time, following Halberstam as well as Muñoz, Freeman, and Freccero (Dunn, "(Queer) Family" 137). Other queer scholarship important to theorizing queer temporality cited by Dunn includes Boellstorff; Castiglia and Reed; Düttmann; Goltz; Morris ("My Old Kentucky Homo"). Also see the special issue of *GLQ: A Journal of Lesbian and Gay Studies* devoted to queer temporalities, especially the introduction by

Freeman and roundtable discussion by Dinshaw, Edelman, Ferguson, Freccero, Freeman, Halberstam, Jagose, Nealon, and Nguyen.

19. This gendering of the models is in line with epistolary novels, which generally represent the gendered seduction of women by men who were "rakes" (Hewitt 44, 124–25; Illouz 46).

20. In the absence of copyright laws and given limited railroads, roads, and mail services, any printer could copy text from another printer's book and sell that text locally; books often included material copied and compiled from other books (Nietz 7; see also Bannet; S. Carr).

21. For further discussion of nineteenth-century invention practices, see Crowley; Rothermel ("Prophets, Friends, Conversationalists").

22. Farrar deemed the entire complete letter-writer genre "a serious evil, and one to be guarded against" (vi). Initiating her critique, Farrar remarked on "The numerous editions which the 'Complete Letter-Writer' has passed through, and the various forms in which it has, again and again, been presented to the public," characterizing these editions as marked by "glaring absurdities and gross faults" (v–vi). She claimed that complete letter writers "are filled with absurdities, vulgarisms, and the flattest nonsense that was ever offered to the public, as a guide to letter-writing" (125). Vulgarity was also an accusation made by *The Epistolary Guide* (1817): "The various works, called *Complete Letter Writers*, are well known for the grossness of their matter, as well as the vulgarity of their manner. . . . Even a volume of essays would answer a better purpose; because it would not mislead, by pretending to exhibit models of genuine letters" (Hardie vii). *The Complete American Letter-Writer* simply refers to other complete letter writers as "ridiculous trash" and "ignorant productions" (iii).

23. *The Art of Correspondence* warns, "Those who attempt to copy wholly the letters of another will find themselves in the position of the rustic who copied a proposal of marriage from a published Letter-Writer and sent it to a young lady, who replied that the negative answer could be found in the same book from which he copied the proposal" (Locke 11–12). A similar story is told in *How to Write Letters* (Westlake 84–85) and *Letter-Writing Simplified* (2).

24. A twentieth-century manual, *Putnam's Phrase Book: An Aid to Social Letter Writing* (1922), offers remarkably detailed instruction for invention through the copying and adapting of models (E. Carr iv, 63, 169).

25. The section on letter writing in Farrar's conduct manual advises young women that "All kissing and caressing of your female friends should be kept for your hours of privacy, and never be indulged in before gentlemen" (*The Young Lady's Friend* 241). For consideration of this line, see Comment ("'When it ceases'"). On Farrar, see also Donawerth ("Poaching on Men's Philosophies"); Huh; Schlesinger; Wood.

26. In rare cases, manuals even marked the gender of writers and readers with "queer effect." Garlinger has identified an eighteenth-century manual that "by mistake" included romantic letters written by men to men. Garlinger explained, "The prescriptive function of the letter-writing manual revealed one of the elements that had been eliminated in the process of (mis)categorizing the model letters. The possibility that male letter writers

might send missives to other men reveals the extent to which homoeroticism appears only by means of its absence" (xxi).

27. See also *The Useful Letter Writer* vii, 159; Turner xiv, 255; *The Pocket Letter Writer* xvii, 171. It is possible that some model romantic letters were placed within "Miscellaneous" sections due to nineteenth-century printing and textbook production practices. Adding new models to earlier editions could be accomplished more easily through appending them in a new section at the end of the book than by rearranging to categorize each new model within existing sections.

28. The same cryptogram was reprinted in Locke's *The Art of Correspondence* (1884). Here the cryptogram was included in the chapter on romantic letters. Locke offered a longer explanatory title for the letter, though he too emphasized ingenuity: "A letter with a double meaning, showing how an ingenious wife deceived an arbitrary, overbearing husband, who compelled her to show him all her letters" (161, emphasis added).

29. To view this cryptogram letter, see VanHaitsma ("Queering 'the language of the heart'").

30. Carmichael mentioned "a truly remarkable collection of early-nineteenth-century cryptograms" found among the papers of a retired professor, whose estate also included "private correspondence to the professor from his best friend, interspersed with some titillating although not raunchy gay pictorial pornography" (89). Perhaps the best-known instance of writing in code about same-sex romantic relations is the English gentlewoman Anne Lister's diary (Pritchard, *Fashioning Lives;* Vicinus, *Intimate Friends;* Whitbread, *I Know My Own Heart; No Priest but Love*). Lister also wrote coded letters to Mariana Belcombe after she married Charles Lawton and he began reviewing all of the women's correspondence (Vicinus, *Intimate Friends* 20).

31. Elsewhere I discuss these feminist methodologies of critical imagination in terms of queer gossip ("Gossip as Rhetorical Methodology").

32. Royster expands on this initial definition with Kirsch (71).

Chapter 2: "To address you *My Husband*"

1. See Comment ("Dickinson's Bawdy"); Doyle; Faderman (*Surpassing the Love of Men; To Believe in Women*); Hart; Katz; Messmer; Morris ("My Old Kentucky Homo"); Norton; Rotundo, "Romantic Friendship"; Smith-Rosenberg; Vicinus.

2. Also see Newkirk, whose collection consists of romantic letters by African Americans.

3. My use of the term "everyday" follows Zboray and Zboray (Everyday Ideas xx). I also use the term in the tradition of de Certeau, in that I underscore the tactical creativity and ingenuity of people in queering cultural norms, genre conventions, and generic boundaries as they learned romantic epistolary rhetoric. For characterizations of Brown and Primus's epistolary practices as "everyday" and "ordinary," see F. Griffin (4); Hansen ("No Kisses" 179). Other sources on everyday rhetoric include Ackerman; Dickinson; Modesti; Nystrand and Duffy; Sinor; Sloop, "People Shopping."

4. Prichard discusses this erasure further in *Fashioning Lives: Black Queers and the Politics of Literacy* (10, 53, 103–04). Exceptions cited by Pritchard include portions of

studies by Malinowitz and by Pough (51). See also Campbell; Chávez (*Queer Migration Politics*); Morrissey; Nakayama; L. Olson; Patton; Ramirez; Squires and Brouwer; Van-Haitsma ("Queering 'the language of the heart'"; "Romantic Correspondence"); Watts.

    5. Pritchard defined "racialized heteronormativity" as "the racialization of gender and sexual practices that position elite, White, cisgender, male, heterosexuality as the model of normativity and the qualifying standard for national identity within the Western state" (Fashioning Lives 26). In the face of racialized heteronormativity, "restorative literacies are a form of cultural labor through which individuals tactically counter acts of literacy normativity through the application of literacies for self- and communal love" (33).

    6. This letter is from Box I of the Primus Family Papers, held at the Connecticut Historical Society. Box I includes Brown's letters to Primus, and Box II includes Primus's letters to family. Within each box, folders are organized by date. I cite letters according to their date.

    7. For more on Primus's involvement in self-education for racial uplift on behalf of formerly enslaved African Americans, see Beeching (*Hopes*); F. Griffin; VanHaitsma ("Romantic Correspondence").

    8. F. Griffin did mention the envelope on the back of which, "in Rebecca's handwriting, is written: 'Addie died at home, January 11, 1870'" (235).

    9. The earliest scholarship on Brown and Primus's letters focused on the history of African Americans in Hartford. White did not go much further than recognizing that the women's relationship was "particularly close" ("Addie Brown's Hartford" 57; see also "Rebecca Primus"). Beeching more fully acknowledged their relationship as a "sentimental and erotic connection" (*Hopes* 141), but maintained that "Whether there was homosexual content is not clear from Addie's letters" ("Primus Papers" 55).

    10. Hansen first discovered the letters when conducting research for her book, *A Very Social Time*. Unless otherwise noted, quotations of Hansen are from her essay, "'No Kisses Is Like Youres.'" Hansen was responsible for having "introduced" F. Griffin to the letters (F. Griffin xiii). Faderman also cited Hansen (*To Believe in Women* 368).

    11. F. Griffin collected, edited, and offered commentary on Brown and Primus's correspondence. Griffin highlighted the importance of their letters for addressing silences within the historical record about the "personal and public" lives of "ordinary" black women not self-censoring in order to write for publication or a white audience (4). Griffin's edited versions of the letters have been cited by R. Harrison and Peiss, and the collection itself has become a subject of analysis by Grasso, who considered how "the letters tell another story as the result of being organized, annotated, placed in the company of other sources, and published in book form" (250).

    12. Hansen explained how the correspondence "fills a gap in the literature about African-American women in the nineteenth century," because the letters are written by "ordinary women" about their "everyday" lives (178–79). Moreover, the correspondence "fills a gap in the literature" about nineteenth-century romantic friendship between women, which at that point focused almost entirely on white middle-class women (179, 202). Here Hansen cited research on middle-class white women by Cott, Faderman (*Surpassing the Love of Men*), and Smith-Rosenberg ("Female World"), as well as her own research on working-class white women (*Very*).

13. For further discussion of the familial terms of address used within romantic letters between women, see Vicinus (*Intimate Friends* 43–45).

14. There were, however, same-sex couples in the nineteenth-century United States whose relationships were understood as "marriage" within their local contexts (Cleves).

15. Brown wrote, "We are to be married at 6 p.m. and leave at 7 whenever take place. Please dont mention to no one" (Oct. 15, 1867). In F. Griffin's words, Brown "welcomes the opportunity to leave her job as a live-in servant and to begin a new life as the wife of her longtime suitor, Joseph Tines. Nonetheless, though she views marriage as an escape from life as a domestic servant, she continues to express some ambivalence and fear about the institution" (236).

16. It is possible that Primus also conceived of their relationship in terms more romantic than her marriage to Charles Thomas. In 1868, Brown married Joseph Tines, and extant correspondence with Primus ceased (F. Griffin 235). When Brown passed away shortly after, in 1870, Primus made note of her death on the outside of an envelope (235). By 1872 Primus had married Thomas (77). Although Primus stayed with Thomas and his wife when teaching in Royal Oak, neither her nor Brown's mentions of him suggest a romantic relation or even flirtation. The Primus Family Papers include two postcards and five letters to Thomas from others; these letters are short, incredibly formal, and for clearly professional and political purposes. Primus saved the romantic letters from Brown—well over a hundred of them—until her own death more than sixty years later, in 1932 (White, "Rebecca Primus" 284). It may also be of note that there is some mystery surrounding the circumstances of Thomas's parting with his first wife and his marriage to Primus (281).

17. As I discuss elsewhere, Brown's repurposing of the romantic letter genre to erotic ends takes on further significance within the context of stereotypes about black women's sexuality that were used to justify violence and often circumscribed black women's expression (Abdur-Rahman; P. Collins; Hansen; Lorde; Pritchard, *Fashioning Lives*; E. Richardson; VanHaitsma, "Romantic Correspondence"). Subverting the "racialized heteronormativity" that "pathologizes Black sexuality," Brown's writing about erotic life amounted to what Pritchard has theorized as "restorative literacy" (65).

18. While I focus on "the language of the heart" in poetry and the novel, Brown and Primus's letters reference texts ranging from novels to antislavery papers, from slave narratives to poetry, from speeches to books on religion, politics, and history.

19. Brown also redeployed phrasing from the Christian Bible in order to express desire and longing for Primus (Aug. 30, 1859; May 24, 1861).

20. F. Griffin similarly noted this shift in style as indicative of copying (64).

21. Nor was Brown's relationship to other texts deferential on the whole. As F. Griffin pointed out, Brown "demonstrates her intellectual independence" when writing about a speech by Henry Ward Beecher (140). Calling Beecher "very plain," Brown wrote, "he says the recent history of the nation may be divided into three periods. . . . I should think it was four" (Oct. 16, 1866).

22. As Beeching wrote, "Addie's letters frequently started off as if she were following a formulae. . . . Once under way, however, Addie's writing conveyed the impression of transcribed speech" ("Primus Papers" 70).

23. With George Pope Morris and Nathaniel Parker Willis, Fay served as an editor of the *New-York Mirror: Devoted to Literature and the Fine Arts*, with which he corresponded while traveling abroad. "Reveries by Night" was published in the *New-York Mirror* under the heading "Original Communications" (1831).

24. Brown also used this invention strategy of interspersing seemingly copied language with epistolary address in more overtly romantic passages (Mar. 30, 1862; also ctd. in Faderman, *To Believe in Women* 104; Grasso 262; R. Harrison 224; Peiss 218).

25. Brown's active process of selection and deletion is further evident in her use of the poem "Alone" (Dec. 8, 1861), another version of which was published in *Peterson's Magazine* (1855) under the name Clarence May.

26. On nineteenth-century autograph albums and rhetorical invention, see Ricker ("(De)Constructing the Praxis").

27. On the racial politics of imitation as practiced by African Americans in the nineteenth century, see Wilson.

28. For further discussion of romantic letters as evidence, as well as approaches to reading and interpreting such texts, see Cloud; Faderman, *To Believe in Women;* Jones; Lystra; Morris, "My Old Kentucky Homo"; Stanley.

29. Nor are such approaches to letters limited to histories of sexuality. As Henkin wrote in his history of the postal age, historians rely on letters as evidence, but "often with the underexamined assumption that letters provide unusually transparent windows into the sincere beliefs or private lives of their authors" (6). In contrast with the assumption described by Henkin, Ruberg has recognized that "it is often not possible for historians to reconstruct actually felt emotions. Since emotions are always represented through a medium (often a text), their discursive character should be taken into account. . . . Letters cannot be taken as straightforward sources unveiling historical reality, but have to be studied as multifaceted and complicated documents. Letters are often composed according to social and cultural rules and written with certain aims in mind. Relationships between sender and receiver are constructed in correspondence, not necessarily reflecting daily relationships outside the correspondence" (208–09).

30. Like letters, K. Harrison has explained, "Diaries . . . do not present pure, unfiltered rhetorical evidence. As readers, we can never know with certainty the slant by which an event was recounted or the details omitted to support a desired image for the writer's own self-narrative or for the benefit of future readers, whether imagined or real. Yet, such uncertainties do not negate the value of evidence found in diaries, especially with a focus on patterns and the writer's context" (*Rhetoric of Rebel Women* 20).

31. The series of letters includes those dated Oct. 20, 27; Nov. 17; Dec. 8, 1867.

32. Here the letter under consideration is from Jan. 21, 1866.

33. For further discussion of how writers used the letter to develop and advance cultural and political critiques, see Carlacio; Favret; Gaul and Harris; Henkin; Hewitt.

Chapter 3: "Somehow or other, queer in the extreme"

1. The Albert Dodd Papers are held by the Yale University Library, Manuscripts and Archives. The Papers consist of three folders: the first is labeled Dodd's "diary"; the second

his "album of poetry"; and the third his "letters" and "obituary." Entries, poems, and letters are generally dated, and I cite them according to their dates.

2. Although Dodd's education was marked by consequential forms of race, class, and gender privilege, his epistolary rhetoric can also be understood as "everyday." Just as the first historian to publish on Brown's writing was dismissive, the first historian to publish on Dodd's denigrated it as an "artless record" (Gay 207; see also White, "Addie Brown's Hartford" 57–58). Along with Brown and Primus, Dodd was included in Zboray and Zboray's large-scale study of everyday letters and diaries by "931 informants" (*Everyday Ideas* xxi, 54, 183, 316). In none of these references, though, are their same-sex romantic epistolary relations acknowledged.

3. For other discussions of queer boundary crossing, pedagogy, and student writing, see Alexander and Rhodes ("Queer: An Impossible Subject"); Waite ("Cultivating the Scavenger").

4. In a dairy entry dated Apr. 27, 1838, Dodd wrote, "Yesterday was my birthday, 19 years old." But other sources conflict regarding the year of his birth. His "Obituary" does not reference his date of birth. *Biographical Record of the Class of 1838 in Yale College* claims he was "Born about 1818" (53), but, as Katz indicated, *Biographical Notes of Graduates of Yale College* states that he "died at the age of 27, in 1844, which means that he was born in 1817" (Dexter 288 ctd. in Katz 354 n. 1).

5. According to the obituary, "a meeting of the citizens of Bloomington and vicinity" was held regarding his death "on Monday the 19th day of June, a.d., 1844." See also *Biographical Record* 53; Dexter 288.

6. Jesse was "a tree and flower enthusiast, a temperance advocate, and a civic leader" (Katz 31). In 1834 he "had begun a friendship and long political association with Abraham Lincoln," and later he "worked hard to win Lincoln the Republican nomination for president" (31). Related to the potential significance of this connection to Lincoln, see Morris ("My Old Kentucky Homo").

7. I have modernized the long s, and I will do so throughout.

8. Soon after beginning his studies at Yale, Dodd joined the secret society Skull and Bones (July 5, 1837). Dodd's other extracurricular involvements at Yale included a less-than positive experience getting published in the *Yale Literary Magazine* (diary July 17, 1837; "The Sea Nymph's Song" 294; poetry album Aug. 1835).

9. Since I conducted my primary research in the brick-and-mortar archives at Yale, Dodd's commonplace book turned diary has been digitized. Readers may find it here: http://digital.library.yale.edu/cdm/ref/collection/1004_8/id/1381.

10. In Katz's view, Dodd here referred to "two sins unwritable among that day's college students, most probably sexual sins, which Dodd represented by long dashes." Katz also speculated about whether "M. O." is "mutual onanism? masturbation? ononism?" (27).

11. The first of these historians to publish about Dodd, Gay briefly attended to Dodd's writing within *The Tender Passion* (206–12). Rotundo considered Dodd's writing alongside that of other young men when seeking to define the characteristics of nineteenth-century romantic friendship between men ("Romantic Friendship"). Rotundo cited Gay's book, however, and did not mention conducting primary research (8; 23 n. 26). Katz offered

the most in-depth discussion of Dodd and his romantic relations. Dodd's diary is widely cited elsewhere as well (Bernard; Quinn; Robb; Robinson; Rotundo, *American Manhood;* Woolverton; Zboray and Zboray, *Everyday Ideas*).

12. Commenting on this entry, Gay continued, "It might in fact be manly and pure, but it was heavily invested with libido, a 'flame,' as Albert Dodd pictured it to himself, 'that was burning' in his heart" (208).

13. Unless otherwise noted, all subsequent citations of Rotundo refer to his article "Romantic Friendship".

14. As Rotundo remarked, "Not only does Albert kiss Anthony Halsey as they embrace in bed . . . but there is an undertone of passion to Albert Dodd's account of his mention of Anthony's 'beloved form' and in his remembrance of the kisses—and the nights—as 'sweet' ones. All these subtle differences take additional erotic force from Albert's confession that he found Anthony 'so handsome'" (7).

15. Like Dodd, Elizabeth Morgan may have experienced "love" for both men and women. Dodd wrote in his diary, "Had some interesting conversation with her . . . among other things, she asked me if I had ever fallen in love at first sight . . . she said she had once so, not meaning love for one of another sex, but of her own" (Apr. 19, 1837).

16. Gay wrote that Dodd's diary moves "without apparent strain from male to female loves," often from one line to the very next, and his "sexual choices" repeatedly "vacillate between women and men" (207–08).

17. For further discussion of the classical orientation of rhetorical education at Yale, see Whitburn ("Rhetorical Theory").

18. Yet, as Johnson has cautioned, scholars should avoid a "classicist stance," which leads to pejorative assessments of nineteenth-century education as "unstable or inherently compromised" to the extent that it deviates from Ciceronian or Aristotelian rhetorical philosophy (*Nineteenth-Century Rhetoric* 12). While I emphasize how Dodd's rhetorical training was classically oriented, it is important to remember that his education was "synthetic," "a composite of classical assumptions and epistemological and belletristic premises initially popularized in the late eighteenth-century English tradition" (19).

19. The Stillman K. Wightman Papers are held by the Yale University Library, Manuscripts and Archives. Here I quote from Wightman's notes, apparently taken during one of Goodrich's lectures, which are in Box 1, Folder 19.

20. While Cicero advanced a Roman history and tradition of rhetoric, the Greek Demosthenes was one of the "prominent models" that Cicero referenced (Enos 108).

21. "Plato's Gorgias" is listed for the third part of junior year, but only as one text among others, "At the option of the student" (*Catalogue* 27).

22. The Goodrich Family Papers are also held by the Yale University Library, Manuscripts and Archives. Here I reference Goodrich's lecture notes in Box 7, Folders 61, 71, 73, 77, and 80. Although less frequently, the notes reference other classical rhetorical theorists as well. In "Lecture on Demosthenes," they reference Plato (Folder 77); in "Lectures on Eloquence," they reference Quintilian (Folder 86). For discussion of Goodrich in relation to the history of public address, see Medhurst (24).

23. Here I reference notes in Box 1, Folder 18 of the Stillman K. Wightman Papers. These student notes also mention Isocrates.

24. Dodd's study of rhetorical treatises was not limited to classical ones, however. Instead, his early nineteenth-century rhetorical education combined the classical with eighteenth-century English and Scottish works—such as those of Blair and Kames—as was common (Johnson, *Nineteenth-Century Rhetoric;* Dodd, Apr. 12, 1842). See also Connors, "Day, Henry Noble" 162; Desmet 133; Goodrich, Folders 62, 70, 86; Goodrich, *Select British Eloquence* iii.

25. Dodd actually wrote the most about studying Greek and Latin language and literature during his period of suspension (Mar. 1, 2, 3, 10, 12, 13, 15, 17; Apr. 8, 30; May 7, 8, 17; June 18, 1837).

26. While I cite Brent's survey and empirical research, the scholarship on transfer is expansive. For work especially relevant to questions of rhetorical education, student writing, and genre, see the following: Anson and Schwegler; Ball, Bowen, and Fenn; Beaufort; Clark and Hernandez; Cleary; Dirk; Downs and Wardle; Fraizer; Miles et al.; Moore; Nowacek; Reiff and Bawarshi; Rounsaville; Rounsaville, Goldberg, and Bawarshi; Wardle.

27. Of course, Dodd's nineteenth-century transfer cannot be characterized with certitude. Even writing studies researchers with the opportunity to ask present-day students about transfer find it difficult to get clear answers. Brent has explained, "To determine whether students have been able to reuse higher level knowledge, we need to search for evidence of prior learning that has been transformed or used as a platform for further learning rather than merely transferred. . . . Of course, searching for transformed knowledge makes our research task more difficult because it is hard to know what such knowledge looks like when it is applied to a new rhetorical context" ("Transfer, Transformation, and Rhetorical Knowledge" 410).

28. See, for instance, Bizzell and Herzberg; Fone; Gunderson; Halperin (*One Hundred Years of Homosexuality*); Hawhee.

29. Book 12 of the *Greek Anthology* is "a collection of over 250 epigrams devoted to pederastic sentiment," including "the earliest anthologies of homoerotic verse, the *Garland of Meleager,*" and "poetry by a wide selection of Greek writers celebrat[ing] love, desire, and sex between adult males and youths, often with great specificity" (Fone 40–44).

30. It is unclear whether Dodd wrote, compiled, or translated this verse.

31. The myth is associated with pederasty and even "abduction" (Fone 16; see also Boswell). But there is nothing in Dodd's verse about the abduction of Ganymede by Zeus, and there are no direct references to pederasty or even Ganymede's age. Nor is there any reason to presume that Dodd participated in pederastic relations. Where Dodd hinted at the age of his romantic interests, they were students within one to three years of his own age (Sept. 21; Oct. 5, 10, 1837).

32. On self-rhetorics, K. Harrison cited V. Collins and Nienkamp (*Civil War Diaries* 15).

33. Additional studies of the diary include Bunkers; Gannett; K. Harrison ("Rhetorical Rehearsals"); McCarthy; Sinor; Sjöblad. As Logan has reminded readers, this "literature on the history of diary-keeping centers on the habits of middle-class white women" (33).

34. Dodd did write about his attractions as similar in that he was attracted to the same (Western, white) physical form in both men and women. After commenting on Morgan's

personality and demeanor, he wrote, "In truth she is a beautiful girl, and I like my first acquaintance with her much. She is handsome, of the style of beauty which I admire, viz: light complexion and hair, and blue eyes;—just like Julia" (Feb. 26, 1837). Then, a few months later, Dodd wrote of Smith: "Went up in the City Hotel with Jabe and slept with him. He is a fine, handsome fellow, and he interests me much, light curly hair, light complexion, blue eyes, handsome [?] countenance, and a slight graceful form" (Apr. 24, 1837). What Dodd found attractive in all three romantic interests, whether female or male, included a "light complexion" and "blue eyes." These similarities do not suggest, however, that his romantic relations were not carried out in gendered ways. Predictably, he described sharing beds and physically intimate space with men but characterized his interactions with women as limited largely to church and calling (Feb. 11, 26; Mar. 15, 27; Apr. 24; May 8, 17; Sept. 9, 21; Oct. 5, 1837; May 23, 1838). See also Gay (210); Katz (30); Morris, "My Old Kentucky Homo" (96–97); Rotundo (10, 13).

35. Gay claimed that "boys aroused" Dodd "even more" than girls did (208–09).

36. For further discussion of commonplace books, see Rothermel ("Prophets, Friends, Conversationalists").

37. The first entry following the preface is an essay-like reflection on time, occasioned by Dodd's anticipation of commencement and the completion of his second year of college (July 31, 1836). The second, "Miss Clifton, as Ernestine," accounts for visiting "the new National Theatre" while vacationing in New York (Sept. 29, 1836). In the entry most like a school-based rhetorical exercise, he began with quotation of a question in Latin that he translated into English. After promising to first "take up the subject literally and analytically," he quoted (again in Latin) a description from Homer, endeavoring to "examine the subject in a metaphorical aspect" and then to "build up an argument for the opposite side" (Oct. 30, 1836). The final commonplace book entry, "Sketches of Travel," characterizes another trip to New York (Nov. 4, 1836).

38. In Logan's study, writers also reported sharing diaries (29, 49).

39. Logan defined the diary as "a text written in the first person with dated, chronological passages in which the writing subject speaks of and comments on certain events" (32). K. Harrison discussed scholarly distinctions between the diary and the journal (*Rhetoric of Rebel Women* 180 n. 15).

40. As Gold explained in his review of Harrison's study, "the rhetoricity of diaries" involves not only how they "illuminated the public rhetorical activities of their authors" but also how diaries functioned "as sites of rhetorical invention in themselves" (385).

41. On the relationship between nineteenth-century epistolary and poetic writing, particularly with respect to Dickinson, see Messmer.

42. For more on the epistolary genre in Latin literature and Horace especially, see de Pretis.

43. Examples include entries dated June 18; June 27; Sept. 3, 1837.

44. In this poem the speaker begins, "I think of thee, Elizabeth," declaring that, "Whatever I do, wherever I roam," the speaker's thoughts turn to "thee at home" (June 1838). The poem returns throughout to versions of the opening refrain, with the final stanza concluding, "I think of thee, I dream of thee. / I sigh for thee, Elizabeth, / Be

thou my friend, my guardian be, / And I will love thee while I've breath. / In good or evil destiny, / Elizabeth, I'll think of thee."

45. In his poem "Epistolary," it is possible Dodd also imitated Byron's epic poem "Don Juan." Unlike Horace, Byron was not referenced directly in Dodd's writing or in Yale's *Catalogue*. Nor is "Don Juan" an epistle verse. Yet "Epistolary" resembles "Don Juan" in terms of Dodd's playful use of parenthesis as well as his rhyme scheme (Barton 15).

46. See Gay (210, 212); Katz (27); Rotundo (8).

47. Dodd essentially instructed Edward to focus on the positive, rather than worrying about what one cannot control, as Dodd himself used to do (Mar. 13, 1844).

48. In response to my inquiries about the provenance of the Albert Dodd Papers, the Manuscripts and Archives staff at Yale University Library confirmed only that, as indicated in the Finding Aide, the papers were a gift of Marion Belden Cook in 1981. Prior to this gift, they were held in a private collection; no further information can be provided.

Conclusion

1. Additional scholarship on Halberstam's queer failure and present-day rhetoric and writing pedagogy includes A. Carr; Gross and Alexander; Rhodes; Waite ("Andy Teaches Me").

2. For another engagement with Halberstam's queer failure with respect to historiography in rhetoric, see Dolmage.

3. See "How to Write"; R. Miller; Biguenet; Chace. The quoted passage is from Miller.

4. See "How to Succeed"; Khazan; Flexman; Hayes.

5. Other popular manuals are less closely tied to the history of rhetoric but nonetheless teach language practices for rhetorically participating in romantic relations (for example, Chapman; Gray).

6. For scholarship on the rhetoric of seduction, see Ballif; Blythin; Brockriede; Erickson and Thomson; Kelley; Tiles; Weaver.

7. For these titles see Davies; Fein and Schneider; Koppel; Silverstein and Lasky.

8. See Berzon; Kaminsky.

9. Homonormativity is theorized across queer studies, including within the work of Conrad; Dinshaw et al.; Duggan; Eng; Muñoz; Stryker.

10. These books are by Easton and Liszt; Matik. See also Taormino; West.

11. Elsewhere I consider classroom opportunities like those Alexander and Wallace call for ("New Archival Engagements").

Works Cited

Abdur-Rahman, Aliyya I. *Against the Closet: Black Political Longing and the Erotics of Race.* Duke UP, 2012.
Ackerman, John. "The Space of Rhetoric in Everyday Life." *Towards a Rhetoric of Everyday Life: New Directions in Research on Writing, Text, and Discourse,* edited by Martin Nystrand and John Duffy, U of Wisconsin P, 2003, pp. 84–120.
Aguilar, Grace. *Women's Friendship: A Story of Domestic Life.* London, 1850. Google Books. Accessed 2 Jan. 2012.
Ahearn, Laura. *Invitations to Love: Literacy, Love Letters, and Social Change in Nepal.* U of Michigan P, 2001.
Albertine, Susan. "Heart's Expression: The Middle-Class Language of Love in Late Nineteenth-Century Correspondence." *American Literary History,* vol. 4, no. 1, 1992, pp. 141–64.
Alexander, Jonathan. *Literacy, Sexuality, Pedagogy: Theory and Practice for Composition Studies.* Utah State UP, 2008.
Alexander, Jonathan, and Michelle Gibson. "Queer Composition(s): Queer Theory in the Writing Classroom." *Journal of Advanced Composition,* vol. 24, no. 1, 2004, pp. 1–21.
Alexander, Jonathan, and Jacqueline Rhodes. "Queer: An Impossible Subject for Composition." *Journal of Advanced Composition,* vol. 31, no. 1/2, 2011, pp. 177–206.
———. "Queer Rhetoric and the Pleasures of the Archive." *Enculturation: A Journal of Rhetoric, Writing, and Culture,* vol. 13, 2012. Accessed 18 June 2015.
Alexander, Jonathan, and Jacqueline Rhodes, editors. *Sexual Rhetorics: Methods, Identities, Publics.* Routledge, 2016.
Alexander, Jonathan, and David Wallace. "The Queer Turn in Composition Studies: Reviewing and Assessing Emerging Scholarship." *College Composition and Communication,* vol. 61, no. 1, 2009, pp. W300–20.
Ali, Kazim. "Genre-Queer: Notes against Generic Binaries." *Bending Genre: Essays on Creative Nonfiction,* edited by Margot Singer and Nicole Walker, Bloomsbury, 2013, pp. 27–39.
Altman, Janet. *Epistolarity: Approaches to a Form.* Ohio State UP, 1982.
The American Lady's and Gentleman's Modern Letter Writer: Relative to Business, Duty, Love, and Marriage. Philadelphia, [185-]. Nietz Collection, U of Pittsburgh, Pennsylvania.

Anderson, Dana. *Identity's Strategy: Rhetorical Selves in Conversation.* U of South Carolina P, 2007.

Anson, Chris M., and Robert A. Schwegler. "Tracking the Mind's Eye: A New Technology for Researching Twenty-First-Century Writing and Reading Processes." *College Composition and Communication,* vol. 64, no. 1, 2012, pp. 151–71.

"Art. XXII.—The Letters of Mrs. Elizabeth Montague, with Some of the Letters of Her Correspondents." *Port Folio,* Mar. 1821, pp. 150–61. American Periodicals Series. Accessed 31 Aug. 2010.

Atwill, Janet. "Rhetoric and Civic Virtue." *The Viability of the Rhetorical Tradition,* edited by Richard Graff, Arthur Walzer, and Janet Atwill, State U of New York P, 2005, pp. 75–92.

Bacon, Jacqueline, and Glen McClish. "Reinventing the Master's Tools: Nineteenth-Century African-American Literary Societies of Philadelphia and Rhetorical Education." *Rhetoric Society Quarterly,* vol. 30, no. 4, 2000, pp. 19–47.

Bakhtin, Mikhail M. "The Problem of Speech Genres." *Speech Genres and Other Late Essays.* Translated by Vern W. McGee, edited by Caryl Emerson and Michael Holquist, U of Texas P, 1986, pp. 60–102.

Ball, Cheryl E., Tia Scoffield Bowen, and Tyrell Brent Fenn. "Genre and Transfer in a Multimodal Composition Class." *Multimodal Literacies and Emerging Genres,* edited by Tracey Bowen and Carl Whithaus, U of Pittsburgh P, 2013, pp. 15–36.

Ballif, Michelle. *Seduction, Sophistry, and the Woman with the Rhetorical Figure.* Southern Illinois UP, 2001.

Bannet, Eve Tavor. *Empire of Letters: Letter Manuals and Transatlantic Correspondence, 1688–1820.* Cambridge UP, 2005.

Barthes, Roland. *A Lover's Discourse: Fragments.* Hill & Wang, 1978.

Barton, Anne. *Byron: Don Juan.* Cambridge UP, 1992.

Bates, Catherine. *The Rhetoric of Courtship: Courting and Courtliness in Elizabethan Language and Literature.* Cambridge UP, 1992.

Bawarshi, Anis S., and Mary Jo Reiff. *Genre: An Introduction to History, Theory, Research, and Pedagogy.* Parlor P, 2010.

Bazerman, Charles. "The Life of Genre, the Life in the Classroom." *Genre and Writing: Issues, Arguments, Alternatives,* edited by Wendy Bishop and Hans Ostrom, Boynton/Cook, 1997, pp. 19–26.

Beaufort, Anne. "*College Writing and Beyond:* Five Years Later." *Composition Forum,* vol. 26, 2012. Accessed 2 Dec. 2014.

Beeching, Barbara J. *Hopes and Expectations: The Origins of the Black Middle Class in Hartford.* State U of New York P, 2017.

———. "The Primus Papers: An Introduction to Hartford's Nineteenth Century Black Community." M.A. thesis, Trinity College, 1995.

Bereiter, Carl. "A Dispositional View of Transfer." *Teaching for Transfer: Fostering Generalization in Learning,* edited by Anne McKeough, Judy Lupart, and Anthony Marini, Lawrence Erlbaum, 1995, pp. 21–34.

Berlant, Lauren. *The Queen of America Goes to Washington City: Essays on Sex and Citizenship.* Duke UP, 1997.

Berlant, Lauren, and Michael Warner. "Sex in Public." *Critical Inquiry*, vol. 24, no. 2, 1998, pp. 547–66.
Berlin, James. *Writing Instruction in Nineteenth-Century American Colleges*. Southern Illinois UP, 1984.
Bernard, Ben. "From the Archives: The Diary of Albert Dodd, 1838." *Q Magazine at Yale*, vol. 29, Mar. 2011. Accessed 16 Apr. 2014.
Berzon, Betty. *Permanent Partners: Building Gay and Lesbian Relationships That Last*. 1988. Plume, 2004.
Bessette, Jean. "An Archive of Anecdotes: Raising Lesbian Consciousness after the Daughters of Bilitis." *Rhetoric Society Quarterly*, vol. 43, no. 1, 2013, pp. 22–45.
———. "Queer Rhetoric *in Situ*." *Rhetoric Review*, vol. 35, no. 2, 2016, pp. 148–64.
Biguenet, John. "A Modern Guide to the Love Letter." *Atlantic*, 12 Feb. 2015. Accessed 5 Mar. 2015.
Biographical Record of the Class of 1838 in Yale College. New Haven, 1879.
Bizzell, Patricia, and Bruce Herzberg, editors. *The Rhetorical Tradition: Readings from Classical Times to the Present*. Bedford St. Martin's, 1990.
Blair, Hugh. *Lectures on Rhetoric and Belles Lettres*. 1783. Philadelphia, [1793]. Early American Imprints. Accessed 9 May 2011.
Blythin, Evan. "'Arguers as Lovers': A Critical Perspective." *Philosophy & Rhetoric*, vol. 12, no. 3, 1979, pp. 176–86.
Boellstorff, Tom. "When Marriage Falls: Queer Coincidences in Straight Time." *GLQ: A Journal of Lesbian and Gay Studies*, vol. 13, no. 2–3, 2007, pp. 227–48.
Bordelon, Suzanne. *A Feminist Legacy: The Rhetoric and Pedagogy of Gertrude Buck*. Southern Illinois UP, 2007.
———. "Participating on an 'Equal Footing': The Rhetorical Significance of California State Normal School in the Late Nineteenth Century." *Rhetoric Society Quarterly*, vol. 41, no. 2, 2011, pp. 168–90.
———. "'Resolved That the Mind of Woman Is Not Inferior to That of Man': Women's Oratorical Preparation in California State Normal School Coeducational Literary Societies in the Late Nineteenth Century." *Advances in the History of Rhetoric*, vol. 15, no. 2, 2012, pp. 159–84.
Boswell, John. *Christianity, Social Tolerance, and Homosexuality: Gay People in Western Europe from the Beginning of the Christian Era to the Fourteenth Century*. U of Chicago P, 1980.
Branstetter, Heather Lee. "Promiscuous Approaches to Reorienting Rhetorical Research." *Sexual Rhetorics: Methods, Identities, Publics*, edited by Jonathan Alexander and Jacqueline Rhodes, Routledge, 2016, pp. 17–30.
Bray, Joe. *The Epistolary Novel: Representations of Consciousness*. Routledge, 2003.
Brent, Doug. "Crossing Boundaries: Co-Op Students Relearning to Write." *College Composition and Communication*, vol. 63, no. 4, 2012, pp. 558–92.
———. "Transfer, Transformation, and Rhetorical Knowledge: Insights from Transfer Theory." *Journal of Business & Technical Communication*, vol. 25, no. 4, 2011, pp. 396–420.
Brereton, John C., editor. *The Origins of Composition Studies in the American College, 1875–1925: A Documentary History*. U of Pittsburgh P, 1995.

Brockriede, Wayne. "Arguers as Lovers." *Philosophy & Rhetoric*, vol. 5, no. 1, 1972, pp. 1–11.

Brookey, Robert Alan. "Speak Up! I Can't Queer You." *Queering Public Address: Sexualities in American Historical Discourse*, edited by Charles E. Morris III, U of South Carolina P, 2007, pp. 195–219.

Brown, Addie. Letters to Rebecca Primus, 1859–1868. Primus Family Papers. MS 44102. Box I. Connecticut Historical Society, Hartford.

Bruce, Emily C. "'Each Word Shows How You Love Me': The Social Literacy Practice of Children's Letter Writing (1780–1860)." *Paedagogica Historica*, vol. 50, no. 3, 2014, pp. 247–64.

Buchanan, Lindal. *Regendering Delivery: The Fifth Canon and Antebellum Women Rhetors*. Southern Illinois UP, 2005.

Bunkers, Suzanne L., editor. *Diaries of Girls and Women: A Midwestern American Sampler*. U of Wisconsin P, 2001.

Burke, Kenneth. *A Rhetoric of Motives*. U of California P, 1950.

Business and Social Correspondence: A Text-book for Use in All Schools in which the Subject is Taught. New York, 1889. Nietz Collection, U of Pittsburgh, Pennsylvania.

Butler, Judith. "Critically Queer." *GLQ: A Journal of Lesbian and Gay Studies*, vol. 1, no. 1, 1993, pp. 17–32.

———. *Gender Trouble: Feminism and the Subversion of Identity*. 1990. Routledge, 2011.

———. "Imitation and Gender Insubordination." *Inside/Out: Lesbian Theories, Gay Theories*, edited by Diana Fuss, Routledge, 1991, pp. 13–31.

Byron, George Gordon. *The Poetical Works of Lord Byron*, vol. 9. Boston, 1871. Google Books. Accessed 15 Apr. 2014.

Campbell, Peter Odell. "Intersectionality Bites: Metaphors of Race and Sexuality in HBO's *True Blood*." *Monster Culture in the 21st Century: A Reader*, edited by Marina Levina and Diem-My T. Bui, Bloomsbury, 2013, pp. 99–114.

Carlacio, Jami. "'Ye Knew Your Duty, But Ye Did It Not': The Epistolary Rhetoric of Sarah Grimké." *Rhetoric Review*, vol. 21, no. 3, 2002, pp. 247–63.

Carmichael, James V., Jr. "'They Sure Got to Prove It on Me': Millennial Thoughts on Gay Archives, Gay Biography, and Gay Library History." *Libraries & Culture*, vol. 35, no. 1, 2000, pp. 88–102.

Carr, Allison D. "In Support of Failure." *Composition Forum*, vol. 27, no. 3, 2013. Accessed 2 Nov. 2016.

———. "'Unbeing and Unbecoming': A Review of Halberstam's *Queer Art of Failure*." *Enculturation: A Journal of Rhetoric, Writing, and Culture*, vol. 15, 20 May 2012. Accessed 2 Nov. 2016.

Carr, Edwin Hamlin. *Putnam's Phrase Book*. New York, 1922. Nietz Collection, U of Pittsburgh, Pennsylvania.

Carr, Jean Ferguson. "Reading School Readers." *Archives of Instruction: Nineteenth-Century Rhetorics, Readers, and Composition Books in the United States*, edited by Jean Ferguson Carr, Stephen L. Carr, and Lucille M. Schultz, Southern Illinois UP, 2005, pp. 81–147.

Carr, Jean Ferguson, Stephen L. Carr, and Lucille M. Schultz. *Archives of Instruction:*

Nineteenth-Century Rhetorics, Readers, and Composition Books in the United States. Southern Illinois UP, 2005.

Carr, Stephen. "Reproducing Rhetorics." *Archives of Instruction: Nineteenth-Century Rhetorics, Readers, and Composition Books in the United States,* edited by Jean Ferguson Carr, Stephen L. Carr, and Lucille M. Schultz, Southern Illinois UP, 2005, pp. 20–80.

Carstarphen, Meta G. "Historicizing Sexual Rhetorics: Theorizing the Power to Read, the Power to Interpret, and the Power to Produce." *Sexual Rhetorics: Methods, Identities, Publics,* edited by Jonathan Alexander and Jacqueline Rhodes, Routledge, 2016, pp. 72–78.

Carter, Julian. *The Heart of Whiteness: Normal Sexuality and Race in America, 1880–1940.* Duke UP, 2007.

Castiglia, Christopher, and Christopher Reed. *If Memory Serves: Gay Men, AIDS, and the Promise of the Queer Past.* U of Minnesota P, 2012.

Catalogue of the Officers and Students in Yale College, 1836–37. New Haven, 1836.

Cavallaro, Alexandra J. "Fighting Biblical 'Textual Harassment': Queer Rhetorical Pedagogies in the Extracurriculum." *Enculturation: A Journal of Rhetoric, Writing, and Culture,* vol. 18, 2015. Accessed 13 Feb. 2015.

Chace, Keely. "How to Write a Love Letter." *Hallmark,* 2015. Accessed 5 Mar. 2015.

Chapman, Gary. *The Five Love Languages: How to Express Heartfelt Commitment to Your Mate.* 1992. Northfield, 2010.

Charland, Maurice. "Constitutive Rhetoric: The Case of the Peuple Québécois." *Quarterly Journal of Speech,* vol. 73, no. 2, 1987, pp. 133–50.

Chartier, Roger, Cecile Dauphin, and Alain Boureau. *Correspondence: Models of Letter-Writing from the Middle Ages to the Nineteenth Century.* Polity P, 1997.

Chauncey, George. *Gay New York: Gender, Urban Culture, and the Makings of the Gay Male World, 1890–1940.* Basic Books, 1994.

Chávez, Karma R. "Beyond Inclusion: Rethinking Rhetoric's Historical Narrative." *Quarterly Journal of Speech,* vol. 101, no. 1, 2015, pp. 162–72.

———. *Queer Migration Politics: Activist Rhetoric and Coalitional Possibilities.* U of Illinois P, 2013.

Chesterfield, Philip Dormer Stanhope, Earl of. *Letters Written by Lord Chesterfield to His Son.* New York, [1889]. Google Books. Accessed 11 Feb. 2013.

Chesterfield's Art of Letter Writing Simplified: Being a Guide to Friendly, Affectionate, Polite and Business Correspondence. New York, 1857. Nietz Collection, U of Pittsburgh, Pennsylvania.

Clair, Robin Patric, and Lindsey B. Anderson. "Portrayals of the Poor on the Cusp of Capitalism: Promotional Materials in the Case of Heifer International." *Management Communication Quarterly,* vol. 27, no. 4, pp. 2013, pp. 537–67.

Clark, Gregory. *Rhetorical Landscapes in America: Variations on a Theme from Kenneth Burke.* U of South Carolina P, 2004.

Clark, Irene, and Andrea Hernandez. "Genre Awareness, Academic Argument, and Transferability." *WAC Journal,* vol. 22, 2011, pp. 65–78.

Cleary, Michelle Navarre. "Flowing and Freestyling: Learning from Adult Students about

Process Knowledge Transfer." *College Composition and Communication*, vol. 64, no. 4, 2013, pp. 661–87.

Cleves, Rachel Hope. *Charity and Sylvia: A Same-Sex Marriage in Early America*. Oxford UP, 2014.

———. "'What, Another Female Husband?': The Prehistory of Same-Sex Marriage in America." *Journal of American History*, vol. 101, no. 4, 2015, pp. 1055–81.

Cloud, Dana. "The First Lady's Privates: Queering Eleanor Roosevelt for Public Address Studies." *Queering Public Address: Sexualities in American Historical Discourse*, edited by Charles E. Morris III, U of South Carolina P, 2007, pp. 23–44.

Collins, Patricia Hill. *Black Feminist Thought: Knowledge, Consciousness, and the Politics of Empowerment*. Routledge, 1991.

Collins, Vicki. "Account of the Experience of Hester Ann Rogers: Rhetorical Functions of a Methodist Mystic's Journal." *The Changing Tradition: Women in the History of Rhetoric*, edited by Christine Mason Sutherland and Rebecca J. Sutcliffe, U of Calgary P, 1999, pp. 109–20.

Comment, Kristin M. "Dickinson's Bawdy: Shakespeare and Sexual Symbolism in Emily Dickinson's Writing to Susan Dickinson." *Legacy*, vol. 18, no. 2, 2001, pp. 167–81.

———. "'When it ceases to be silly it becomes actually wrong': The Cultural Contexts of Female Homoerotic Desire in Rose Terry Cooke's 'My Visitation.'" *Legacy*, vol. 26, no. 1, 2009, pp. 26–47.

The Complete American Letter-Writer. New York, 1807. Nietz Collection, U of Pittsburgh, Pennsylvania.

The Complete Art of Polite Correspondence, or, New Universal Letter-Writer. Philadelphia, 1857. Nietz Collection, U of Pittsburgh, Pennsylvania.

The Complete Letter-Writer, Containing Familiar Letters on the Most Common Occasions in Life. Boston, 1790. Early American Imprints. Accessed 15 Apr. 2014.

The Complete Letter Writer, or, The Art of Correspondence. Trenton, 1811. Nietz Collection, U of Pittsburgh, Pennsylvania.

Connors, Robert. *Composition-Rhetoric: Backgrounds, Theory, and Pedagogy*. U of Pittsburgh P, 1997.

———. "Day, Henry Noble (1808–1898)." *Encyclopedia of Rhetoric and Composition: Communication from Ancient Times to the Information Age*, edited by Theresa Enos, Garland, 1996, pp. 161–63.

Conrad, Ryan, editor. *Against Equality: Queer Revolution, Not Mere Inclusion*. AK P, 2014.

Constable, Nicole. *Romance on a Global Stage: Pen Pals, Virtual Ethnography, and "Mail Order" Marriages*. U of California P, 2003.

Conquergood, Dwight. "Rethinking Elocution: The Trope of the Talking Book and Other Figures of Speech." *Text and Performance Quarterly*, vol. 20, no. 4, 2000, pp. 325–41.

Cook, Elizabeth Heckendorn. *Epistolary Bodies: Gender and Genre in the Eighteenth-Century Republic of Letters*. Stanford UP, 1996.

Cott, Nancy. *The Bonds of Womanhood: "Woman's Sphere" in New England, 1780–1835*. Yale UP, 1977.

Cox, Matthew B., and Michael J. Faris. "An Annotated Bibliography of LGBTQ

Rhetorics." *Present Tense: A Journal of Rhetoric in Society*, vol. 4, no. 2, 2015. Accessed 17 June 2015.

Cram, E. "Archival Ambience and Sensory Memory: Generating Queer Intimacies in the Settler Colonial Archive." *Communication and Critical/Cultural Studies*, vol. 13, no. 2, 2016, pp. 109–29.

Crowley, Sharon. *The Methodical Memory: Invention in Current-Traditional Rhetoric*. Southern Illinois UP, 1990.

Cvetkovich, Ann. *An Archive of Feelings: Trauma, Sexuality, and Lesbian Public Cultures*. Duke UP, 2003.

Davidson, Cathy N. *The Book of Love: Writers and Their Love Letters*. Pocket Books, 1992.

Davies, Laurie. *Love @ First Click: The Ultimate Guide to Online Dating*. Simon & Schuster, 2013.

De Certeau, Michel. *The Practice of Everyday Life*. U of California P, 1984.

Decker, William Merrill. *Epistolary Practices: Letter Writing in America before Telecommunications*. U of North Carolina P, 1998.

Denman, William. "Rhetoric, the 'Citizen-Orator,' and the Revitalization of Civic Discourse in American Life." *Rhetorical Education in America*, edited by Cheryl Glenn, Margaret Lyday, and Wendy Sharer, U of Alabama P, 2004, pp. 3–17.

DePalma, Michael-John. "Rhetorical Education for the Nineteenth-Century Pulpit: Austin Phelps and the Influence of Christian Transcendentalism at Andover Theological Seminary." *Rhetoric Review*, vol. 31, no. 1, 2012, pp. 1–20.

De Pretis, Anna. *"Epistolarity" in the First Book of Horace's Epistles*. Gorgias P, 2004.

Derrida, Jacques. *The Post Card: From Socrates to Freud and Beyond*. U of Chicago P, 1987.

Derrin, Daniel. "Engaging the Passions in John Donne's Sermons." *English Studies*, vol. 93, no. 4, 2012, pp. 452–68.

Desmet, Christy. "Henry Home, Lord Kames (1696–1782)." *Eighteenth-Century British and American Rhetorics and Rhetoricians: Critical Studies and Sources*, edited by Michael Moran, Greenwood, 1994, pp. 132–41.

Devitt, Amy. "Generalizing about Genre: New Conceptions of an Old Concept." *College Composition and Communication*, vol. 44, no. 4, 1993, pp. 573–86.

Dexter, Franklin. *Biographical Notes of Graduates of Yale College*. New Haven, 1913.

Dickinson, Greg. "Joe's Rhetoric: Finding Authenticity at Starbucks." *Rhetoric Society Quarterly*, vol. 32, no. 4, 2002, pp. 5–27.

Diggs, Marylynne. "Romantic Friends or a 'Different Race of Creatures'? The Representation of Lesbian Pathology in Nineteenth-Century America." *Feminist Studies*, vol. 21, no. 2, 1995, pp. 317–40.

Dinshaw, Carolyn, Lee Edelman, Roderick A. Ferguson, Carla Freccero, Elizabeth Freeman, Jack [Judith] Halberstam, Annamarie Jagose, Christopher S. Nealon, Tan Hoang Nguyen. "Theorizing Queer Temporalities: A Roundtable Discussion." *GLQ: A Journal of Lesbian and Gay Studies*, vol. 13, no. 2–3, 2007, pp. 177–95.

Dirk, Kerry. "The 'Research Paper' Prompt: A Dialogic Opportunity for Transfer." *Composition Forum*, vol. 25, 2012. Accessed 1 Dec. 2014.

Dodd, Albert. Albert Dodd Papers, 1836–1844. MS 1343. Manuscripts and Archives, Yale U Library, New Haven.

Dolmage, Jay Timothy. *Disability Rhetoric*. Syracuse UP, 2013.

Donawerth, Jane. *Conversational Rhetoric: The Rise and Fall of a Women's Tradition, 1600–1900*. Southern Illinois UP, 2012.

———. "Nineteenth-Century United States Conduct Book Rhetoric by Women." *Rhetoric Review*, vol. 21, no. 1, 2002, pp. 5–21.

———. "Poaching on Men's Philosophies of Rhetoric: Eighteenth- and Nineteenth-Century Rhetorical Theory by Women." *Philosophy & Rhetoric*, vol. 33, no. 3, 2000, pp. 243–58.

Downs, Douglas, and Elizabeth Wardle. "Teaching about Writing, Righting Misconceptions: (Re)Envisioning 'First-Year Composition' as 'Introduction to Writing Studies.'" *College Composition and Communication*, vol. 58, no. 4, 2007, pp. 552–84.

Doyle, David D., Jr. "'A Very Proper Bostonian': Rediscovering Ogden Codman and His Late-Nineteenth-Century Queer World." *Journal of the History of Sexuality*, vol. 13, no. 4, 2004, pp. 446–76.

Driskill, Qwo-Li. *Asegi Stories: Cherokee Queer and Two-Spirit Memory*. U of Arizona P, 2016.

Duggan, Lisa. *The Twilight of Equality?: Neoliberalism, Cultural Politics, and the Attack on Democracy*. Beacon P, 2003.

Dunn, Thomas R. "(Queer) Family Time: *Brothers & Sisters* and Managing Temporal Anxieties." *Western Journal of Communication*, vol. 79, no. 2, 2015, pp. 133–50.

———. *Queerly Remembered: Rhetorics for Representing the GLBTQ Past*. U of South Carolina P, 2016.

Düttmann, Alexander García. *At Odds with AIDS: Thinking and Talking about a Virus*. Stanford UP, 1996.

Easton, Dossie, and Catherine Liszt. *The Ethical Slut: A Guide to Infinite Sexual Possibilities*. Greenery, 1997.

Edelman, Lee. *No Future: Queer Theory and the Death Drive*. Duke UP, 2004.

Elshtain, Jean Bethke. *Public Man, Private Woman: Women in Social and Political Thought*. Princeton UP, 1993.

Eng, David. *The Feeling of Kinship: Queer Liberalism and the Racialization of Intimacy*. Duke UP, 2010.

Enoch, Jessica. *Refiguring Rhetorical Education: Women Teaching African American, Native American, and Chicano/a Students, 1865–1911*. Southern Illinois UP, 2008.

Enos, Richard. "Marcus Tullius Cicero." *Classical Rhetorics and Rhetoricians: Critical Studies and Sources*, edited by Michelle Ballif and Michael Moran, Praeger, 2005, pp. 101–10.

Erickson, Keith, and Stephanie Thomson. "Seduction Theory and the Recovery of Feminine Aesthetics: Implications for Rhetorical Criticism." *Communication Quarterly*, vol. 52, no. 3, 2004, 300–19.

Faderman, Lillian. *Surpassing the Love of Men: Romantic Friendship and Love between Women from the Renaissance to the Present*. William Morrow, 1981.

———. *To Believe in Women: What Lesbians Have Done for America—A History*. Houghton Mifflin Harcourt, 2000.

Farrar, Eliza Ware Rotch. *The Young Lady's Friend.* New York, 1857. Google Books. Accessed 24 Apr. 2010.

———. *The Youth's Letter-Writer; or the Epistolary Art; Made Plain to Beginners through the Example of Henry Morton.* New York, 1836. Google Books. Accessed 24 Apr. 2010.

The Fashionable American Letter Writer, or, The Art of Polite Correspondence. Brookfield, [MA], 1832. Nietz Collection, U of Pittsburgh, Pennsylvania.

Favret, Mary. *Romantic Correspondence: Women, Politics and the Fiction of Letters.* Cambridge UP, 1993.

Fay, Theodore Sedgwick. "Reveries by Night." *Dreams and Reveries of a Quiet Man,* vol. 2. New York, 1832, pp. 194–97. Google Books. Accessed 15 Apr. 2014.

Fein, Ellen, and Sherrie Schneider. *The Rules for Online Dating: Capturing the Heart of Mr. Right in Cyberspace.* Pocket Books, 2002.

Flexman, Jamie. "6 Proven Ways to Succeed with Online Dating." *Lifehack.* Accessed 5 Mar. 2015.

Fone, Byrne, editor. *The Columbia Anthology of Gay Literature: Readings from Western Antiquity until the Present Day.* Columbia UP, 1998.

Foucault, Michel. *The History of Sexuality.* Translated by Robert Hurley, vol. 1, Pantheon, 1978.

Fraizer, Dan. "First Steps beyond First Year: Coaching Transfer after FYC." *Writing Program Administration,* vol. 33, no. 3, 2010, pp. 34–57.

France, Peter, editor. *The Oxford Guide to Literature in English Translation.* Oxford UP, 2000.

Fraser, Nancy. "Rethinking the Public Sphere: A Contribution to the Critique of Actually Existing Democracy." *Social Text,* vol. 25/26, 1990, pp. 56–80.

Freccero, Carla. "Queer Times." *South Atlantic Quarterly,* vol. 106, no. 3, 2007, pp. 485–94.

Freeman, Elizabeth. "Introduction: Queer Temporalities." *GLQ: A Journal of Lesbian and Gay Studies,* vol. 13, no. 2–3, 2007, pp. 159–76.

Fuller, Wayne. *The American Mail: Enlarger of the Common Life.* U of Chicago P, 1972.

Gage, John. "Vestiges of Letter Writing in Composition Textbooks, 1850–1914." *Letter-Writing Manuals and Instruction from Antiquity to the Present: Historical and Bibliographic Studies,* edited by Carol Poster and Linda C. Mitchell, U of South Carolina P, pp. 200–29.

Gannett, Cinthia. *Gender and the Journal: Diaries and Academic Discourse.* State U of New York P, 1992.

Gardiner, Judith Kegan. "Queering Genre: Alison Bechdel's *Fun Home: A Family Tragicomic* and *The Essential Dykes to Watch Out For.*" *Contemporary Women's Writing,* vol. 5, no. 3, 2011, pp. 188–207.

Garlinger, Patrick Paul. *Confessions of the Letter Closet: Epistolary Fiction and Queer Desire in Modern Spain.* U of Minnesota P, 2005.

Gaul, Theresa Strouth, and Sharon Harris, editors. *Letters and Cultural Transformation in the United States, 1760–1860.* Ashgate, 2009.

Gay, Peter. T*he Tender Passion,* vol. 2 of *The Bourgeois Experience: Victoria to Freud.* Oxford UP, 1986.

"Genrequeer." *Cream City Review*, vol. 39, no. 1, 2015, pp. 97–98.

Gere, Anne Ruggles. "Kitchen Tables and Rented Rooms: The Extracurriculum of Composition." *College Composition and Communication*, vol. 45, no. 1, 1994, pp. 75–92.

Gibson, Michelle, Martha Marinara, and Deborah Meem. "Bi, Butch, and Bar Dyke: Pedagogical Performances of Class, Gender, and Sexuality." *College Composition and Communication*, vol. 52, no. 1, 2000, pp. 69–95.

Gilroy, Amanda, and W. M. Verhoeven, editors. *Epistolary Histories: Letters, Fiction, Culture*. UP of Virginia, 2000.

Glenn, Cheryl. "Rhetorical Education in America (A Broad Stroke Introduction)." *Rhetorical Education in America*, edited by Cheryl Glenn, Margaret Lyday, and Wendy Sharer, U of Alabama P, 2004, pp. vii–xvi.

Glenn, Cheryl, Margaret Lyday, and Wendy Sharer, editors. *Rhetorical Education in America*. U of Alabama P, 2004.

Gold, David. *Rhetoric at the Margins: Revising the History of Writing Instruction in American Colleges, 1873–1947*. Southern Illinois UP, 2008.

———. Rev. of *The Rhetoric of Rebel Women: Civil War Diaries and Confederate Persuasion*, by Kimberly Harrison. *Rhetoric Society Quarterly*, vol. 44, no. 4, 2014, pp. 383–86.

Gold, David, and Catherine Hobbs. *Educating the New Southern Woman: Speech, Writing, and Race at the Public Women's Colleges, 1884–1945*. Southern Illinois UP, 2014.

Goltz, Dustin Bradley. *Queer Temporalities in Gay Male Representation: Tragedy, Normativity, and Futurity*. Routledge, 2010.

Gonçalves, Zan Meyer. *Sexuality and the Politics of Ethos in the Writing Classroom*. Southern Illinois UP, 2005.

Goodrich, Chauncey. Goodrich Family Papers, 1732–1905. MS 242. Manuscripts and Archives, Yale U Library, New Haven.

———. *Select British Eloquence*. New York, 1852. Google Books. Accessed 11 Feb. 2013.

Graff, Richard, Arthur Walzer, and Janet Atwill, editors. *The Viability of the Rhetorical Tradition*. State U of New York P, 2005.

Grasso, Linda. "Edited Letter Collections as Epistolary Fictions: Imagining African American Women's History in *Beloved Sisters and Loving Friends*." *Letters and Cultural Transformation in the United States, 1760–1860*, edited by Theresa Strouth Gaul and Sharon Harris, Ashgate, 2009.

Gray, John. *Men Are from Mars, Women Are from Venus: The Classic Guide to Understanding the Opposite Sex*. 1992. Harper Collins, 2009.

Gregory, John. *A Father's Legacy to His Daughters*. London, 1774. Google Books. Accessed 18 Dec. 2014.

———. *A Father's Legacy to His Daughters*. Boston, 1834. Google Books. Accessed 18 Dec. 2014.

Greene, Robert. *The Art of Seduction*. 2001. Penguin, 2003.

Griffin, Cindy L. "The Essentialist Roots of the Public Sphere: A Feminist Critique." *Western Journal of Communication*, vol. 60, no. 1, 1996, pp. 21–39.

Griffin, Farah Jasmine, editor. *Beloved Sisters and Loving Friends: Letters from Rebecca Primus of Royal Oak, Maryland, and Addie Brown of Hartford, Connecticut, 1854–1868*. Ballantine, 1999.

Gring-Pemble, Lisa M. "Writing Themselves into Consciousness: Creating a Rhetorical Bridge between the Public and Private Spheres." *Quarterly Journal of Speech*, vol. 84, no. 1, 1998, pp. 41–61.

Gross, Daniel M., and Jonathan Alexander. "Frameworks for Failure." *Pedagogy*, vol. 16, no. 2, 2016, pp. 273–95.

Gunderson, Erik. *Declamation, Paternity, and Roman Identity: Authority and the Rhetorical Self*. Cambridge UP, 2003.

———. *Staging Masculinity: The Rhetoric of Performance in the Roman World*. U of Michigan P, 2000.

Halberstam, Jack [Judith]. *In a Queer Time and Place: Transgender Bodies, Subcultural Lives*. New York UP, 2005.

———. "Perverse Presentism: The Androgyne, the Tribade, the Female Husband, and Other Pre-Twentieth-Century Genders." *Female Masculinity*. Duke UP, 1998, pp. 45–73.

———. *The Queer Art of Failure*. Duke UP, 2011.

Halloran, S. Michael. "Rhetoric in the American College Curriculum: The Decline of Public Discourse." *Pre/Text*, vol. 3, no. 3, 1982, pp. 245–69. Reprinted in *Pre/Text: The First Decade*, edited by Victor J. Vitanza, U of Pittsburgh P, 1993, pp. 93–115.

Halloran, S. Michael, and Gregory Clark. *Oratorical Culture in Nineteenth-Century America: Transformations in the Theory and Practice of Rhetoric*. Southern Illinois UP, 1993.

Halperin, David. *How to Do the History of Homosexuality*. U of Chicago P, 2002.

———. *One Hundred Years of Homosexuality: And Other Essays on Greek Love*. Routledge, 1990.

Halttunen, Karen. *Confidence Men and Painted Women: A Study of Middle-Class Culture in America, 1830–1870*. Yale UP, 1982.

Hansen, Karen. "'No *Kisses* Is Like Youres': An Erotic Friendship between Two African-American Women during the Mid-Nineteenth Century." *Lesbian Subjects*, edited by Martha Vicinus, Indiana UP, 1996, pp. 178–207.

———. *A Very Social Time: Crafting Community in Antebellum New England*. U of California P, 1994.

Hardie, James. *The Epistolary Guide*. New York, 1817. Nietz Collection, U of Pittsburgh, Pennsylvania.

Harrison, Kimberly. *The Rhetoric of Rebel Women: Civil War Diaries and Confederate Persuasion*. Southern Illinois UP, 2013.

———. "Rhetorical Rehearsals: The Construction of Ethos in Confederate Women's Civil War Diaries." *Rhetoric Review*, vol. 22, no. 3, 2003, pp. 243–63.

Harrison, Renee. *Enslaved Women and the Art of Resistance in Antebellum America*. Palgrave Macmillan, 2009.

Hart, Ellen. "The Encoding of Homoerotic Desire: Emily Dickinson's Letters and Poems to Susan Dickinson, 1850–1886." *Tulsa Studies in Women's Literature*, vol. 9, no. 2, 1990, pp. 251–72.

Hauser, Gerard. "Rhetorical Democracy and Civic Engagement." *Rhetorical Democracy: Discursive Practices of Civic Engagement*, edited by Gerard Hauser and Amy Grim, Lawrence Erlbaum, 2004, pp. 1–14.

Hawhee, Debra. *Bodily Arts: Rhetoric and Athletics in Ancient Greece.* U of Texas P, 2004.

Hawkins, Ames. "Exhuming Transgenre Ties." *Enculturation: A Journal of Rhetoric, Writing, and Culture,* vol. 21, 2016. Accessed 29 Nov. 2016.

Hayes, Jason. "Everything You Need to Know about Online Dating." *New Yorker,* 4 Mar. 2015. Accessed 5 Mar. 2015.

Heath, Robert L. "A Rhetorical Theory Approach to Issues Management." *Public Relations Theory II,* edited by Carl H. Botan and Vincent Hazleton, Lawrence Erlbaum, 2006, pp. 55–87.

Henkin, David. *The Postal Age: The Emergence of Modern Communications in Nineteenth-Century America.* U of Chicago P, 2006.

Hesford, Wendy. "Global Turns and Cautions in Rhetoric and Composition Studies." *PMLA,* vol. 121, no. 3, 2006, pp. 787–801.

Hewitt, Elizabeth. *Correspondence and American Literature, 1770–1865.* Cambridge UP, 2004.

Hill, Thomas. *Hill's Manual of Social & Business Forms: A Guide to Correct Writing.* Chicago, 1883. Hathi Trust Digital Library. Accessed 15 Apr. 2014.

Horner, Winifred Bryan. *Nineteenth-Century Scottish Rhetoric: The American Connection.* Southern Illinois UP, 1993.

Horowitz, Helen Lefkowitz. *Alma Mater: Design and Experience in the Women's Colleges from Their Nineteenth-Century Beginnings to the 1930s.* U of Massachusetts P, 1993.

Hoshor, John P. "Lectures on Rhetoric and Public Speaking by Chauncey Allen Goodrich." *Speech Monographs,* vol. 14, no. 1–2, 1947, pp. 1–37.

"How to Succeed at Online Dating." *wikiHow.* Accessed 5 Mar. 2015.

"How to Write a Love Letter." *wikiHow.* Accessed 5 Mar. 2015.

Huh, Joonok. "Elizabeth Ware Rotch Farrar." *American National Biography,* edited by John A. Garraty and Mark C. Carnes, vol. 7, Oxford UP, 1999, pp. 737–38.

Illouz, Eva. *Consuming the Romantic Utopia: Love and the Cultural Contradictions of Capitalism.* U of California P, 1997.

Inness, Sherrie A. "Mashes, Smashes, Crushes, and Raves: Woman-to-Woman Relationships in Popular Women's College Fiction, 1895–1915." *National Women's Studies Association Journal,* vol. 6, no. 1, 1994, pp. 48–68.

Jasinski, James. "Constitutive Framework for Rhetorical Historiography: Toward an Understanding of the Discursive (Re)constitution of 'Constitution' in The Federalist Papers." *Doing Rhetorical History: Concepts and Cases,* edited by Kathleen J. Turner, U of Alabama P, 1998, pp. 72–92.

John, Richard. *Spreading the News: The American Postal System from Franklin to Morse.* Harvard UP, 1995.

Johnson, Nan. *Gender and Rhetorical Space in American Life, 1866–1910.* Southern Illinois UP, 2002.

———. *Nineteenth-Century Rhetoric in North America.* Southern Illinois UP, 1991.

Jones, Constance, editor. *The Love of Friends: An Anthology of Gay and Lesbian Letters to Friends and Lovers.* Simon & Schuster, 1997.

Kaminsky, Neil. *Man Talk: The Gay Couple's Communication Guide.* 2007. Routledge, 2012.

Karkulehto, Sanna. "In-Between: Genre and Gender Hybridity, and Pirkko Saisio's Novel *Punainen erokirja.*" *Nordic Journal of Feminist and Gender Research,* vol. 20, no. 3, 2012, pp. 199–214.

Kates, Susan. *Activist Rhetorics and American Higher Education, 1885–1937.* Southern Illinois UP, 2001.

Katz, Jonathan. *Love Stories: Sex between Men before Homosexuality.* U of Chicago P, 2001.

Kauffman, Linda. *Discourses of Desire: Gender, Genre, and Epistolary Fictions.* Cornell UP, 1986.

Kelley, William. "Rhetoric as Seduction." *Philosophy & Rhetoric,* vol. 6, no. 2, 1973, pp. 69–80.

Khazan, Olga. "A Psychologist's Guide to Online Dating." *Atlantic,* 11 Dec. 2013. Accessed 5 Mar. 2015.

Kitzhaber, Albert. *Rhetoric in American Colleges, 1850–1900.* Southern Methodist UP, 1990.

Koppel, Dale. *The Intelligent Woman's Guide to Online Dating.* Peterman, Samuelson, 2008.

Kopelson, Karen. "(Dis)Integrating the Gay/Queer Binary: 'Reconstructed Identity Politics' for a Performative Pedagogy." *College English,* vol. 65, no. 1, 2002, pp. 17–35.

Kraemer, Don J. "Between Motion and Action: The Dialectical Role of Affective Identification in Kenneth Burke." *Advances in the History of Rhetoric,* vol. 16, no. 2, 2013, pp. 141–64.

Lazar, David. "Queering the Essay." *Bending Genre: Essays on Creative Nonfiction,* edited by Margot Singer and Nicole Walker, Bloomsbury, 2013, pp. 15–20.

Lee, Christina H. "The Rhetoric of Courtship in Lope De Vega's *Novelas a Marcia Leonarda.*" *Bulletin of Spanish Studies,* vol. 80, no. 1, 2003, pp. 13–31.

Legg, Emily. "Daughters of the Seminaries: Re-landscaping History through the Composition Courses at the Cherokee National Female Seminary." *College Composition and Communication,* vol. 66, no. 1, 2014, pp. 67–90.

Leslie, Eliza. *Miss Leslie's Behaviour Book: A Guide and Manual for Ladies.* Philadelphia, 1839. Google Books. Accessed 18 June 2015.

———. *Selections from Eliza Leslie,* edited by Etta M. Madden, U of Nebraska P, 2011. Google Books. Accessed 18 June 2015.

Leslie, Miss. "Eliza Farnham; or, The Love Letters: Part the First." *Godey's Lady's Book, and Ladies' American Magazine,* May 1841, pp. 217–20. ProQuest American Periodicals. Accessed 20 Nov. 2014.

———. "Eliza Farnham; or, The Love Letters: Part the Second." *Godey's Lady's Book, and Ladies' American Magazine,* June 1841, pp. 245–50. ProQuest American Periodicals. Accessed 20 Nov. 2014.

"Letter Writing." *Spirit of the Times; A Chronicle of the Turf, Agriculture, Field Sports, Literature,* 14 Aug. 1847, p. 289. American Periodicals Series. Accessed 2 Sept. 2010.

"Letter-Writing." *The Recreative Magazine, or Eccentricities of Literature and Life,* 1 Apr. 1822, p. 289. American Periodicals Series. Accessed 31 Aug. 2010.

Letter-Writing Simplified, by Precept and Example. New York, 1844. Nietz Collection, U of Pittsburgh, Pennsylvania.

Lipari, Lisbeth. "The Rhetoric of Intersectionality: Lorraine Hansberry's 1957 Letters to the *Ladder*." *Queering Public Address: Sexualities in American Historical Discourse*, edited by Charles E. Morris III, U of South Carolina P, 2007, pp. 220–48.

Lipson, Carol, and Roberta Binkley, editors. *Rhetoric Before and Beyond the Greeks*. State U of New York P, 2004.

Locke, John. *The Art of Correspondence: How to Construct and Write Letters According to Approved Usage*. Boston, 1884. Nietz Collection, U of Pittsburgh, Pennsylvania.

Logan, Shirley Wilson. *Liberating Language: Sites of Rhetorical Education in Nineteenth-Century Black America*. Southern Illinois UP, 2008.

Loomis, Henry T. *Practical Letter Writing*. Cleveland, 1897. Nietz Collection, U of Pittsburgh, Pennsylvania.

Lorde, Audre. *Sister Outsider: Essays & Speeches by Audre Lorde*. 1984. Crossing P, 2007.

Love, Heather. *Feeling Backward: Loss and the Politics of Queer History*. Harvard UP, 2007.

Lystra, Karen. *Searching the Heart: Women, Men, and Romantic Love in Nineteenth-Century America*. Oxford UP, 1989.

Mahoney, Deirdre M. "'More Than an Accomplishment': Advice on Letter Writing for Nineteenth-Century American Women." *Huntington Library Quarterly*, vol. 66, no. 3/4, 2003, pp. 411–23.

Malinowitz, Harriet. *Textual Orientations: Lesbian and Gay Students and the Making of Discourse Communities*. Heinemann, 1995.

Masten, Jeffrey. "Toward a Queer Address: The Taste of Letters and Early Modern Male Friendship." *GLQ: A Journal of Gay and Lesbian Studies*, vol. 10, no. 3, 2004, pp. 367–84.

Matik, Wendo-O. *Redefining Our Relationships: Guidelines for Responsible Open Relationships*. Defiant Times, 2004.

May, Clarence. "Alone." *Peterson's Magazine*, vol. 27, no. 6, 1855, p. 397. Google Books. Accessed 7 Sept. 2012.

McCarthy, Molly. "A Pocketful of Days: Pocket Diaries and Daily Record Keeping among Nineteenth-Century New England Women." *New England Quarterly*, vol. 73, no. 2, 2000, pp. 274–96.

McClish, Glen. "'To Furnish Specimens of Negro Eloquence': William J. Simmons's *Men Of Mark* as a Site of Late-Nineteenth-Century African American Rhetorical Education." *Rhetoric Society Quarterly*, vol. 44, 1, 2014, pp. 46–67.

Medhurst, Martin J. "The History of Public Address as an Academic Study." *The Handbook of Rhetoric and Public Address*, edited by Shawn J. Parry-Giles and J. Michael Hogan, Blackwell, 2010, pp. 19–66.

Mendenhall, Annie S. "Joseph V. Denney, the Land-Grant Mission, and Rhetorical Education at Ohio State: An Institutional History." *College English*, vol. 74, no. 2, 2011, pp. 131–56.

Messmer, Marietta. *A Vice for Voices: Reading Emily Dickinson's Correspondence*. 2001. U of Massachusetts P, 2010.

Miles, Libby, et al. "Interchanges: Commenting on Douglas Downs and Elizabeth Wardle's 'Teaching about Writing, Righting Misconceptions.'" *College Composition and Communication*, vol. 59, no. 3, 2008, pp. 503–11.

Miller, Carolyn. "Genre as Social Action." *Quarterly Journal of Speech*, vol. 70, 1984, pp. 151–67.

Miller, Rachel Wilkerson. "15 Tips for Writing an Amazing Love Letter." *BuzzFeed*, 6 Feb. 2015. Accessed 5 Mar. 2015.

Miller, Susan. *Assuming the Positions: Cultural Pedagogy and the Politics of Commonplace Writing*. U of Pittsburgh P, 1998.

Modesti, Sonja. "Home Sweet Home: Tattoo Parlors as Postmodern Spaces of Agency." *Quarterly Journal of Speech*, vol. 72, no. 3, 2008, pp. 197–212.

Monson, Connie, and Jacqueline Rhodes. "Risking Queer: Pedagogy, Performativity, and Desire in Writing Classrooms." *Journal of Advanced Composition*, vol. 24, no. 1, 2004, pp. 79–91.

Montague, Mary Wortley. *The Poetical Works of the Right Honorable Lady Mary Wortley Montague*. Philadelphia, 1769. Early American Imprints. Accessed 5 Dec. 2010.

Moore, Jessie. "Mapping the Questions: The State of Writing-Related Transfer Research." *Composition Forum*, vol. 26, 2012. Accessed 1 Dec. 2014.

Morris, Charles E., III. "Archival Queer." *Rhetoric & Public Affairs*, vol. 9, no. 1, 2006, pp. 145–51.

———. "Context's Critic, Invisible Traditions, and Queering Rhetorical History." *Quarterly Journal of Speech*, vol. 101, no. 1, 2015, pp. 225–43.

———. "Introduction: Portrait of a Queer Rhetorical/Historical Critic." *Queering Public Address: Sexualities in American Historical Discourse*, edited by Charles E. Morris III, U of South Carolina P, 2007, pp. 1–19.

———. "Milk Memory's Queer Rhetorical Futurity." *Sexual Rhetorics: Methods, Identities, Publics*, edited by Jonathan Alexander and Jacqueline Rhodes, Routledge, 2016, pp. 79–92.

———. "My Old Kentucky Homo: Abraham Lincoln, Larry Kramer, and the Politics of Queer Memory." *Queering Public Address: Sexualities in American Historical Discourse*, edited by Charles E. Morris III, U of South Carolina P, 2007, pp. 93–120.

Morris, Charles E., III, editor. *Queering Public Address: Sexualities in American Historical Discourse*. U of South Carolina P, 2007.

Morris, Charles E., III, and K. J. Rawson. "Queer Archives/Archival Queers." *Theorizing Histories of Rhetoric*, edited by Michelle Ballif, Southern Illinois UP, 2013, pp. 74–89.

Morrissey, Megan E. "Rape as a Weapon of Hate: Discursive Constructions and Material Consequences of Black Lesbianism in South Africa." *Women's Studies in Communication*, vol. 36, no. 1, 2013, pp. 72–91.

Muñoz, José Esteban. *Cruising Utopia: The Then and There of Queer Futurity*. New York UP, 2009.

Murphy, James. *Rhetoric in the Middle Ages: A History of Rhetorical Theory from St. Augustine to the Renaissance*. U of California P, 1974.

Nakayama, Thomas K. "Show/Down Time: 'Race,' Gender, Sexuality, and Popular Culture." *Critical Studies in Mass Communication*, vol. 11, no. 2, 1994, pp. 162–79.

Narayan, Madhu. "At Home with the Lesbian Herstory Archives." *Enculturation: A Journal of Rhetoric, Writing, and Culture*, vol. 15, 2013. Accessed 19 June 2015.

Nelson, Brent. *Holy Ambition: Rhetoric, Courtship, and Devotion in the Sermons of John Donne*. Arizona Center for Medieval and Renaissance Studies, 2005.

Nestle, Joan, Riki Wilchins, and Clare Howell, editors. *Genderqueer: Voices from Beyond the Sexual Binary*. Alyson Books, 2002.

The New Parlor Letter Writer. Auburnn, [NY], [1853]. Nietz Collection, U of Pittsburgh, Pennsylvania.

Newkirk, Pamela, editor. *A Love No Less: More Than Two Centuries of African American Love Letters*. Doubleday, 2003.

Newman, Samuel. *A Practical System of Rhetoric, or, the Principles and Rules of Style, Inferred from Examples of Writing*. Andover, 1836. Hathi Trust Digital Library. Accessed 15 Apr. 2014.

Nienkamp, Jean. *Internal Rhetorics: Toward a History and Theory of Self-Persuasion*. Southern Illinois UP, 2001.

Nietz, John. *Old Textbooks: Spelling, Grammar, Reading, Arithmetic, Geography, American History, Civil Government, Physiology, Penmanship, Art, Music, as Taught in the Common Schools from Colonial Days to 1900*. U of Pittsburgh P, 1961.

Norton, Rictor. *My Dear Boy: Gay Love Letters through the Centuries*. Leyland, 1998.

Nowacek, Rebecca S. *Agents of Integration: Understanding Transfer as a Rhetorical Act*. Southern Illinois UP, 2011.

Nystrand, Martin, and John Duffy, editors. *Towards a Rhetoric of Everyday Life: New Directions in Research on Writing, Text, and Discourse*. U of Wisconsin P, 2003.

"Obituary." *Hartford Daily Times*, June 1844. Albert Dodd Papers. MS 1343. Manuscripts and Archives, Yale U Library, New Haven.

"Odds and Ends from a Portfolio." *United States Magazine, and Democratic Review*, Aug. 1847, p. 150. American Periodicals Series. Accessed 2 Sept. 2010.

Olson, Christa J. "Places to Stand: The Practices and Politics of Writing Histories." *Advances in the History of Rhetoric*, vol. 15, no. 1, 2012, pp. 77–100.

Olson, Lester C. "The Personal, the Political, and Others: Audre Lorde Denouncing 'The Second Sex Conference.'" *Philosophy & Rhetoric*, vol. 33, no. 3, 2000, pp. 259–85.

———. "Traumatic Styles in Public Address: Audre Lorde's Discourse as Exemplar." *Queering Public Address: Sexualities in American Historical Discourse*, edited by Charles E. Morris III, U of South Carolina P, 2007, pp. 249–82.

"On Letters and Letter-Writers." *Literary Gazette; or, Journal of Criticism, Science, and the Arts*, 27 Oct. 1821, p. 685. American Periodicals Series. Accessed 31 Aug. 2010.

Parker, Andrew, Mary Russo, Doris Sommer, and Patricia Yaeger, editors. "Introduction." *Nationalisms & Sexualities*. Routledge, 1992, pp. 1–20.

Patton, Cindy. "In Vogue: The 'Place' of 'Gay Theory.'" *Pre/Text: A Journal of Rhetorical Theory*, vol. 13, no. 3/4, 1992, pp. 151–57.

Peary, Alexandria. "Eliza Leslie's 1854 *The Behaviour Book* and the Conduct of Women's Writing." *Rhetoric Review*, vol. 31, no. 3, 2012, pp. 219–35.

———. "Walls with a Word Count: The Textrooms of the Extracurriculum." *College Composition and Communication*, vol. 66, no. 1, 2014, pp. 43–66.

Peiss, Kathy Lee. *Major Problems in the History of American Sexuality: Documents and Essays*. Houghton Mifflin, 2002.

Works Cited

Perelman, Chaïm, and Lucie Olbrechts-Tyteca. *The New Rhetoric: A Treatise on Argumentation.* U of Notre Dame P, 1969.

Plato. "Gorgias." *The Rhetorical Tradition: Readings from Classical Times to the Present,* edited by Patricia Bizzell and Bruce Herzberg, Bedford St. Martin's, 1990, pp. 61–112.

———. "Phaedrus." *The Rhetorical Tradition: Readings from Classical Times to the Present,* edited by Patricia Bizzell and Bruce Herzberg, Bedford St. Martin's, 1990, pp. 113–43.

The Pocket Letter Writer: Consisting of Letters on Every Occurrence in Life, with Complimentary Cards, etc. 1836. 4th ed., Providence, 1840. Nietz Collection, U of Pittsburgh, Pennsylvania.

Poster, Carol. "The Case of the Purloined Letter-Manuals: Archival Issues in Ancient Epistolary Theory." *Rhetoric Review,* vol. 27, no. 1, 2008, pp. 1–19.

———. "A Conversation Halved: Epistolary Theory in Greco-Roman Antiquity." *Letter-Writing Manuals and Instruction from Antiquity to the Present: Historical and Bibliographic Studies,* edited by Carol Poster and Linda C. Mitchell, U of South Carolina P, 2007, pp. 21–51.

———. "Introduction." *Letter-Writing Manuals and Instruction from Antiquity to the Present: Historical and Bibliographic Studies,* edited by Carol Poster and Linda C. Mitchell, U of South Carolina P, 2007, pp. 1–6.

Poster, Carol, and Linda C. Mitchell, editors. *Letter-Writing Manuals and Instruction from Antiquity to the Present: Historical and Bibliographic Studies.* U of South Carolina P, 2007.

Pough, Gwendolyn. *Check It While I Wreck It: Black Womanhood, Hip Hop Culture, and the Public Sphere.* Northeastern UP, 2004.

Poulakis, Takis, and David Depew, editors. *Isocrates and Civic Education.* U of Texas P, 2004.

Powell, Malea. 'This is a Story about a Belief . . .' "Octalog III: The Politics of Historiography in 2010." *Rhetoric Review,* vol. 30, no. 2, 2010, pp. 120–22.

Primus, Rebecca. Letters to her family, 1854–1869. Primus Family Papers. MS 44102. Box II. Connecticut Historical Society, Hartford.

Pritchard, Eric Darnell. "'As Proud of Our Gayness, as We Are of Our Blackness': Raceing Sexual Rhetorics in the National Coalition of Black Lesbians and Gays." *Sexual Rhetorics: Methods, Identities, Publics,* edited by Jonathan Alexander and Jacqueline Rhodes, Routledge, 2016, pp. 159–71.

———. *Fashioning Lives: Black Queers and the Politics of Literacy.* Southern Illinois UP, 2017.

———. "'Like signposts on the road': The Function of Literacy in Constructing Black Queer Ancestors." *Literacy and Composition Studies,* vol. 2, no. 1, 2014, pp. 29–56.

———. "'This Is Not an Empty-Headed Man in a Dress': Literacy Misused, Reread and Rewritten in Soulopoliz." *Southern Communication Journal,* vol. 74, 3, 2009, pp. 278–99.

Quinn, D. Michael. *Same-Sex Dynamics among Nineteenth-Century Americans: A Mormon Example.* U of Illinois P, 1996.

Radhakrishnan, R. "Nationalism, Gender, and the Narrative of Identity." *Nationalisms & Sexualities,* edited by Andrew Parker, Mary Russo, Doris Sommer, and Patricia Yaeger, Routledge, 1992, pp. 77–95.

Ramirez, John. "The Chicano Homosocial Film: Mapping the Discourses of Sex and Gender in *American Me.*" *Pre/Text: A Journal of Rhetorical Theory,* vol. 16, no. 3/4, 1995, pp. 260–74.

Rand, Erin J. *Reclaiming Queer: Activist and Academic Rhetorics of Resistance.* U of Alabama P, 2014.

Rawson, K.J. "Archive This! Queering the Archive." *Practicing Research in Writing Studies: Reflexive and Ethically Responsible Research,* edited by Katrina M. Powell and Pamela Takayoshi, Hampton P, 2012, pp. 237–50.

———. "Queering Feminist Rhetorical Canonization." *Rhetorica in Motion: Feminist Rhetorical Methods & Methodologies,* edited by Eileen Schell and K. J. Rawson, U of Pittsburgh P, 2010, pp. 39–52.

Reiff, Mary Jo, and Anis S. Bawarshi. "Tracing Discursive Resources: How Students Use Prior Genre Knowledge to Negotiate New Writing Contexts in First-Year Composition." *Written Communication,* vol. 28, no. 3, 2011, pp. 312–37.

"Reveries by Night." *New-York Mirror: Devoted to Literature and the Fine Arts,* 30 June 1832, p. 410. Google Books. Accessed 15 Apr. 2014.

"Reviews. Some Letter-Writing of Men-of-Letters." *The Critic: A Weekly Review of Literature and the Arts,* 21 July 1888, p. 25. American Periodicals Series. Accessed 2 Sept. 2010.

Rhodes, Jacqueline. "The Failure of Queer Pedagogy." *The Writing Instructor,* Mar. 2015. Accessed 31 July 2017.

Richardson, Elaine. "'To Protect and Serve': African American Female Literacies." *College Composition and Communication,* vol. 53, no. 4, 2002, pp. 675–704.

Richardson, Malcolm. "The *Ars dictaminis,* the Formulary, and Medieval Epistolary Practice." *Letter-Writing Manuals and Instruction from Antiquity to the Present: Historical and Bibliographic Studies,* edited by Carol Poster and Linda C. Mitchell, U of South Carolina P, pp. 52–66.

Ricker, Lisa Reid. "'Ars Stripped of Praxis': Robert J. Connors on Coeducation and the Demise of Agonistic Rhetoric." *Rhetoric Review,* vol. 23, no. 3, 2004, pp. 235–52.

———. "(De)Constructing the Praxis of Memory-Keeping: Late Nineteenth-Century Autograph Albums as Sites of Rhetorical Invention." *Rhetoric Review,* vol. 29, no. 3, 2010, pp. 239–56.

Robb, Graham. *Strangers: Homosexual Love in the Nineteenth Century.* W. W. Norton, 2003.

Robinson, Paul. "Love, Love, Hooray for Love." Rev. of *The Tender Passion,* by Peter Gay. *New York Times,* 16 Mar. 1986. Accessed 16 Apr. 2014.

Ronald, Kate. "A Reexamination of Personal and Public Discourse in Classical Rhetoric." *Rhetoric Review,* vol. 9, no. 1, 1990, pp. 36–48.

Rothermel, Beth Ann. "Prophets, Friends, Conversationalists: Quaker Rhetorical Culture, Women's Commonplace Books, and the Art of Invention, 1775–1840." *Rhetoric Society Quarterly,* vol. 43, no. 1, 2013, pp. 71–94.

———. "A Sphere of Noble Action: Gender, Rhetoric, and Influence at a Nineteenth-Century Massachusetts State Normal School." *Rhetoric Society Quarterly*, vol. 33, no. 1, 2003, pp. 35–64.

Rothman, Ellen. *Hand and Hearts: The History of Courtship in America*. Basic Books, 1984.

Rotundo, E. Anthony. *American Manhood: Transformations in Masculinity from the Revolution to the Modern Era*. Basic Books, 1993.

———. "Romantic Friendship: Male Intimacy and Middle-Class Youth in the Northern United States, 1800–1900." *Journal of Social History*, vol. 23, no. 1, 1989, 1–25.

Rounsaville, Angela. "Selecting Genres for Transfer: The Role of Uptake in Students' Antecedent Genre Knowledge." *Composition Forum*, vol. 26, 2012. Accessed 25 Nov. 2014.

Rounsaville, Angela, Rachel Goldberg, and Anis S. Bawarshi. "From Incomes to Outcomes: FYW Students' Prior Genre Knowledge, Meta-Cognition, and the Question of Transfer." *Writing Program Administration*, vol. 32, no. 1/2, 2008, pp. 97–112.

Royster, Jacqueline Jones. *Traces of a Stream: Literacy and Social Change among African-American Women*. U of Pittsburgh P, 2000.

Royster, Jacqueline Jones, and Gesa E. Kirsch. *Feminist Rhetorical Practices: New Horizons for Rhetoric, Composition, and Literacy Studies*. Southern Illinois UP, 2012.

Ruberg, Willemijn. "Epistolary and Emotional Education: The Letters of an Irish Father to His Daughter, 1747–1752." *Paedagogica Historica*, vol. 44, no. 1/2, 2008, pp. 207–18.

Rufo, Kenneth, and R. Jarrod Atchison. "From Circus to Fasces: The Disciplinary Politics of Citizen and Citizenship." *Review of Communication*, vol. 11, no. 3, 2011, pp. 193–215.

Runge, Laura L. "Beauty and Gallantry: A Model of Polite Conversation Revisited." *Eighteenth-Century Life*, vol. 25, no. 1, 2001, pp. 43–63.

Schultz, Lucille M. "Letter-Writing Instruction in 19th Century Schools in the United States." *Letter Writing as Social Practice*, edited by David Barton and Nigel Hall, John Benjamins North America, 1999, pp. 109–31.

Schlesinger, Elizabeth Bancroft. "Two Early Harvard Wives: Eliza Farrar and Eliza Follen." *New England Quarterly*, vol. 38, no. 2, 1965, pp. 147–67.

Scruggs, Charles. "Jean Toomer and Kenneth Burke and the Persistence of the Past." *American Literary History*, vol. 13, no. 1, 2001, pp. 41–66.

"The Sea Nymph's Song." *Yale Literary Magazine*, vol. 2, no. 8, July 1837, pp. 294–95.

Sedgwick, Eve Kosofsky. *Epistemology of the Closet*. U of California P, 1990.

Sedinger, Tracey. "Women's Friendship and the Refusal of Lesbian Desire in the Faerie Queene." *Criticism*, vol. 42, no. 1, 2000, pp. 91–113.

Seidman, Steven. *Romantic Longings: Love in America, 1830–1980*. Routledge, 1991.

Shepard, Sylvanus. *The Natural Letter-Writer: Divided into Five Chapters*. [Montpelier, VT], 1813. Nietz Collection, U of Pittsburgh, Pennsylvania.

Shields, Sarah Annie Frost. *Frost's Original Letter-Writer*. New York, 1867. Nietz Collection, U of Pittsburgh, Pennsylvania.

Silverstein, Judith, and Michael Lasky. *Online Dating for Dummies: A Reference for the Rest of Us*. Wiley, 2004.

Singer, Margot, and Nicole Walker, editors. *Bending Genre: Essays on Creative Nonfiction*. Bloomsbury, 2013.

Sinor, Jennifer. *The Extraordinary Work of Ordinary Writing: Annie Ray's Diary.* U of Iowa P, 2002.

Sjöblad, Christina. "From Family Notes to Diary: The Development of a Genre." *Eighteenth-Century Studies,* vol. 31, no. 4, 1998, pp. 517–21.

Sloop, John M. "Lucy Lobdell's Queer Circumstances." *Queering Public Address: Sexualities in American Historical Discourse,* edited by Charles E. Morris III, U of South Carolina P, 2007, pp. 149–73.

———. "People Shopping." *Rhetoric, Materiality, Politics,* edited by Barbara Biesecker and John Lucaites, Peter Lang P, 2009, pp. 67–98.

Smith-Rosenberg, Carroll. "Diaries and Letters." *Lesbian Histories and Cultures: An Encyclopedia,* edited by Bonnie Zimmerman, Garland, 2000, pp. 234–36.

———. "Discourses of Sexuality and Subjectivity: The New Woman, 1870–1936." *Hidden from History: Reclaiming the Gay and Lesbian Past,* edited by Martin Bauml Duberman, Martha Vicinus, and George Chauncey Jr., New American Library, 1989, pp. 264–80.

———. "The Female World of Love and Ritual." *Disorderly Conduct: Visions of Gender in Victorian America.* Oxford UP, 1985, pp. 53–76.

Somerville, Siobhan B. *Queering the Color Line: Race and the Invention of Homosexuality in American Culture.* Duke UP, 2000.

Southey, Robert. *The Poetical Works of Robert Southey, with a Memoir.* Vol. 3, Houghton, Osgood, 1880. Google Books. Accessed 15 Apr. 2014.

Spring, Suzanne B. "'Seemingly Uncouth Forms': Letters at Mount Holyoke Female Seminary." *College Composition and Communication,* vol. 59, no. 4, 2008, pp. 633–75.

———. "A Meditation on the Value of Liberty: Mary Ann Shadd, Anti-Slavery Conscience, and the Labor of the Public Letter." *Argumentation & Discourse Analysis,* vol. 5, 2010. Accessed 15 Apr. 2014.

Squires, Catherine R., and Daniel C. Brouwer. "In/Discernible Bodies: The Politics of Passing in Dominant and Marginal Media." *Critical Studies in Media Communication,* vol. 19, no. 3, 2002, pp. 283–310.

Stanley, Liz. "Romantic Friendship? Some Issues in Researching Lesbian History and Biography." *Women's History Review,* vol. 1, no. 2, 1992, pp. 193–216.

Stock, David. "Recuperating John Bascom's Contributions to Nineteenth-Century Rhetoric and Contemporary Rhetorical Education." *Rhetoric Society Quarterly,* vol. 45, no. 1, 2015, pp. 65–83.

Stryker, Susan. "Transgender History, Homonormativity, and Disciplinarity." *Radical History Review,* vol. 100, 2008, pp. 145–57.

Stuckey, Zosha. *A Rhetoric of Remnants: Idiots, Half-Wits, and Other State-Sponsored Inventions.* State U of New York P, 2014.

Sullivan, Robert G. "Classical Epistolary Theory and the Letters of Isocrates." *Letter-Writing Manuals and Instruction from Antiquity to the Present: Historical and Bibliographic Studies,* edited by Carol Poster and Linda C. Mitchell, U of South Carolina P, pp. 7–20.

Taormino, Tristan. *Opening Up: A Guide to Creating and Sustaining Open Relationships.* Cleis, 2008.

Thames, Richard H. "The Meaning of the Motivorum's Motto: 'Ad Bellum Purificandum' to 'Tendebantque Manus Ripae Ulterioris Amore.'" *KB Journal*, vol. 8, no. 1, 2012. Accessed 3 Nov. 2014.

Thomas, Kate. *Postal Pleasures: Sex, Scandal, and Victorian Letters*. Oxford UP, 2012.

Tiles, J. E. "Logic and Rhetoric: An Introduction to Seductive Argument." *Philosophy & Rhetoric*, vol. 28, no. 4, 1995, pp. 300–15.

Trasciatti, Mary Anne. "Letter Writing in an Italian Immigrant Community: A Transatlantic Tradition." *Rhetoric Society Quarterly*, vol. 39, no. 1, 2009, pp. 73–94.

Turner, R. *The Parlour Letter-Writer: And Secretary's Assistant: Consisting of Original Letters on Every Occurrence in Life*. Philadelphia, 1835. Nietz Collection, U of Pittsburgh, Pennsylvania.

The Useful Letter Writer: Comprising a Succinct Treatise on the Epistolary Art, and Forms of Letters for All the Ordinary Occasions of Life. New York, 1844. Nietz Collection, U of Pittsburgh, Pennsylvania.

VanHaitsma, Pamela. "Gossip as Rhetorical Methodology for Queer and Feminist Historiography." *Rhetoric Review*, vol. 35, no. 2, 2016, pp. 135–47.

———. "New Archival Engagements: Student Inquiry and Composing in Digital Spaces." *College English*, vol. 78, no. 1, 2015, pp. 34–55.

———. "Queering 'the language of the heart': Romantic Letters, Genre Instruction, and Rhetorical Practice." *Rhetoric Society Quarterly*, vol. 44, no. 1, 2014, pp. 6–24.

———. "Romantic Correspondence as Queer Extracurriculum: The Self-Education for Racial Uplift of Addie Brown and Rebecca Primus." *College Composition and Communication*, vol. 69, no. 2, 2017, pp. 182–207.

Vicinus, Martha. *Intimate Friends: Women Who Loved Women, 1778–1928*. U of Chicago P, 2004.

———. "'They Wonder to Which Sex I Belong': The Historical Roots of the Modern Lesbian Identity." *Feminist Studies*, vol. 18, 1992, pp. 467–97.

Waite, Stacey. "Andy Teaches Me to Listen: Queer Silence and the Problem of Participation." *Writing on the Edge*, vol. 24, no. 1, 2013, pp. 63–74.

———. "Becoming the Loon: Performance Pedagogy and Female Masculinity." *Writing on the Edge*, vol. 19, no. 2, 2009, pp. 53–68.

———. "Cultivating the Scavenger: A Queerer Feminist Future for Composition and Rhetoric." *Peitho*, vol. 18, no. 1, 2015, pp. 51–71.

———. *Teaching Queer: Radical Possibilities for Writing and Knowing*. U of Pittsburgh P, 2017.

Walker, Jeffrey. *The Genuine Teachers of This Art: Rhetorical Education in Antiquity*. U of South Carolina P, 2011.

Walzer, Arthur. 'Rhetoric as a History of Education and Acculturation.' "Octalog III: The Politics of Historiography in 2010." *Rhetoric Review*, vol. 30, no. 2, 2010, pp. 123–25, 132.

———. "Teaching 'Political Wisdom': Isocrates and the Tradition of *Dissoi Logoi*." *The Viability of the Rhetorical Tradition*, edited by Richard Graff, Arthur Walzer, and Janet Atwill, State U of New York P, 2005, 113–24.

Wan, Amy. "In the Name of Citizenship: The Writing Classroom and the Promise of Citizenship." *College English*, vol. 74, no. 1, 2011, pp. 28–49.

Wardle, Elizabeth. "'Mutt Genres' and the Goal of FYC: Can We Help Students Write the Genres of the University?" *College Composition and Communication,* vol. 60, no. 4, 2009, pp. 765–89.

Watts, Eric King. "'Paul's Committed Suicide': A Utopist Tragedy in Wallace Thurman's *Infants of the Spring.*" *Hearing the Hurt: Rhetoric, Aesthetics, and Politics of the New Negro Movement,* edited by Eric King Watts, U of Alabama P, 2012, pp. 140–65.

———. "Queer Harlem: Exploring the Rhetorical Limits of a Black Gay 'Utopia.'" *Queering Public Address: Sexualities in American Historical Discourse,* edited by Charles E. Morris III, U of South Carolina P, 2007, pp. 174–94.

Weaver, Maggie. "Seductive Rhetoric and the Communicative Art of Neo-Burlesque." *Present Tense: A Journal of Rhetoric in Society,* vol. 5, no. 1, 2015. Accessed 19 May 2016.

West, Celeste. *Lesbian Polyfidelity.* Booklegger, 1995.

Westlake, James Willis. *How to Write Letters.* Philadelphia, 1886. Nietz Collection, U of Pittsburgh, Pennsylvania.

Wetzel, Grace. "Winifred Black's Teacherly Ethos: The Role of Journalism in Late-Nineteenth-Century Rhetorical Education." *Rhetoric Society Quarterly,* vol. 44, no. 1, 2014, pp. 68–93.

Whitbread, Helena, editor. *I Know My Own Heart: The Diaries of Anne Lister, 1791–1840.* New York UP, 1992.

———. *No Priest But Love: The Journals of Anne Lister from 1824–1826.* New York UP, 1993.

Whitburn, Merrill D. "Invention in James M. Hoppin's *Homiletics:* Scope and Classicism in Late Nineteenth-Century American Rhetoric." *Advances in the History of Rhetoric,* vol. 10, 2007, pp. 105–29.

———. "Rhetorical Theory in Yale's Graduate Schools in the Late Nineteenth Century: The Example of William C. Robinson's Forensic Oratory." *Rhetoric Society Quarterly,* vol. 34, no. 4, 2004, pp. 55–70.

White, David. "Addie Brown's Hartford." *Connecticut Historical Society Bulletin,* vol. 41, no. 2, 1976, pp. 56–64.

———. "Rebecca Primus in Later Life." *Beloved Sisters and Loving Friends: Letters from Rebecca Primus of Royal Oak, Maryland, and Addie Brown of Hartford, Connecticut, 1854–1868,* edited by Farah Jasmine Griffin, Ballantine, 1999, pp. 279–84.

Wightman, Stillman. Stillman King Wightman Papers, 1803–1899. MS 1079. Manuscripts and Archives, Yale U Library, New Haven.

Wilchins, Riki. "A Certain Kind of Freedom: Power and the Truth of Bodies—Four Essays on Gender." *Genderqueer: Voices from Beyond the Sexual Binary,* edited by Joan Nestle, Riki Wilchins, and Clare Howell, Alyson Books, 2002, pp. 23–66.

Wilson, Kirt H. "The Racial Politics of Imitation in the Nineteenth Century." *Quarterly Journal of Speech,* vol. 89, no. 2, 2003, pp. 89–108.

"Woman's Genius in Letter-Writing." *The Chautauquan; A Weekly Newsmagazine,* Jan. 1895, p. 478. American Periodicals Series. Accessed 2 Sept. 2010.

Wood, Mary E. "'With Ready Eye': Margaret Fuller and Lesbianism in Nineteenth-Century American Literature." *American Literature,* vol. 65, no. 1, 1993, pp. 1–18.

Woolverton, John. *The Education of Phillips Brooks.* U of Illinois P, 1995.

Works Cited

Zaczek, Barbara. *Censored Sentiments: Letters and Censorship in Epistolary Novels and Conduct Material.* U of Delaware P, 1997.

Zboray, Ronald, and Mary Saracino Zboray. *Everyday Ideas: Socioliterary Experience among Antebellum New Englanders.* U of Tennessee P, 2006.

———. "Is It a Diary, Commonplace Book, Scrapbook, or Whatchamacallit?: Six Years of Exploration in New England's Manuscript Archives." *Libraries & the Cultural Record,* vol. 44, no. 1, 2009, pp. 101–23.

Zwagerman, Sean. *Wit's End: Women's Humor as Rhetorical and Performative Strategy.* U of Pittsburgh P, 2010.

Index

Abdur-Rahman, Aliyya I., 119n17
abolitionism, 51
activism, 107
Adam, Alexander, 81
Aeneid (Virgil), 81–82
Aeschylus, 81
African Americans, Hartford (CT) community, 51, 71, 118n9
African American women: citizenship rights denied to, 21; in cross-class relationships, 54; freeborn, 49–50; historical erasure of, 50; marriage as economic stability for, 59; rhetoric of, 46, 61; scholarship on, 118n12; sexual stereotypes about, 119n17. *See also* Brown, Addie; Brown/Primus correspondence; Primus, Rebecca
Aguilar, Grace, 66–68
Ahern, Laura, 106
Albert Dodd Papers, 120–21n1, 125n48
Alexander, Jonathan, 7, 107, 109n5, 110–11n15, 125n1, 125n11
Ali, Kazim, 13, 75, 85, 111n18
Althusser, Louis, 110n10
Altman, Janet, 113n2
American Lady's and Gentleman's Modern Letter Writer, The, 32, 114n10
American Manhood (Rotundo), 122n11
Anabasis (Xenophon), 81
Anacreon, 81
Anderson, Dana, 110n10
Anthony, Susan B., 49
Antigone (Sophocles), 81
antislavery newspapers, 119n18
Aristotle, 88, 122n18

ars dictaminis, 17, 24
Art of Correspondence, The (Locke), 30, 34, 116n23, 117n28
Art of Seduction, The (Greene), 104–5
Atchison, R. Jarrod, 110n9
Atlantic (monthly), 102
Atwill, Janet, 7

Bakhtin, Mikhail M., 10, 11, 37
Ballif, Michelle, 112n24
Bannet, Eve Tavor, 24, 25, 28, 31, 114n7, 114n8, 115n12, 116n20
Barthes, Roland, 112n28
baseness, 33–35
Bates, Catherine, 15, 104, 112n25
Bazerman, Charles, 10
Beecher, Henry Ward, 119n21
Beeching, Barbara, 52, 118n9, 119n22
Beers, Julia, 78, 86–87, 90, 93–95, 107, 124n34
Belcombe, Mariana, 117n30
Beloved Sisters and Loving Friends (Griffin), 53
Bereiter, Carl, 84
Berlant, Lauren, 8, 10, 32, 110n8, 110n13
Berlin, James, 114n4
Bernard, Ben, 122n11
Bessette, Jean, 7
Bible, 119n19
Binkley, Roberta, 106
Biographical Notes of Graduates of Yale College (Dexter), 80, 121n4
Biographical Record of the Class of 1838 in Yale College, 80, 121n4

blackness, 27–28
Blair, Hugh, 2, 17, 24, 113n4, 114n7, 123n24
Bloomington (IL), 80, 121n5
Boellstorff, Tom, 115n18
"bosom sex," 53, 60–61, 70
Boureau, Alain, 114n6
bourgeois logic, 33
Branstetter, Heather Lee, 109n5
Bray, Joe, 113n2
Brent, Doug, 84–85, 87–88, 123nn26–27
Brereton, John C., 7, 17, 79, 83
Brookey, Robert Alan, 109n5
Brown, Addie, 4; citizenship rights of, 21; death of, 75, 118n8, 119n16; family/education of, 51–52, 53, 75; financial situation of, 60; "language of the heart" adapted by, 50; marriage of, 52, 58–60, 119nn15–16; political commentary of, 61–62; queer rhetorical practices of, 11–12, 13–14; romantic relationships of, 20, 78. *See also* Brown/Primus correspondence
Brown/Primus correspondence, 52; archival holdings of, 118n6; author's research on, 4, 16, 21, 52, 53; complete letter writers and, 50, 68–69, 99; cross-category romantic epistolary address in, 55–58; duration of, 52; genre conventions used in, 54–55; interpretive difficulty of, 53–54, 71–72, 120nn29–30; invention strategies with queer effects, 63–69, 119–20nn17–25; pacing/intensity of, 56–58; postal age and, 16; queer failure and, 98, 99–100, 107; queer rhetorical practices in, 11–12, 50, 54–63, 72–73, 74, 99–100; scholarship on, 101, 118nn9–12, 121n2; spelling/punctuation in, 52–53, 63, 64
Bruce, Emily C., 114n6
Buchanan, Lindal, 112n27
Bunkers, Suzanne L., 123n33
Burke, Edmund, 9
Burke, Kenneth, 15, 110n10, 111–12n23, 112n26
Butler, Judith, 111n18
BuzzFeed, 102
Byron, Lord, 65, 125n45

capitalism, late, 110n7, 110n14
Captivi (Plautus), 81

Carmichael, James V., Jr., 117n30
Carr, Allison D., 125n1
Carr, Edwin Hamlin, 116n24
Carr, Jean Ferguson, 47, 114n8
Carr, Stephen, 47, 114n8, 115n15, 116n20
Carstarphen, Meta G., 109n5
Carter, Julian, 27
Castiglia, Christopher, 115n18
Catalogue of the Officers and Students in Yale College, 1836–37, 77, 80–81, 82, 83, 85, 92, 122n21
Cavallaro, Alexandra J., 109n5
Certeau, Michel de, 117n3
Charland, Maurice, 110n10
Chartier, Roger, 114n6
Chávez, Karma R., 7, 8, 101, 106, 109n6
Chesterfield, Philip Dormer Stanhope, Earl of, 81
Chesterfield's Art of Letter Writing Simplified, 34, 36; invention strategies taught in, 38–39, 40–41, 42–43; "miscellaneous" letters in, 44; popularity of, 114n8
Chinese women, 106
Cicero, 7, 17, 24, 80, 81, 122n18, 122n20
cisgender normativity, 118n5
citizenship, 21, 101, 103, 106–7, 110nn7–9
civic engagement: queer failure and, 101, 106–7; rhetorical education for, 9, 79–85, 95; rhetoric and, 7, 8, 101; romantic engagement vs., 110n11
civic/romantic distinction, queering of, 7, 8–9
civil rights, 110n7
Civil War, 16, 49–50
Clark, Gregory, 7, 110n10
class, 3, 27, 31, 40–41, 49–50, 75, 114n10
Cloud, Dana, 109n5, 109n6, 110n11
Collectanea Graeca Minora (Dalzel), 81
Collins, Patricia Hill, 119n17
colonialism, 114n9
commonplace books, 88, 92. *See also* Dodd, Albert, and commonplace book/diary of
comparison, 86–87
Complete American Letter-Writer, The, 26, 116n22
Complete Art of Polite Correspondence, The, 26
Complete Letter Writer, The, 40, 115n15

Index

complete letter writers: affordability of, 16; "American" emphasis in, 26, 114n9; author's research on, 4, 25; British predecessors of, 24, 26; Brown/Primus correspondence and, 50, 68–69, 99; contents/organization of, 25–26, 32, 43, 99, 114n8; critiques of, 116nn22–23; epistolary culture and, 23–24, 113n2; feminist histories of, 45–46, 47; heteronormative genre instruction in, 10–12, 31–37, 46, 54, 56–57, 70–71, 99, 116–17n26; homoeroticism and, 116–17n26; imagined as pedagogical failures, 45–48; invention strategies taught in, 37, 50, 63, 116nn22–24; "miscellaneous" letters in, 44, 117n27; model letter sharing among, 114n8, 115n15, 116n20; model romantic letters in, 14, 116n19; pedagogical paradox of, 24–25; popularity of, 3, 14, 24, 114n8; queer failure and, 99; queer scholarship on, 47; rhetorical tradition and, 24; romantic epistolary rhetoric instruction in, 2–3, 16, 23–24; scholarship on, 28; social conventions modeled in, 26–28, 114–15nn10–11; use of term, 23. *See also specific letter writer*
Composition-Rhetoric (Connors), 114n4
composition textbooks, 23, 113–14n4
Connecticut Historical Society (Hartford, CT), 52, 118n6
Connors, Robert, 7, 79, 114n4
Conquergood, Dwight, 115n11
Conrad, Ryan, 110n14, 125n9
Constable, Nicole, 106
Cook, Elizabeth Heckendorn, 113n2
Cook, Marion Belden, 125n48
copying, 3
copyright laws, 116n20
"coquette" (literary figure), 104
Cott, Nancy, 118n12
courtship: evolving definition of, 104, 112n25; in marriage *telos*, 10, 35, 99; pacing/intensity of, 57, 58; rhetoric of, 111–12n23, 112nn25–26
courtship letter, 115n12
Cox, Matthew B., 109n5
Cram, E., 109n5
critical imagination, 45, 46, 47, 117n31

"crush notes," 111n16
cryptograms, 44–45, 47, 58, 117n28, 117n30
cultural context, 106–7

Dalzel, A., 81
dating sites/apps, 102, 105
Dauphin, Cecile, 114n6
Davidson, Cathy N., 115n13
Day, Jeremiah, 79
debates, 82, 83
deception, 1–2, 3, 15–16, 29–31, 36–37
Decker, William Merrill, 16, 72–73, 110n6
declamations, 82, 83, 103
definition, 86–87
delivery, 112n27
Demosthenes, 80, 81, 85, 122n20, 122n22
Denman, William, 7
De Oratore (Cicero), 80, 81
Depew, David, 7
Derrida, Jacques, 112n28
Devitt, Amy, 10, 11, 37
Dexter, Franklin, 80, 121n4
diaries: defined, 124n39; generic shifts using, 89; interpretive difficulty of, 120n30; rhetorical education and, 78; rhetoricity of, 124n40; scholarship on, 121n2, 123n33; sharing, 124n38
Dickinson, Anna, 49
Dickinson, Emily, 49
Dickinson, Susan Gilbert, 49
Diggs, Marylynn, 20
digital age, 102, 104, 105
digression, 94
Dinshaw, Carolyn, 110n14, 116n18, 125n9
Dodd, Albert, 5; archival holdings of, 120–21n1, 125n48; author's research on, 19, 21, 77; birth of, 121n4; civic orientation of, 79–80; death of, 75, 97, 121nn4–5; epistolary rhetoric of, as "everyday," 121n2; extracurricular activities of, 121n8; familial correspondence of, 95–96, 121n1; genre awareness of, 96–98; heterosexual romantic relationships of, 78, 86–87, 122n15, 122n16, 123–24n34, 124–25n44; multigenre epistolary rhetoric of, 75, 77–78, 87, 95–98; poetry album of, 13, 74, 81–82, 86, 92–95, 120–21n1, 124–25nn44–45; queer failure and, 98,

Dodd, Albert (*continued*)
99, 107; queer rhetorical practices of, 12–14, 19, 21, 74, 75, 85; rhetorical education of, 21, 75, 76–77, 79–85, 95, 96–97, 100, 121n2, 122n18, 123n24; romantic relationships of, 20; same-sex romantic relationships of, 75–76, 77–78, 86–87, 88–89, 96–97, 121n6, 122n12, 122n14, 122n16, 123n31, 124nn34–35; scholarship on, 95–98, 101, 121n2, 121–22nn10–11; suspension period of, 82–83

Dodd, Albert, and commonplace book/diary of: digitalization of, 121n9; in Dodd archival holdings, 120n1; early writings in, 76, 124n37; as genre-crossing text, 12–13, 74–75, 87–89; genre-queer practices for romantic engagement in, 85–87, 90–92; male/female romantic interests recorded in, 122n16; rhetorical education detailed in, 80–81; rhetorical precedents for, 88; scholarship on, 95–96, 122n11; self-censorship in, 77

Dodd, Albert, and genre-queer practices for romantic engagement: commonplace book/diary as enactor of romantic epistolary rhetoric, 90–92; commonplace book/diary shift, 87–89; epistolary/poetic address/exchange mixed, 92–95; rhetorical education repurposed for, 75, 85, 97–98; self-rhetorics of literary representations of same-sex erotic relationships, 85–87

Dodd, Edward, 80, 96
Dodd, Julius, 81, 82, 96
Donawerth, Jane, 18–19, 28, 45–46
"Don Juan" (poem; Byron), 125n45
Douglas, Alfred, 49
Douglass, Frederick, 62
Doyle, Peter, 49
Dreams and Reveries of a Quiet Man (Fay), 65
Driskill, Qwo-Li, 106
Duggan, Lisa, 110n14, 125n9
Dunn, Thomas R., 7, 33, 115n18
Düttmann, Alexander García, 115n18

Edelman, Lee, 115–16n18
education, 3; democratization of, 16–18. *See also* rhetorical education

Electra (Sophocles), 81
Elizabethan language/literature, 104
Ellsworth (legal scholar), 79
elocutionary manuals, 115n11
elopements, 42, 59
Elshtain, Jean Bethke, 109n6
Eng, David, 110n7, 110n14, 125n9
engagement: broken, 99; in marriage *telos*, 10
Enlightenment, 88
Enoch, Jessica, 7
Enos, Richard, 122n20
epistle verse, 92, 125n45
"Epistolary" (poem; Dodd), 93–95, 125n45
epistolary address, gendered, 10, 31–32. *See also* romantic epistolary address
epistolary culture, 23–24, 113n2
Epistolary Guide, The, 116n22
epistolary logic, 13, 92
epistolary novels, 23, 29, 112–13n35, 113n2
epistolary rhetoric: of "everyday" people, 49–50; gender and, 18–19, 112–13n35; instruction in principles of, in manuals, 25; of literary/political figures, 49; multigenre, 75, 77–78; romantic letters as, 14–16, 21–22, 69–73, 100; same-sex, 49–50; Western histories of, 1
epistolary writing, 112n28
Erasmus, 24
erotic interactions, 53, 60–61, 70–71, 116n25
Ethical Slut, The, 105
etiquette guides, 25, 40
Euripides, 81
Everyday Ideas (Zboray and Zboray), 117n3, 121n2, 122n11
exhibitions, 82–83, 84
extramarital affairs, 36

Facebook, 102
Faderman, Lillian, 20, 118n10, 118n12
failure, 11, 99, 100. *See also* queer failure
Faris, Michael J., 109n5
Farrar, Eliza Ware Rotch, 38, 116n22, 116n25
Fashionable American Letter Writer, The: contents/organization of, 25, 26; invention strategies taught in, 44–45; "language of the heart" in, 14, 23, 29;

Index

marriage *telos* in, 35; popularity of, 114n8; social conventions modeled in, 27
Fashioning Lives (Pritchard), 50, 117–18nn4–5, 119n17
Father's Legacy to His Daughters, A (Gregory), 115n15
Favret, Mary, 19, 110n6, 112n35, 113n2
Fay, Theodore Sedgwick, 65, 120n23
Fell, Jesse W., 75–76, 97, 121n6
feminist rhetorical scholarship, 3, 18–19, 28, 45–46
feminist theory, 8, 47, 104–5, 117n31
Ferguson, Roderick A., 116n18
Filipinas, 106
flattery, 29, 30–31, 36–37
flirtation, 60–61
Folsom, Charles, 81
Fone, Byrne, 85, 123n31
Foucault, Michel, 19
France, Peter, 92
Fraser, Nancy, 109n6
Freccero, Carla, 115–16n18
Freeman, Elizabeth, 115–16n18
Frost's Original Letter-Writer (Shields), 26, 29, 30, 35–36, 38, 115n15
futurism, reproductive, 115n18

Gage, John, 18, 114n4
Gannett, Cinthia, 123n33
Ganymede myth, 85–87, 123n31
Garlinger, Patrick Paul, 15, 70, 111n21, 116–17n26
Garnett, Henry Highland, 62
Gaul, Theresa Strouth, 112n29
Gay, Peter, 76, 77, 95–97, 121n2, 121n11, 122n12, 122n16, 124n35
gay relationships, 105
gender, 3; deception/flattery and, 29–31, 116n19; letter-writing and, 18–19, 112–13n35; queer practices involving crossing of, 40–41; racialization of, 118n5; romantic epistolary address and, 31–32, 37, 40–41; romantic relationships and, 115n12
Gender and Rhetorical Space in American Life, 1866–1910 (Johnson), 19, 109n6, 115n12
gender performativity, 111n18

genre instruction: heteronormative, 10–12, 31–37, 46, 50, 54; in pacing/intensity, 32–35, 37, 41–43, 46, 56–58; queer practices and, 10–12, 37, 54–63; in rhetorical purpose, 35–37, 43–45, 46–47, 58–63; in romantic epistolary address, 31–32, 37, 40–41, 46, 54–56; romantic letters learned through, 50
genre-queer texts, 13, 85, 111n18
Gere, Anne Ruggles, 24
Gibson, Michelle, 109n5
Gillett (Yale student), 84
Gilroy, Amanda, 110n6, 112n35, 113n2
Glenn, Cheryl, 7, 9
globalization, 106–7
GLQ: A Journal of Lesbian and Gay Studies, 115–16n18
Godey's Lady's Book (Leslie), 21; authorship of, 109n1 (Pref.); digital-age imagining of, 101–2, 105; marriage *telos* in, 3, 99; queer failure and, 107; readership of, 3; romantic epistolary rhetoric instruction in, 1–3, 23
Gold, David, 7, 124n40
Goltz, Dustin Bradley, 115n18
Gonçalves, Zan Meyer, 8
Goodrich, Chauncey A., 79, 81, 122n19
Goodrich Family Papers, 122n22
Google, 102
Gorgias (Plato), 112n24, 122n21
gossip, 117n31
Grasso, Linda, 118n11
Greco-Roman literature, 80, 81–82, 84, 85, 103, 123n25
Greek Anthology, 81, 85, 123n29
Greek Grammar (Goodrich), 81
Greene, Robert, 104–5
Gregory, John, 115n15
Griffin, Cindy L., 109n6
Griffin, Farah Jasmine, 51, 52, 53, 61, 69, 70, 71, 72, 118n8, 118n10, 118n11, 119nn15–16, 119nn20–21
Gring-Pemble, Lisa M., 19
Gross, Daniel M., 109n5, 125n1
Gunderson, Erik, 103

Halberstam, Jack, 10, 11, 33, 47, 57, 69, 98, 99, 100, 101, 110n14, 115–16n18, 125n1

Hall, Radclyffe, 49
Hallmark, 102
Halloran, S. Michael, 6, 7
Halsey, Anthony, 77–78, 86–87, 90, 91–92, 107, 122n14
Hansen, Karen, 52, 53, 60, 69, 70, 71, 72, 78, 118n10, 118n12, 119n17
Hardie, James, 114n7, 116n22
Harris, Sharon, 112n29
Harrison, Kimberly, 86, 120n29, 123n33, 124nn39–40
Harrison, Renee, 118n11
Hartford (CT), 51, 52, 61–62, 71, 75, 118n9. See also Washington College (Hartford, CT)
Hartford Freedmen's Aid Society, 51
hastiness, precautions against, 34
Hauser, Gerard, 7
Heath, John, 76, 77, 78, 86–87, 88–89, 90–91, 93, 107
Hebe and Ganymede (medieval poem), 86
Henkin, David, 16, 120n29
Hesford, Wendy, 106
heteronormativity, 30; failure of, 47; genre instruction based in, 1, 10–12, 31–37, 46, 50, 70–71, 99, 116–17n26; heterosexuality vs., 10; marriage *telos* and, 2, 35–37; queer challenges to, 50; "racialized," 118n5, 119n17; use of term, 10, 110n13
heterosexuality: heteronormativity vs., 10; "national," 32, 110n8, 118n5; normalization of, 10, 31
Hewitt, Elizabeth, 27, 110n6, 113n2
Hill's Manual of Social and Business Forms, 36, 66
historical erasure, 50, 117–18n4 (Ch. 2)
historiography, 6–7, 100–101
History of Sexuality, The (Foucault), 19
Hoang Nguyen, Tan, 110n14, 116n18
Homer, 81, 85, 124n37
homoeroticism, 85, 103, 116–17n26, 123n29
homonormativity, 105–6, 110n14, 125n9
Horace, 19, 81, 82, 92
Hoshor, John P., 79
How to Write Letters (Westlake), 43–44, 114n7, 116n23

Hunt, Violet, 49

Iliad (Homer), 81, 85
Illinois State Legislature, 80
immigrants, 27, 28
In a Queer Time and Place (Halberstam), 10, 33, 57
Intelligent Woman's Guide to Online Dating, The, 105
interdisciplinary studies, 106
Internet, 106
invention strategies with queer effects: category-crossing address forms, 40–41, 46; copying/adaptation and, 37–40, 46; "language of the heart" adaptations from novels, 66–69, 119n18; "language of the heart" adaptations from poetry, 63–66, 119n18; pacing/intensity, 41–43, 46; repurposing and, 43–45, 46–47
Invitations to Love (Ahern), 106
Irish immigrants, 27
Isocrates, 7, 80, 103, 122n23
Italian immigrants, 28

Jagose, Annamarie, 116n18
Jasinski, James, 110n10
Johnson, Andrew, 61–62
Johnson, Nan, 19, 28, 45–46, 109n6, 114n8, 122n18, 123n24
Jones, Constance, 49
journals, 124n39

Kames, Henry Home, Lord, 123n24
Kates, Susan, 7
Katz, Jonathan, 75–76, 77, 78, 87, 95–96, 97, 121n4, 121–22nn10–11
Kauffman, Linda, 113n2
Kelley, William, 112n24
Kirsch, Gesa E., 117n32
Kitzhaber, Albert, 7, 17
Kopelson, Karen, 8

"language of the heart," 50; copying/adaptation of, 37–40; deception/flattery and, 29–31; invention strategies with novels, 66–69, 119n18; invention strategies with poetry, 63–66, 119n18; romantic letters as composed using, 2–3, 23, 29–31

Index

language practices, 9, 16, 24, 102–3, 104, 105–7
Latin Grammar (Andrews and Stodard), 81
Lawton, Charles, 117n30
Lectures on Rhetoric and Belles Lettres (Blair), 17, 113n4
Lee, Mr. (Brown suitor), 59
lesbian relationships, 105
Leslie, Miss, 21, 23, 109n1 (Pref.)
letter(s): defined, 24, 25, 114n7; familial, 96–97; gender and, 18–19, 112–13n35; genre-queer practices involving, 92; as historical sources, 95–96, 120n29; interpretations of, 111n22; model, in manuals, 3, 25–26, 27–28, 116n19; as "open closets," 111n21; rhetorics of, 2; scholarship on, 121n2; Western histories of, 1; writing instruction, during postal age, 17–18, 113–14nn1–4, 114n6. *See also* epistolary rhetoric; romantic letters
letter-writing manuals. *See* complete letter writers
Letter-Writing Manuals and Instruction from Antiquity to the Present (Poster and Mitchell), 24
Letter-Writing Simplified, 29–30, 36, 115n15, 116n23
LGBTQ people, 11, 50, 110n14
liberal assimilationism, 110n7
Lifehack, 102
Lincoln, Abraham, 20, 49, 111n22, 121n6
Lipari, Lisbeth, 109n5, 109n6
Lipson, Carol, 106
Lister, Anne, 117n30
literacy, 16
literature: Greco-Roman, 80, 81–82, 84, 85, 103, 123n25; self-rhetorics of representations of same-sex erotic relationships in, 85–87. *See also* novel; poetry
Livy (Folsom), 81
Locke, John, 30, 34, 116n23, 117n28
Logan, Shirley Wilson, 7, 61, 78, 86, 123n33, 124nn38–39
Loomis, Henry, 25, 38, 113n4, 114n7
Lorde, Audre, 119n17
Love @ First Click, 105
Love of Friends, The (ed. Jones), 49
Lystra, Karen, 14, 15

Mahoney, Deirdre M., 18, 19, 28, 45–46, 113n2, 115n12
"mail order" companies, 106
Malinowitz, Harriet, 8, 118n4
Man Talk: The Gay Couple's Communication Guide, 105
Marinara, Martha, 109n5
marriage, civil rights via, 110n7
marriage *telos*, 28; elopements and, 42; heteronormativity and, 2, 99; queer failure and, 100; queer repurposing and, 43–45, 46–47; as rhetorical purpose of romantic letters, 35–37, 54, 71; same-sex romantic relationships and, 57; "straight time" and, 10, 57
Masten, Jeffrey, 114n7
McCarthy, Molly, 123n33
Meem, Deborah, 109n5
meta-commentary, 89, 94–95
Miller, Carolyn, 10, 26, 28, 45
Miller, Susan, 88, 113n35, 115n12
Mitchell, Charles B., 61
Mitchell, Linda C., 24
Monson, Connie, 109n5
Montague, Mary Wortley, 113n3
Morgan, Elizabeth, 78, 90, 107, 122n15, 123–24n34, 124–25n44
Morris, Charles E., III, 6, 7–8, 20, 107, 109n6, 115n18
Morris, George Pope, 120n23
Muñoz, José Esteban, 110n14, 115n18, 125n9
Murphy, James, 114n6

Narayan, Madhu, 109n5
National Theatre (New York, NY), 124n37
nation and sexuality, 8, 110n8
Natural Letter-Writer, The (Shepard), 29, 30, 36–37
Nealon, Christopher S., 116n18
New Haven (CT), 76–77
Newman, Samuel, 114n4
New Parlor Letter Writer, The, 115n15
New York (NY), 124n37
New Yorker, 102
New York Mirror, 65, 120n23
Nietz, John, 114n8, 116n20
Nietz Collection (Univ. of Pittsburgh), 4, 25

Nineteenth-Century Rhetoric in North America (Johnson), 122n18, 123n24
"'No *Kisses* Is Like Yours'" (Hansen), 118n10
nonmonogamous relations, 105–6
novel: epistolary, 23, 29, 112–13n35, 113n2; "language of the heart" adaptations from, 50, 66–69, 119n18

Olbrechts-Tyteca, Lucie, 86
Olson, Christa J., 110n10
Olson, Lester C., 8
online dating, 102, 105
Online Dating for Dummies, 105
oral dialogues, 103
oratory, 82–83, 84
Ovid, 92

Parlour Letter-Writer, The (Turner), 27, 35, 40
pedagogy: cultural significance of, 21–22; "failure" of, 45–48; queer failure and, 107; shaping of subjects through, 9; writing, 125n1
pederasty, 123n31
Peiss, Kathy Lee, 118n11
Pennington, James, 51
Perelman, Chaïm, 86
periodical articles, 23, 113nn1, 3
Permanent Partners: Building Gay and Lesbian Relationships That Last, 105
Phaedrus (Plato), 112n24
Plato, 15, 80, 103, 104, 112n24, 122n21, 122n22
Plato, Ann, 51
Plautus, 81
Pocket Letter Writer, The, 27–28, 32, 33–34, 35, 41–42, 115n15
"poetique," 93
poetry: in complete letter writers, 30; genre-queer practices involving, 92–95; homoerotic, 123n29; "language of the heart" adaptations from, 50, 63–66, 119n18
political/personal distinction, queering of, 6–7
politics, 80
Postal Act (1845), 16
Postal Act (1851), 16

postal age: defined, 16; letters as historical sources for, 120n29; letter-writing and women's rhetoric during, 18–19; letter-writing instruction during, 17–18, 113–14nn1–4, 114n6; same-sex romantic friendships during, 19–20; scholarship on, 112n29, 120n29
Poster, Carol, 14, 24
Post Office Act (1792), 16
Pough, Gwendolyn, 118n4
Poulakis, Takis, 7
Powell, Malea, 106
Practical Letter Writing (Loomis), 25, 38, 113n4
Practical System of Rhetoric, A (Newman), 114n4
Primus, Rebecca, 4, 75; citizenship rights of, 21; envelope notations of, 54–55, 57, 118n8; family/education of, 51; letters to family from, 52, 56, 57; marriage of, 52, 58–59, 119n16; Maryland teaching job of, 51, 57, 61, 119n16; political commentary of, 61; queer rhetorical practices of, 11–12, 13–14; romantic relationships of, 20, 78. *See also* Brown/Primus correspondence
Primus Family Papers, 118n6, 119n16
Prince Hall Masonic Lodge (Hartford, CT), 51
print culture, 17, 116n20
Pritchard, Eric Darnell, 8, 50, 117n30 (Ch. 1), 117–18n4 (Ch. 2), 118n5, 119n17
Prometheus (Aeschylus), 81
proposals, 41–42
psychoanalytic theory, 103
public/private distinction: Brown/Primus correspondence and, 72–73; oversimplification of, 8; queering of, 7; queer/feminist scholarship on, 109–10n6
public speaking, 17–18, 82–83
Putnam's Phrase Book (E. Carr), 116n24

"queer" as term: "same-sex" vs., 12; use of, 11, 12
Queer Art of Failure, The (Halberstam), 11, 47, 69, 98, 100
"queer effect," 11, 37. *See also* invention strategies with queer effects

queer failure: Brown/Primus correspondence and, 99–100; civic engagement and, 101; complete letter writers and, 3, 11, 45, 47–48, 99; Dodd and, 98, 99, 100; movement toward, 100–107; scholarship on, 125n1; use of term, 11
queer gossip, 117n31
queer historiography, 11
queer liberalism, 110n7
queer politics, 110n7
queer rhetorical practices, 5; cross-category romantic epistolary address, 55–56, 62; defined, 11–12, 74, 110–11n15; epistolary exchanges with urgency/intensity, 57–58, 62; generic categories and, 54, 111n19; repurposing to erotic/political ends, 58–63, 72–73
queer rhetorical scholarship, 11, 47, 109–10nn5–7, 115–16n18
queer studies, 125n9
queer temporality, 33, 115–16n18
queer theory, 8, 11, 104–5
"queer time," 33
Quinn, D. Michael, 122n11
Quintilian, 80, 88, 122n22

race: complete letter writers and, 3, 27–28, 31; cross-race erotic interactions, 61; historical erasure and, 49–50, invention strategies with queer effects and, 66; "restorative literacies" and, 118n5; rhetorical education and, 75, 115n11
"racialized heteronormativity," 118n5, 119n17
racial politics, 61–63
"rake" (literary figure), 29, 104, 116n19
Rand, Erin J., 8
Rawson, K. J., 8
Reconstruction Era, 61
Redefining Our Relationships: Guidelines for Responsible Open Relationships, 105
Reed, Christopher, 115n18
Renaissance, 88
reproductive futurism, 115n18
"restorative literacies," 118n5, 119n17
restraint, studied, 33–35, 41–43, 46, 54, 57, 58
"Reveries by Night" (poem; Fay), 65, 120n23

rhetoric: civic engagement and, 8, 101; college-level training in, 24; constitutive, 9, 110n10; of courtship, 111–12n23, 112nn25–26; defined, 9; of diaries, 124n40; feminist histories of, 3; Greco-Roman tradition of, 6, 7, 80–81, 85, 112n24; historians of, 100–101; homoeroticism and, 85; instruction in principles of, in manuals, 25; present-day, 125n1; queer scholarship on, 109–10nn5–7; as seduction, 15–16, 104, 112n24; Western histories of, 1; women's, and letter-writing, 18–19; written vs. oral, 17
rhetorical education: British/Scottish works in, 123n24; for civic engagement, 7, 79–85, 95; "classicist stance" on, 122n18; commonplace books and, 88; defined, 9, 103; delivery, 112n27; diaries and, 78; expanded view of, 21–22; feminist histories of, 46, 47; future studies on, 104–7; Greco-Roman tradition of, 6, 123n24; histories of, 4, 21, 103; in oratory, 82–83; during postal age, 16, 17–18, 113–14nn1–4; queer failure and, 100–100, 102, 103–7; queer reconception of, 5, 47, 107; repurposing of, 84–85, 95, 123nn26–27; for romantic engagement, 9, 20–22, 69, 72, 84–85, 101–7; scholarship on, 122n18, 123n26; in writing, 83–84
rhetorical purpose: queer repurposing to erotic ends, 58–61, 119nn17–19; queer repurposing to political ends, 61–63, 119n21
rhetorical thinking, 87–88, 98
Rhetoric of Rebel Women, The (K. Harrison), 86, 124n39
rhetoric textbooks, 23
Rhodes, Jacqueline, 7, 8, 109n5, 110–11n15, 125n1
Richardson, Elaine, 61, 119n17
Robb, Graham, 122n11
Robinson, Paul, 122n11
Roman Antiquities (Adam), 81
Romance on a Global Stage (Constable), 106
romantic engagement: civic engagement vs., 110n11; rhetorical education for, 9, 20–22, 50, 69, 72, 84–85, 95, 101–7; rhetorical practices of, 50; use of term, 9

romantic epistolary address: category-crossing address forms of, 40–41, 46, 54–56; heteronormative genre instruction in, 11, 50, 54; invention strategies with queer effects, 90–95; queer failure and, 101–2; queer rhetorical practices, 11–12, 13

romantic epistolary rhetoric: address and, 31–32, 40–41, 46; author's research on, 11, 102–3; civic dimensions of, 4–5; commonplace understandings of, 14; complete letter writers and instruction in, 2–3, 16, 23–24; defined, 9–10; digital-age instruction in, 102; *Godey's Lady's Book* as cautionary tale about, 1–2; "language of the heart" and, 2–3, 29, 37–38; learning/practice of, 54; pacing of, 10, 32–35, 41–43, 46; queer practices in, 11–12, 19, 37–45, 46–48, 90–92, 117n3; repurposed to nonnormative ends, 43–45; same-sex, 49–50; scholarship on, 28

romantic friendships, 111n22; debates about, 100; erotic interactions and, 53; of "everyday" people, 49–50, 117n3, 118n12; histories of, 70, 72, 118n12; of literary/political figures, 49; same-sex, during postal age, 19–20. *See also* Brown/Primus correspondence

Romanticism, 65

romantic letters: author's research on, 103; commonplace understandings of, 14, 69–70; complete letter writers and instruction in, 115n12; courtship, 115n12; dating, 32–33, 34, 54, 56–57; digital-age instruction in, 102; as epistolary rhetoric, 14–16, 21–22, 69–73, 100; heteronormative conception of, 54, 71; interpretive difficulty of, 71–72; "language of the heart" and, 29–31; learning of, through genre instruction, 50; marriage *telos* as rhetorical purpose for, 35–37, 54, 71; model, in manuals, 14, 29; pacing of, 32–35, 37, 40–41, 56–58; repurposed to nonnormative ends, 58–63, 71; as rhetorical practices, 54; "skeletons" of, 41; timelessness of, 115n13

romantic relationships: cross-class, 27, 40–41, 54; gendering of, 115n12;

normative temporality for, 33–35; same-class, 114n10

Roosevelt, Eleanor, 111n22

Rotundo, E. Anthony, 77, 95–96, 121–22n11, 122nn13–14

Royal Oak (MD), 51, 57, 61, 62, 119n16

Royster, Jacqueline Jones, 46, 61, 117n32

Ruberg, Willemijn, 120n29

Rufo, Kenneth, 110n9

Rules for Online Dating, The, 105

Sallust, 81

salutation lines, 54, 55–56

same-sex epistolary rhetoric, 54

same-sex romantic friendships, 111n22; code-writing about, 117n30; local contexts of, 119n14; during postal age, 19–20

same-sex romantic relationships: gay/lesbian, 105; literary representations of, 85–87. *See also under* Dodd, Albert

Sappho, 93

schools, common, 16

Schultz, Lucille M., 28, 47, 112n29

seduction, 16, 104–5, 112n24

self-censorship, 77

self-education, 88

self-rhetorics: defined, 86; of literary representations of same-sex erotic relationships, 85–87

sentimental literature, 23, 113n2

sexual identity, 11, 19–20

sexuality, 3; black women's, 119n17; historiography of, 15, 69, 95–96, 100; national, 8, 110n8; overfocus on, in letters, 69–70; queer rhetorical scholarship on, 7–8; same-sex romantic friendships, 19–20

Shepard, Sylvanus, 29, 30, 36–37

Shields, Sarah Annie Frost, 26, 29, 30, 35–36, 115n15. *See also Frost's Original Letter-Writer* (Shields)

Singer, Margot, 111n19

Sinor, Jennifer, 123n33

Sjöblad, Christina, 123n33

Skull and Bones (Yale secret society), 121n8

slave narratives, 23, 119n18

Sloop, John M., 109n5

Index

Smith, Jabez, 78, 87, 90, 107, 124n34
Smith-Rosenberg, Caroll, 20, 69, 70, 113n38, 118n12
Snapchat, 102
social media, 102
sophistry, 112n24
Sophocles, 81
Southey, Robert, 65
speeches, 83, 119n18
Speed, Joshua, 20, 49
Spring, Suzanne B., 13, 19, 74–75
Stillman K. Wightman Papers, 122n19, 122n23
St. Louis (MO), 80
Stowe, Harriet Beecher, 51–52
"straight time": defined, 10; heteronormative genre instruction and, 10, 41, 46, 57, 99; heteronormative relationship development according to, 33, 37; invention strategies subverting, 43, 46, 58, 99–100; queer failure and, 99, 100
Stryker, Susan, 110n14, 125n9
Symposium (Plato), 112n24

Tacitus, 81
Talcott Street Congregational Church (Hartford, CT), 51, 62
Teaching Queer (Waite), 47, 100
temporality: normative, 10, 33–35, 37, 56–57; queer, 115–16n18. *See also* "straight time"
Tender Passion, The (Gay), 121n11
Thomas, Charles, 52, 119n16
Thomas, Kate, 11, 37, 41, 45
Tinder, 102
Tines, Joseph, 52, 59, 119nn15–16
"To Elizabeth" (poem; Dodd), 93
transportation, 116n20
Trasciatti, Mary Anne, 28, 115n12
Trimble (Tennessee colonel), 62
Trinity College (Hartford, CT), 75. *See also* Washington College (Hartford, CT)
Turner, R., 27, 35, 40

Uncle Tom's Cabin (Stowe), 51–52
United States: liberal assimilationism in, 110n7; "national heterosexuality" in, 110n8

University of Pittsburgh, 4, 25
Useful Letter-Writer, The, 31, 35, 114n7

Van Buren, Martin, 80
VanHaitsma, Pamela, 109n5, 117n31, 119n17, 125n11
Verhoeven, W. M., 110n6, 112n35, 113n2
Very Social Time, A (Hansen), 118n10
Vicinus, Martha, 117n30
Virgil, 81–82, 85
vulgarity, 116n22

Waite, Stacey, 8, 47, 100, 125n1
Walker, Jeffrey, 7, 9
Walker, Nicole, 111n19
Wallace, David, 107, 109n5, 125n11
Walzer, Arthur, 7, 9, 28
Wan, Amy, 110n9
Warner, Michael, 8, 10, 32, 110n8, 110n13
Washington College (Hartford, CT): commonplacing at, 88; Dodd multigenre epistolary rhetoric developed at, 75, 78; Dodd rhetorical education at, 21, 76, 88, 95, 123n25; Dodd suspended while at, 82–83
Watts, Eric King, 109n5
Webster, Daniel, 83
Westlake, James Willis, 43–44, 114n7, 116n23
Whitbread, Helena, 117n30
White, David, 52, 118n9, 119n16
whiteness, 27, 28, 115n11, 118n5
Whitman, Walt, 49
Wightman, Stillman, 79, 81, 122n19, 122n23
wikiHow, 102
Wilchins, Riki, 111n18
Wilde, Oscar, 49
Willis, Nathaniel Parker, 120n23
women, 21, 112n24, 118n12. *See also* African American women
Women's Friendship (Aguilar), 66–68
women's rhetoric, 18–19, 46, 61
women's schools, 111n16
Woolverton, John, 122n11
writing instruction, 83–84

Xenophon, 81

Yale College: Dodd commonplace book entries while at, 124n37; Dodd extracurricular activities at, 121n8; Dodd graduation from, 96; Dodd rhetorical education at, 21, 75, 76–77, 80–81, 85, 96–97; required reading at, 81, 85
Yale Literary Magazine, 121n8
Yale University, 75; Library, 5, 120–21n1, 122n19, 122n22, 125n48
Young Lady's Friend, The (Farrar), 116n25
Youth's Letter-Writer, The (Farrar), 38

Zboray, Mary Saracino, 89, 117n3, 121n2, 122n11
Zboray, Ronald, 89, 117n3, 121n2, 122n11
Zeus/Ganymede myth, 85–87, 123n31
Zion Methodist Church (Hartford, CT), 51
Zwagerman, Sean, 112n26